RIP VAN WINKLE'S NEIGHBORS

SUNY SERIES,
AN AMERICAN REGION:
STUDIES IN THE HUDSON VALLEY

THOMAS S. WERMUTH, EDITOR

RIP VAN WINKLE'S NEIGHBORS

The Transformation of Rural Society in the Hudson River Valley, 1720–1850

THOMAS S. WERMUTH

STATE UNIVERSITY OF NEW YORK PRESS

Cover art: oil painting of Joseph Jefferson as "Rip Van Winkle" by George W. Waters, New York, 1871. Printed with permission of Historic Hudson Valley, Tarrytown, New York.

Published by
STATE UNIVERSITY OF NEW YORK PRESS, ALBANY

© 2001 State University of New York

For information, contact State University of New York Press, Albany, NY
www.sunypress.edu

Production and book design, Laurie Searl
Marketing, Patrick Durocher

Library of Congress Cataloging-in-Publication Data

Wermuth, Thomas S., 1962–
    Rip Van Winkle's neighbors : the transformation of rural society in the Hudson River Valley, 1720–1850 / Thomas S. Wermuth.
      p. cm. — (SUNY series, an American region)
    Includes bibliographical references and index (p.).
    ISBN 0-7914-5083-X (alk. paper) — ISBN 0-7914-5084-8 (pbk. : alk. paper)
      1. Hudson River Valley (N.Y. and N.J.)—Economic conditions. 2. Hudson River Valley (N.Y. and N.J.)—Social conditions. I. Title. II. Series.

HC107.N72 H85 2001
303.4'09747'3—dc21
                                                                                                    00-054909

        10   9   8   7   6   5   4   3   2   1

Contents

═══════════════

ACKNOWLEDGMENTS

Several scholars and friends have read all or portions of this book and their assistance in helping me to clarify my thinking and writing is deeply appreciated. In particular, Douglas Ambrose, James Lemon, Cathy Matson, Michael Merrill, Jennifer Miller, Joseph McArtin, Ben McTernan, Greg Nobles, Edwin Perkins and Mike Zuckerman, read chapters or commented on conference papers that later became chapters. Special thanks to the suggestions and comments from reviewers at SUNY Press: Edward Countryman, James Henretta, George Rappaport, and one anonymous reader. In addition, I owe a great deal of gratitude to Thomas Dublin, who oversaw the dissertation from which this book originated some ten years ago.

Special thanks to audiences that commented on papers I delivered at the McNeill Center for Early American Studies (1992), the Organization of American Historians (1994), the Economic and Business Historical Society (1999), and the New York History Conference (2000). I also want to thank the staffs of the New York Historical Society, the Ulster County Clerk's Office, the New York State Library, the New York State Archives, the Kingston Senate House, and the Huguenot Historical Society for their assistance.

My colleagues and students at Marist College assisted me in a variety of ways. Special thanks to Bill Olson, Robyn Rosen, Sally Dwyer and Jerry White for their collegiality and support—one of the many reasons Marist is such a wonderful place to work. Ed Woell gave timely computer assistance at a critical stage. The staff at SUNY Press made the process of publishing this book as smooth as it possibly could be. In particular I would like to thank Laurie Searl and Ronald Helfrich at the Press for their attentiveness and professionalism.

Finally, but most important, this book is dedicated to my parents, Kathleen and Robert, who have always supported and encouraged my work.

Introduction

When the Hudson Valley's most famous fictional resident, Rip Van Winkle, set out from his small, mid-valley village for an afternoons' hunting in the Catskills, he left, in Washington Irving's romantic revisioning, a contented, quiet town characterized by a "drowsy tranquility" that had little contact with the larger "outside" world. Indeed, Rip lived in a veritable "Sleepy Hollow," "a peaceful spot . . . found here and there embosomed in the great State of New York, that population, manners, and customs remain fixed; while the great torrent of migration and improvement, which is making such incessant changes in other parts of this restless country, sweeps by them unobserved."

Rip's typical Hudson Valley neighbor was, in Irving's fictional reconstruction, a "thriving, contented, liberal-hearted farmer" who tended to be somewhat provincial:

> seldom, it is true, sent either his eyes or his thoughts beyond the boundaries of his own farm; but within those everything was snug, happy, and conditioned. He was satisfied with his wealth, but not proud of it; and piqued himself upon the hearty abundance, rather than the style in which he lived.

Upon return from his hunting trip some twenty years later (or the next day by Rip's own calculations), Van Winkle found a new and different world. Not surprisingly, the village had "altered; it was larger and more populous." More significantly, "the very character of the people seemed changed. There was a busy, bustling, disputatious tone about it, instead of the accustomed phlegm and drowsy tranquility."

Although Washington Irving was an author of fiction, and "Rip Van Winkle" and "The Legend of Sleepy Hollow" really transplanted European folktales, Irving was also a thoughtful social observer and commentator. What Irving was commenting on in many of his writings was the character and speed of the economic change that transformed the rural North, and in particular, his beloved Hudson River Valley, in the years following the American Revolution. Indeed, Rip Van Winkle, by sleeping some twenty years, is the ideal observer and commentator on these changes. Although on the one hand befuddled and disoriented by the dramatic change he discovers, he is nonetheless one of the few people who can truly measure the magnitude of the transformation. Having missed twenty years, he can witness in stark contrast the "new" society with the "old."

Rip Van Winkle's eighteenth century Hudson Valley was clearly a romanticized one constructed by Irving for fictional purposes; a simple, uncomplicated society dominated by small self-sufficient farms, hearty yeomen, and isolated, but close-knit, communities. Quite simply, there were few "sleepy hollows" on the eve of the American Revolution, valley towns in which the "population, manners, and customs remain fixed" and change "sweeps by them unobserved." Further, Irving exaggerated the "disputatious" character of the new society in his attempt to clarify the change that had taken place. Nevertheless, even if Irving romaniticized and fictionalized the valley, he was essentially correct in his observations that the society and economy of the northern United States, including the Hudson Valley, was undergoing substantial and profound change in the late eighteenth and early nineteenth centuries.

Although Irving's fictional account of this transformation is the most famous (and most entertaining) commentary on this process, he was not the only observer detailing the economic transformation that was reshaping the northeastern countryside, and the lives of the agricultural population. Reflecting upon the then current condition of agriculture in New York, the president of the state's agricultural society commented in 1851 that while early settlers in the region had produced "for self-consumption," no farmer in the mid-nineteenth century could "find it profitable 'to do everything within himself.'" The self-sufficiency of eighteenth-century New York farmers, if they truly ever achieved it, had become, by the middle of the nineteenth century, already a romantic memory. As the president observed, "Time and Labor have become cash articles and [the farmer] neither lends them or barters them" but "now sells for money."[1]

Although the society's president had no statistics to cite at his fingertips, and, like Irving, possibly romanticized the activities of earlier farmers, he accurately described many of the changes taking place during his lifetime. New York, like much of the northeastern United States generally, was undergoing significant structural and institutional changes. All of these affected the state's residents, but certainly no group more than the agricultural population. Farmers saw changes in the transportation systems that carried their goods to new, distant markets; they also witnessed changes in the methods they employed to produce and exchange goods.

The growing market-oriented behavior outlined by the society's president was essentially precipitated by the wide-scale structural changes that dramatically transformed the world of the nineteenth century American farm family. The general outline of this transformation is fairly clear. In the colonial period, most farm families in the Hudson Valley, and the northeast generally, lived on small freehold farms located in rural, agrarian communities. Although families produced much of what they ate and wore, they traded with neighbors for goods they needed, but because of limitations in labor and capital, could not produce. Although farmers regularly sent surplus to commercial markets, much of the farm production in northeastern households in this early period was neither market-directed nor coordinated, but was attuned to the local needs of families and communities.[2]

During the second half of the eighteenth century, and accelerating rapidly during the nineteenth century, northeastern communities became immersed in the developing market system, as both producers and consumers. Although historians continue to debate the various meanings market participation had for farm families, there is general agreement that early national farmers increased their commercial production, participated more regularly in commodity trade, and purchased more manufactured goods than they had during the colonial and revolutionary periods. Studies of areas as diverse as Massachusetts and Pennsylvania reveal the extraordinary distances farmers traveled to receive the most profitable returns for the sale of their produce, and their enthusiastic response to the thriving market economy and to the expanding rural industry that offered them opportunities for profit.[3] Clearly, many farmers responded positively to the opportunities offered by the expanded marketplace and shared its benefits.

Although this picture is straightforward, many questions remain concerning rural economic life, the commercial behavior of farmers, and the ways farmers reconciled new opportunities with traditional family and community considerations. Although northern farmers increased their market production, the ways in which they did so, and the meanings these changes had for farm families, as well as farm communities, are less clear. Did all farmers become market producers, and share the same attitudes and tolerance toward risk? Did local, community-oriented trade and productive systems such as those that had existed in the colonial period continue, and if so, how were they affected by, and how did *they* affect, farmers' considerations on where to send their farm produce?[4]

For several years, a spirited debate among historians has addressed the character of early American economic and social life. There are, at the risk of some oversimplification, two schools of thought. One, the so-called market school, has tended to emphasize the significance of commercial markets in early American life, even the "entrepreneurial" character of Colonial American society. Winifred Rothenberg, one of the foremost exponents of this interpretation, believes northeastern farmers' economic beliefs were characterized by "a commercial *mentalité*, an entrepreneurial spirit, an individualistic ethic of private gain."[5] Historical geographer James Lemon has argued that limits in economic activity "were set by conditions rather more than by any moral or legislative injunctions" that early Americans farmers were generally capitalists, even liberal in the classical sense, "placing individual freedom and material gain over that of public interests."[6]

An alternative school of thought has tended to emphasize the relative weakness of commercial markets, the role of neighborhood trade and labor systems in shaping everday life, and the importance of "community" in early America. These scholars, most notably James Henretta and Michael Merrill, believe that the economic worldview of early Americans was circumscribed by the prevailing social and economic conditions, conditions that dictated more subsistence-oriented agriculture and local trade.[7] Although economic gain was important, Henretta believes eighteenth-century farm families were enmeshed in a "web of social relationships and cultural expectations that inhibited the free play of market forces," and that the primary goal of rural farm families was to satisfy the needs of the household and to sustain community and kin social relations.[8]

Most studies of rural economic practices in the North have focused on Massachusetts and Pennsylvania, two of the leading centers of market agriculture.[9] However, the evidence and conclusions are often contradictory. Winifred Rothenberg's rigorous quantitative analysis of the market orientation of Massachusetts's farmers emphasizes the importance of markets and commercial production for these farmers in the late eighteenth and early nineteenth centuries.[10] Rothenberg's research has revealed the extent of price convergence, the extraordinary distances many farmers willingly traveled in order to receive the most lucrative returns for their produce, and the emergence of a market for wage labor.[11]

In contrast, Christopher Clark's study of Western Massachusetts reveals a farm society that geared its economic planning toward family and community needs "rather than the demands of production for profit in the marketplace." Based on more than a mere absence of cash, this system had a "deeper cultural attachment to kinship and neighborhood ties and the spirit of mutual cooperation."[12] Daniel Vickers's analysis of Essex County, in Eastern Massachusetts, finds evidence of both types of behavior, and argues that neither long-distance commodity production for markets, nor surplus production traded with neighbors on essentially noncommercial markets, should necessarily be viewed as mututally exclusive.[13]

Paul G. E. Clemens's intensive research into southeastern Pennsylvania from the mid-eighteenth century through the early nineteenth century has uncovered a thriving market economy in that important middle state, where farm families regularly exported wheat and flaxseed, with a variety of secondary products entering the regional market. In addition, a growing rural industry characterized local economic development, providing "profit-making opportunities for a significant number of entrepreneurially inclined farmers."[14]

In addition to disagreements among historians over the timing of economic changes, many questions remain concerning rural economic life, the commercial behavior of farmers, and the ways farmers reconciled new opportunities with traditional family and community considerations. Although northern farmers increased their market production, the ways in which they did so, and the meanings these changes had for farm families, as well as farm communities, are less clear. Did all farmers become market producers and share the same attitudes and tolerance toward risk? Did local, community-oriented trade and productive systems such as those that had existed in the colonial period continue, and if so, how were they affected by, and how did *they* affect, farmers' considerations on where to send their farm produce?[15]

If commercial markets began dictating much of the production and exchange of many farm families by the early nineteenth century, does this mean that capitalism, as a social and productive system, with all of its specific values, beliefs, and attitudes, dominated everyday life for these rural farmers? Were there alternative systems to the new commercial ones, and in some areas, did more traditional and customary systems meld with the new commercial, capitalist ones? Were there regions where the older systems still dictated and residents "built" capitalism into previously existing systems of production and exchange?[16]

Further, the activities of the multitude of smaller farmers who traded locally and sold on regional markets has received scant attention. Several recent studies have highlighted the role of those farmers who were at the vanguard of commercial production. Many of these studies, such as those of Winifred Rothenberg, are based on information culled from farm account books, records that tend to be disproportionately representative of larger commercial producers, or in the words of Gloria Main, the "records of busy, successful men."[17] The behavior and perspective of smaller farmers, whose decisions were as important to the nature and character of the rural economy as those of the larger producers, remain largely unexplored.

Other questions concerning the impact of the market revolution on northern families remain. To what extent did the community structures within which these farmers lived, worked, and traded shape their economic activities? Some scholars have focused almost exclusively on the relationship of farmers to commercial markets, downplaying other, noneconomic considerations, which presumably had some impact on farmers' market behavior and attitudes.[18] Other studies have emphasized the importance of local trade networks and the interdependence among neighbors and kin, but have paid less attention to the local community institutions that helped shape daily life in rural America, such as town governments, churches, and economic structures.[19]

Curiously, although New England and Pennslavania have received significant attention from historians, scholars have largely ignored the market behavior of farmers from New York, even though it was precisely during this period that the region emerged as the hub of American commercial activity.[20] Consequently, existing studies have produced a fragmented picture of rural life in the United States. The existence of significant differences in land-ownership patterns, availability of labor, cultural and ethnic backgrounds of residents, and material opportunities for market involvement—all crucial factors in shaping the market behavior of rural families—cast doubt on the wisdom of generalizing findings from one region to the other.

The Hudson River Valley, the rich grain-producing hinterland of the New York City market, offers an ideal locale for a study exploring the economic culture, and economic behavior, of rural farm families. Agricultural producers in the mid-valley county of Ulster, located some sixty miles north of New York City, enjoyed a variety of options when exchanging and selling their goods, and many of them participated in both long-distance and local trading systems. Exploring farmers' behavior as both producers and consumers provides insight into the factors that guided their choices when producing, trading, and selling. By situating this behavior in the context of the community structures in which these farmers lived, worked, and traded, one gains a fuller understanding of the ways in which individual households attempted to improve their living standards while carefully negotiating community needs and demands.

The first half of this book explores the economic activities and practices of Ulster County farmers and the rural social and economic culture that took shape and dictated their behavior in the eighteenth century. The essence of this economic culture was householders' attempts to balance individual concerns for profit and security, or, as they described it, a "comfortable subsistence," with broader community demands for stability and growth. Essentially, valley farm families combined and alternated their economic strategies, employing the complementary strategies of production for consumption, local exchange with neighbors, and commercial export. Their goals were to subsist, acquire consumer goods, increase landholdings, and transmit legacies to their heirs.

Central to the economic behavior of rural valley farmers was the existence of a vibrant, community-based economy that linked farmers, artisans, and shopkeepers in bonds of interdependence. While participants in the thriving Hudson River trade, much of farmers' economic activity was oriented toward local markets. Although the commercial market offered profitable opportunities to valley residents, it was only one consideration, albeit an important one, in farmers' decisions about production, sale, and trade. Valley residents' decisions in these areas were just as often shaped by community, family, and institutional concerns as by market opportunities.

This community economy was sustained by an intricate network of social, cultural, and political institutions that shaped community life, providing both the opportunities and limitations for economic activity. Eighteenth-century farmers were connected in a series of "horizontal" as well as "vertical" linkages with other farmers, tradesmen, and shopkeepers, linkages that transcended mere economic bonds but extended into the social, political, and religious spheres as well.[21] These linkages structured relationships among town residents into bonds of mutuality and reciprocity, giving form to the economic culture and behavior of rural New Yorkers in the eighteenth century.

Further, eighteenth century rural New Yorkers did not live in a world of "free enterprise" or "laissez-faire." Town governments regulated prices and wages, as well as various forms of economic behavior by forbidding usury or monopolization, and many other acquisitive practices that were believed to endanger the public good. Although no "moral economy" existed in rural New York, at least not in the way so well articulated by E. P. Thompson for eighteenth-century England, neither did a market economy solely dictate behavior or beliefs. Local economic practices were just as often shaped by social concerns and obligations as they were market demands. Indeed, during times of economic distress and crisis, rural residents demanded careful market regulation and participated in food riots against "price-gouging" merchants and farmers.[22]

The second half of this book explores the mid-valley's economic and social development from the last third of the eighteenth, through the middle of the nineteenth century, the age of the "market revolution." A variety of events challenged the social and economic order that had taken shape in the eighteenth century, restructuring the nature of community and diversifying local economic practices. The American Revolution spawned a democratic politics that challenged the old social and political order, and the transportation and commercial revolutions had, by mid-century, as the agricultural president's address reported, restructured the economy of New York, compelling farmers to develop more aggressive productive and marketing techniques in order to keep pace with new, western competition.[23]

The market revolution had substantial implications for the nature and character of community, as well. During the first half of nineteenth century the economic and social interdependence of town residents eroded as the valley's economy diversified. Although agriculture had once enjoyed uncontested preeminence in the economic sphere, farmers now competed with manufacturers, tradesmen, and others to shape the economic policies of their towns. Where eighteenth-century towns had emphasized public policies that negotiated the appropriate balance between individual economic interests and the community's public good, nineteenth-century towns adopted policies arguing that the public good could be best achieved through private commercial interests competing with one another. Although far from a world of "free trade," public policy was increasingly shaped by the belief that the competitive, *unregulated* market, not a market controlled by town governments, provided the best setting for prosperity and security.

Although it would be easy to characterize these developments as simple community-declension, it would be far more accurate to view this process as a reshaping of the nature of community. Indeed, a new voluntarism and booster-ism emerged within nineteenth-century northern communities as town residents recognized their future economic prosperity depended upon intense economic competition with other towns and communities in the region and beyond. Although many competing economic interests still existed within towns, residents generally joined together to obtain control over regional transportation systems or commercial manufactories.

There was still much continuity with the past throughout the period under discussion, however. Though manufacturing moved into the region, the valley remained predominantly agricultural and, in the years before the Civil War, the region did not replicate the scope or scale of New England's industrialization. Furthermore, while New England families gradually became dependent on the wages paid for merchant-controlled "outwork," valley farm families developed new forms of nonagricultural production to maintain their households as independent and autonomous economic units.

In addition, although the social and economic circumstances had changed significantly, farmers and tradesmen employed the new economic opportunities to meet familiar family and household needs. Even though local economies were no longer the self-sustaining, economic communities they had been earlier, and formal market controls had been signifcantly reduced, neighborhood trade networks continued to play an important role in residents' lives, and families continued to rely on customary economic behavior when dealing with one another.

Rip Van Winkle was ambivalent about the changes that took place in his fictional lifetime. He was certainly frightened and confused by the new bustling economy, and the "disputatious" character of the people. This undoubtedly reflects the attitudes of Rip's creator, Washington Irving, who sharply criticized many of the developments of his own day: the industry, railroads, and other forms of "improvement" that "spoiled" his beautiful river valley

On the other hand, Rip was much happier in his new environs than when he left twenty years earlier. Further, Irving himself lauded certain aspects of "progress" such as steamboat travel and the completion of the Delaware & Hudson Canal (which he named "the artificial river") for bringing economic opportunity to hitherto neglected regions of the valley.[24] In this area, the fictional "Rip Van Winkle" was probably much like his "real" valley neighbors who saw both good and bad, as well as opportunity and challenge, in the developments that transformed their society in the years between the American Revolution and Civil War.

Disagreements about the proper balance between competing social and economic visions have characterized much of American history. As we enter the twenty-first century, these debates have intensified, as plans for industrial and commercial growth often clash with environmental and preservation concerns. The Hudson River Valley, both a commercial hub and a historically rich scenic landscape, has been at the center of debates involving, on the one side, the desire for more industry and jobs, and on the other, the threat many see in this growth to community life and the natural landscape.[25]

Understanding the economic and social milieu of the Hudson River Valley during the period of the "market revolution" tells us much about the ways rural families in an earlier time structured community life, as well as the ways they negotiated and debated the benefits and costs of economic expansion. Americans in the early national period lived in a "transitional" economy—still partly governed by community values even while becoming more engaged in commercial market development—and they attempted to shape their economic policies accordingly. The strategies and tactics they employed at the household, neighborhood, and town level offer a unique opportunity to understand how these communities balanced family and community needs with the opportunities offered by market growth.

CHAPTER ONE

"A Very Beautiful and Fertile Wheatland"

THE SEVENTEENTH-CENTURY SETTLEMENT OF THE HUDSON RIVER VALLEY

On June 10, 1749, Swedish traveler and naturalist Peter Kalm left New York City for a voyage up the Hudson River to Albany, about five days' journey. Kalm commented at length about the local scenery along the river, the topography of the land, the fauna and growth on the river's banks, and his impressions of the landscape. Kalm's journal records in detail the condition of agriculture and husbandry, the specialties of the region, and the condition of various villages along the shore.

By mid-valley, about sixty miles up the Hudson, Kalm took special note of the very diverse landscapes he saw on either side of him. While the eastern shore (Dutchess County) consisted of gentle slopes peaceful and pleasing to the eye, and "well cultivated soil . . . fine plowed fields, well built farms and good orchards," the west bank (Ulster County) loomed out in stark contrast with its rough, rocky, and jagged shore, "covered with woods with one or two little settlements." Some twenty years later, in May 1769, Richard Smith, a second traveler recording his impressions of the river's natural beauty, noted that while Ulster County, located in the mid-valley's west bank, might one day "be a place of Consequence" because of its fertile hinterland, the soil seemed "broken, stony and few places proper for the Plow."[1]

Of greater significance in these two travelers' accounts, however, is that both commented on the state of agricultural production in the area. Although the west bank lagged behind the east in terms of serene landscapes, it stood above its cross river rival in cultivation. Indeed, Kalm stated boldly that "wheat flour" from Kingston on the west bank was "reckoned the best in all North America." Smith concurred, adding that the Kingston area, the "granary" of the valley, was the greatest supplier of wheat to New York City. Both commented that the area produced superb cheese and dairy products as well.[2]

In addition to the exceptional grain and dairy production, the central valley lay perched on one of the most important natural transportation systems in North America. Cutting from the Adirondack Mountains through the eastern part of New York, the Hudson River flows due south where it empties into the Atlantic Ocean at New York City, creating a convenient, accessible route for commercial navigation. In addition, with its connection to the Mohawk River at Cohoes, it penetrates west across the state toward the Great Lakes.

However, even with these excellent opportunities for agricultural production and trade, settlement along the Hudson progressed slowly. While New England and the mid-Atlantic colonies developed rapidly following the initial European settlement, settlement in New York lagged. The first shipload of Dutch settlers to "New Netherland" arrived five years before the "Great Migration" to New England, yet in the 1650s, while Massachusetts claimed a population of some 40,000 settlers, the population of New Netherland (soon to be New York) numbered barely 4,000.[3] An overview of the history of seventeenth-century European colonization of the valley, the various groups that settled there, and the changing nature of social and economic life supply the background for the settlements that took shape in the late seventeenth century.

The original appeal the Hudson Valley held for Europeans was first and foremost the fur trade, and second, the lush, fertile, farmland that lined both sides of the river. Even people who settled as farming families in the seventeenth century did so with an eye toward the profitable peltry that local Indians were willing to trade. The first European settlers in the region were sponsored by the Dutch West India Company, which had exclusive powers over Dutch colonization in North America, and for whom long-term settlement was not a preeminent concern. Indeed, the company saw its developing colony as a commercial enterprise centered around the fur trade, not as an agricultural colony.[4]

Although the exploitation of both fur and land began immediately from the time of first settlement, most settlers, whether individually or as families sent over by the West India Company, were primarily interested in the potential profits of the fur trade. Adriaen Van der Donck echoed this state of affairs in 1646 when he complained that New Netherland "had a superabundance of Petty Traders" but suffered from "a want of farmers and farm servants." Since the trappers and traders moved with the fur supply, they had little need for long-term communities or settlements and made few attempts to construct them. Through the 1660s only three communities of note existed in New Netherland: New Amsterdam at the mouth of the Hudson, the fur-trading town of Beverwyck located 140 miles upriver, and Esopus, a small trading post about halfway between the two. As late as 1650, New Netherland's population was just a little over 3,000, with less than one-third of this number residing in the valley.[5]

The standard interpretation of these seventeenth-century fur-trading towns is that they were generally contentious, disharmonious places where greed and economic individualism took precedence over community needs. The town of Schenectady, although located about ten miles west of the Hudson in the Mohawk Valley, is the stereotypical seventeenth-century New York town. According to its chronicler, Schenectady was founded by people who "viewed the village less as a new home and community than as a profit-seeking investment." Indeed, this fur-trading village "suffered from a severe structural atrophy, lacking the autonomous political, economic, and even religious institutions of community."[6]

Although this portrayal of provincial and village life is accurate for many communities in the seventeenth century, when New York was populated primarily by company employees and fur traders, by the 1670s towns and communities based on long-term settlement, composed primarily of farm families and shaped along a collective sense of social organization, had begun to develop throughout the valley. By the late seventeenth century, the fur trade was moving north and west, and the valley began to take on a new appearance as farming became the principal employment.

The mid-valley town of Kingston reflects, in microcosm, this changing social and economic orientation of the valley, and the way the changing economy revealed itself in a maturing nature of community. Originally named Esopus, this village was settled by Dutch farmers/traders in the 1650s, although a small trading post had existed there since the 1640s. Blessed with an excellent port, the original purpose of this post was to service the transient traders and trappers and ship their pelts downriver. From its beginnings, Kingston was a point of commerce and trade, a characteristic it never lost even as it became oriented toward other economic pursuits.

With the decline of the fur trade in the mid-valley, Kingston began to settle into more stationary agricultural pursuits. Laurentius Van Gaasbeck described the Kingston area in 1679 as a "very beautiful and fertile wheatland, which here grows so abundantly" that the area is considered the "granary of the whole New Netherlands, and the adjacent places." Indeed, by the 1680s, the town was populated primarily by farm families producing grain both for themselves and exporting their surplus downriver. Furthermore, the town was exhibiting all of the characteristics of a growing agricultural community: an expanding population of farm families, cleared farm- and pasture lands, a mill, and a small, yet bustling port.[7]

Although Kingston's development was characteristic of Hudson Valley communities that began settlement before, or during, the heyday of the fur trade, most towns like New Paltz, Rochester, Marbletown, and New Windsor were settled *after* the decline of the fur trade, and were founded as farming villages settled by families with ambitions of creating long-term communities. Although the fur trade continued to exist as a "by-industry" until the very end of the century, none of these towns enjoyed significant commercial benefits from the trade. Like the people who began to settle in Kingston in the 1670s, the people who settled these towns did so after the most unstable period of settlement had already taken place.

These communities that took shape in the mid-valley did so for different reasons, and were settled by groups with different heritages. Although New England tended to be settled by families sharing a religious, ethnic, and linguistic background, New York's Hudson Valley was a far more heterogenous region. Within the county of Ulster alone, and Ulster was generally representative of other New York regions, the three most populous and leading communities, Kingston, New Paltz, and New Windsor, were settled by three distinct ethnic groups (Dutch, French, English) separated by custom, religion, and language. Even though these towns shared important economic and political characteristics by the early eighteenth century, their original settlement patterns and histories were significantly different.

Although few, if any, of the families that established Kingston in the 1650s knew each other before settling the town, the French Huguenot families that settled the town of New Paltz twelve miles to the southwest came together in 1678 to settle a planned community. These families shared a common religious, ethnic, and cultural past, and established a farming community based on a collective vision of society. In order to maintain social order and their vision of cooperative democracy, they established the "Duzine," a governing board to which each of the original families sent a representative. The Duzine owned land in common, was responsible for land distribution, and possessed judicial authorities.[8]

Before 1700, immigration to the valley was small. Several reasons account for this. First, the Hudson Valley was considered the frontier, and the fear of Indian attacks significantly reduced the attractiveness of the fertile farmland. Second, the West India Company's establishment of "Patroonships" in the 1630s, ostensibly intended to increase settlement, actually accomplished the reverse. These large grants of land, under the control of a single, favored "lord," never attracted more than a smattering of tenants, and except for one, Rensselaerswyck, did not survive into the English period. As Governor Robert Bellomont of New York observed, a man would have to be "a fool" to become a tenant in New York when he could "purchase a good freehold in the Jersies for a 'song.'"[9]

During the 1670s, small groups of English, French, and Germans began applying to the New York governor for land grants, settling in the valley, and beginning the slow, laborious process of building villages and towns. Others who settled in the valley were internal migrants, families moving south from Albany, Schenectady, and Rensselaerswyck. These families, either fearful of the frontierlike conditions in those places, or desirous of better farmland, resettled to Ulster County.[10]

Of much significance about who came was, of course, why they came. Some scholars have argued that the men and women who settled in New England in the seventeenth century "came to the New World to get ahead."[11] This could probably be said of all willing immigrants to North America, including the Hudson Valley. What is most important, then, is to determine what it meant to a Colonial American to "get ahead." Ulster County's Cadwallader Colden wrote of his neighbors that their "hopes of having land of their own and becoming independent of Landlords . . . is what chiefly induces people into America."[12] Indeed, some of the families who applied to the New York Congress for incorporation as the town of Kingston did so to escape the tenancy of Johannes Van Rensalaer. Many who came throughout the colonial period, whether to the Hudson Valley or other parts of North America, did so to achieve the economic opportunity, political freedom, or religious toleration that eluded them in Europe.

The people who settled the central valley's west bank were primarily Dutch. About two-thirds of the Ulster population before the mid-eighteenth century were of clear Dutch descent, with much of the remainder generally English, but a significant French minority existed as well.[13] Most towns maintained ethnic and religious homogeneity through the early nineteenth century, while others became mixed from a very early period. For example, Kingston, founded by the Dutch, remained predominantly Dutch, with a growing English minority, throughout the eighteenth century. Right through 1774 many of the town court records were kept in Dutch, the Dutch Reformed church dominated, and Dutch was commonly spoken. The same was true of Marbletown and Rochester, where Dutch was regularly spoken through the early nineteenth century.[14]

Other towns, however, reveal a strong intercultural mixing. Although New Paltz was settled by French Huguenots, a large number of Dutch settlers moved into the area, and by the early eighteenth century, French, Dutch, and English were regularly spoken and used in business transactions and legal proceedings. Most revealing, even the records of the New Paltz Huguenot church, originally kept in French, were later recorded in Dutch, and only by the late eighteenth century, English. Even the name of the town government established by the Huguenots, the "Duzine," was taken from the Dutch word for dozen, *dozijn*.[15]

By the late seventeenth century, these new valley settlers went about the business of clearing farms, building roads, and founding towns. However, through the 1750s the population of these towns remained relatively small, with Kingston the largest at about 1,500 people. These communities, much like small towns in New England, regulated land ownership, distribution, division, and sale. Although the methods adopted varied from town to town, these communities shared several basic strategies and premises. First, after receiving a patent from the governor, town proprietors divided land among the original incorporating families and put the bulk of remaining land aside for later use. Although these divisions were not democratic, they were roughly equal.[16]

Second, the original grantees kept land aside for future generations. For example, the small farming community of New Paltz, settled by French Huguenots in 1678, put the process of land distribution under the control of the Duzine, the representatives of the twelve families that had originally settled the town. The Duzine drew up detailed methods of dividing and subdividing the common holdings.[17] We must keep in mind that these towns were agricultural communities, absolutely dependent on the ability to provide easy access to good, fertile land for the present family and future generations.

Third, some land was reserved for common use, rentals, and future sale. Through this method, newcomers could become landowners, and people who could not afford to buy, and therefore could not become freemen, could still farm or practice a trade and live within the township. In addition, this method offered the town a form of revenue through rents on the common land.

Other similarities to New England, and even Pennsylvania townships, existed. For example, the original grants incorporating the towns of New Paltz, Rochester, and Kingston required male residents to labor several weeks per year building and repairing the roads, fences, bridges, and mills necessary for the community to survive and prosper. In addition, men had to serve a variety of elected offices such as town clerk, surveyor, fence viewer, constable, market inspector, and assessor.[18]

Although these original incorporations shared certain similarities to those of New England, important and distinct differences existed. First, there was no formal covenant as the original seventeenth-century New England towns understood it. The incorporation was a contract, but it did not contain the moral overtones or responsibilities that the Puritan covenants did. Second, little sense of religious purpose bonded these Hudson Valley residents together. Although like-minded men and women of similar religious backgrounds founded towns in the mid-valley, this was never an explicit part of the original act of incorporation.

Finally, these grants were not exclusionary, at least not in the way the Puritan covenants were. Although these acts bestowed preferential status on the original proprietors, families, and their descendants, these towns were not "closed"—not even in the earliest years. These towns were neither religious refuges nor cities "upon a hill." They were communities of people who shared similar ethnicities, national origins, and religious orientation; however, they were not settled for these reasons alone. Although these towns were clearly more than mere economic adventures, they were certainly much less than "holy experiments," and little sense of "mission" shaped the activities of these early valley farm families.

By the early eighteenth century, six incorporated towns existed in Ulster County. The oldest town in the county, and one of the oldest in New York, was Kingston. A bustling port town, Kingston balanced its primarily agrarian character with its position as the leading entrepôt on the Hudson between Albany and New York. By balancing its economic interests, and by encouraging the production of its rural hinterland for trade downriver, Kingston was representative of other valley towns of similar size such as Poughkeepsie and Newburgh.

Few Hudson Valley communities, however, whether in Ulster County or the neighboring counties of Orange and Dutchess, enjoyed good ports and therefore relied on general diversified farming. The rural, backwater towns of New Paltz, New Windsor, Rochester, Marbletown, and Hurley differed widely in their geographic location, relation to the Hudson River, and general topography. While New Paltz was praised as a "very beautiful and fertile wheatland," and Kingston as a place where "broad meadows are seen stocked w/ffne cattle" and "fruits are flourishing in exuberant plenty," land in the New Windsor area was described by one contemporary as being "stony, rocky hard soil . . ." where ". . . the farms were rough, the farming implements rude, and the people generally poor."[19]

By the early eighteenth century, the nature and meaning of community in the mid–Hudson Valley had altered significantly. Farm families established long-term settlements on a basis far more secure than the temporary lodgings of the transient fur traders of the mid-seventeenth century. These growing, agricultural communities generally enjoyed fertile land, expanding populations, and access to river trade. Quite different from the contentious seventeenth-century settlements, where fur traders were in active competition with one another for the Indian trade, these towns were consciously structuring communities "in Search of Peace and Harmony." This goal was no attempt to replicate the religious or social utopias of New England's "Peaceable Kingdoms," but a practical attempt to construct stable, and therefore prosperous, communities.[20]

Furthermore, the people who settled these communities were not attempting to escape European society, culture, or customs. Indeed, they often went to great lengths to replicate, albeit with significant alterations in their new environment, the societies and villages they had left behind. Nor were these settlers hoping to avoid participation in the Atlantic market, since from the very earliest period of settlement they participated in the long-distance trade of fur and grain. However, the behavior and conduct they exhibited in their economic dealings with neighbors and fellow townspeople can only be understood within the framework of the community institutions that shaped everyday life in the eighteenth-century Hudson Valley. An overview of the social, economic, and political institutions that structured the communities in which these residents lived, worked, and traded provides context for the rural economic culture that took shape in the countryside.

CHAPTER TWO

"One Body Corporate and Politique"

Politics, Society, and Community in the Eighteenth-Century Valley Towns

On the afternoon of February 13, 1761, the freeholders of the Corporation of Kingston, Ulster County, celebrated the accession of George III to the throne of the British Empire. Abraham Low, High Sheriff of Ulster, "attended by all of the officers of the Horse and Foot Militia, the Justices, and Trustees of this Town-Corporate, and several of the principal Freeholders and Inhabitants" marched in "regular procession" to the courthouse, where "His most Royal and Sacred Majesty was proclaimed in the Presence of a numerous Audience of People."[1]

A series of toasts and cannonade allowed Kingstonians to publicly demonstrate both their allegiance to, and their recognized subordinate place within, the hierarchical chain connecting their small town to the Crown itself. The first toast to the King was followed by toasts to "all the Royal Family," to Generals Jeffrey Amherst and Thomas Gage and finally to "Our worthy President" (the President of the Kingston Corporation). The people of Kingston were proud subjects of the British Empire, and loyal supporters of the pyramidical structure of which the King was the *top*, and their small village one part of a large base that stretched around the globe.

The afternoon's celebration revealed Kingston's symbolic connection to a world much larger than their small community of 1,500 people located almost 80 miles up the Hudson River from New York City. Although a rural farming community, Kingston was no "sleepy hollow" isolated from the larger political and social events structuring the Atlantic world. Indeed, as their toasts recognized, there was a direct connection between the leading political and judicial officials of their town with those of the Crown itself. Furthermore, the day's activities recognized the more practical connection between the mid-valley and the Empire. The valley militia units that paraded on this day had campaigned in Canada during the French and Indian Wars, local residents had sacrificed their lives for their King, and valley farms fed and supplied His Majesty's troops. The day's activities were a clear recognition and celebration of the integral role valley towns believed they occupied in the larger Imperial system.

The way these valley residents chose to demonstrate their allegiance is of significance as well, revealing local, social purposes in addition to larger, Imperial ones. These people were "Freeholders and Inhabitants" who celebrated together as a "Town-Corporate." More than a celebration of the King's coronation, this day was a celebration of community itself, a richly orchestrated ritual publicly reaffirming the vibrant communal life that was eighteenth-century Kingston. The procession wound its way through the streets of town stopping at each of Kingston's central social institutions offering toasts and cannonade. Beginning at Abraham Low's house and progressing northward, past the Dutch Reformed Church of Kingston, the town's central worshiping place, as well as by the public market, the focus of town commerce. The primary stop was at the courthouse, which housed the office of the Board of Trustees of the Kingston Corporation. After several celebratory toasts and additional cannonade, the "numerous audience" followed the parade of trustees and "leading freeholders" to its starting point where several more toasts and cannonade concluded the day's events.

Even if the people of Kingston celebrated and honored their King together, as "One Body Corporate," they did not do so as equals. Local political, judicial, and military authorities led the parade, followed by "principal freeholders and inhabitants." Although there was a large number of onlookers, they followed in the rear, behind Kingston's elite. When the procession returned to its starting point, it did so "in order," an observation concerned less with the orderliness of the parade than with the proper deference that the "numerous audience" showed to their leading citizens by allowing them to march first. Regardless of private resentments that undoubtedly existed, the people of Kingston publicly recognized significant distinctions and gradations in rank, status, and wealth, distinctions dramatically reinforced on this day.

Similar celebrations, although on a much smaller scale, took place in the other mid-valley towns of New Paltz, Marbletown, and New Windsor. Only in the last community did most residents bear English names or worship in the English church now headed by the new monarch. Fifteen years later each of these communities participated in similar communal celebrations sundering the very bonds of monarchy and Empire they so enthusiastically celebrated on this day.

This celebration reflects, in somewhat dramatic form, the nature of public, community life in rural, eighteenth-century New York. The object of the day's celebration was Kingston's identification with a world of great symbolic importance located some distance from the daily activities of residents' everyday lives. Even if Kingstonians were several thousand miles away from the site of the coronation, the nature of the day's activities reveals the extent to which the community identified its political and legal legitimacy with the King and Empire. Equally important was the communal unity that structured daily existence and the hierarchical order that shaped and dictated their social and political life.

Of course, this celebration quite possibly represented an idealized vision of what some Kingstonians wanted community life to be like, not necessarily an accurate portrayal of the social reality of the 1760s. Indeed, at the time of this celebration, political and religious strife was challenging the harmonious vision publicly demonstrated on this day. Nevertheless, the ideal of a society reflects much about the images and goals that guided daily existence, revealing what was *hoped* for if not actually *achieved*.[2]

This chapter explores both the ideal vision valley residents held of what the nature of community should be, but more important, what the reality of community life was. Although Hudson Valley communities were something less than harmonious "Peaceable Kingdoms" they were something more than mere assortments of residents who happened to live near one another. These towns were composed of neighbors, friends, and kin who worshiped together at local churches, constructed roads, docks, and public buildings in community work details, served in civic and public office, fought together in local militias, and shared labor and traded goods on one another's farms. An overview of the nature of political, social, and economic life in these towns reveals how these rural farm families made such communities their homes.

"One Body Corporate and Politique"
HUDSON VALLEY COMMUNITIES
IN THE EIGHTEENTH CENTURY

Of equal importance to the larger world of Atlantic politics celebrated on this day were the local communities of eighteenth-century New Yorkers. The locus of social, political, and economic life for Ulster County residents was not in London or New York City, although both of these were important, but the small towns and communities in which the farm families lived, worked, participated in political affairs, and attended church services. The immediate social and economic context of valley residents was the network of family, friends, and neighbors they relied upon for trade, labor, and support throughout their lives.

More than mere civil constructions, rural New York communities were woven together by bonds of kinship, shared religious beliefs, social duties, and civic responsibilities. Eighteenth-century valley towns were organic communities whose original charters linked their residents together in a series of interdependent obligations shaped by mutual political and social concerns, and shared economic interests and goals. These collective interests consisted of maintaining the social and economic stability necessary to allow households, the basic unit of social organization within these towns, to work, subsist, trade, prosper, and transmit legacies to their heirs.

The late seventeenth-century charters that incorporated Ulster County communities established these towns as corporate entities, in which the freeholders and inhabitants were joined together into legal and political bodies, under the power of a town government or board. Although the powers these boards possessed varied from town to town, they generally included power over local lawmaking, civil and criminal jurisdiction, disposal of common lands, support of the poor, and regulation of markets and local commerce. According to the original acts of incorporation, these powers were to be passed on successively and generationally from the original proprietors to "their Heirs and Successors forever."[3]

Kingston's 1687 charter illustrates the corporate ideal that shaped the founding and structure of valley communities. Issued by Governor Thomas Dongan, the patent established the once small fur-trading outpost as "One Body Corporate and Politique in deed and name," effectively turning the town into a municipal corporation. The governor's patent chartered the Kingston Corporation, which empowered the town to act as a single legal and judicial unit with municipal responsibilities and authority, including the "Powers Libertyes Privilidges & Immunityes" for "Regulating and Well Governing the ffreeholders & Inhabitants of Kingston."[4]

The Patent named the seven original Kingston proprietors to act as trustees of the corporation for the first year, but stated that twelve trustees were to be elected annually from among the freeholders. These twelve were given civil authority to make the laws and ordinances for their town, with the only restriction being that these laws be "in noew wayes Repugnant to the Laws of England & of this province."[5] In addition, the twelve trustees were to designate five of their members to hold court each month with both civil and criminal jurisdiction in the town.

Throughout the eighteenth century, the Board of Trustees was the political and judicial arm of the corporation. Although Kingston, like all New York communities, was subject to the jurisdiction of the New York Assembly, and, after

1703, to the Ulster County Board of Supervisors, the Trustees maintained local authority over legal, political, and judicial matters into the first decade of the nineteenth century. The Board passed local ordinances and laws, and prosecuted violators before the "corporation court."[6] These laws varied from such mundane codes as setting the height of fences, controlling the activities of swine and live-stock, or regulating residents' activities on the Sabbath, to far more significant laws concerning the management of the town's common lands, interest rates on loans, poor relief, and regulating market exchanges. Like other valley communi-ties that had been chartered by the Colonial Assembly, one of the central roles of the Corporation was to act as the town government and court.[7]

The primary authority these towns possessed flowed from their control over, and their right to grant, private landholdings, and their authority to regulate the existing common properties and woodlands. The New Paltz Duzine, the elected governing board of twelve freeholders in that town, granted individual landhold-ings and regulated common lands. In Kingston, the corporation had the addi-tional power of control over fisheries, mines, quarries, hunting, fowling, as well as all "Rents Services Proffitts Commodityes & Emolum(ts) & Heriditaments whatsoever to the said Tract of Land and Premissess belonging to . . . the Trustees of the freeholders & Commonality of Kingston." Throughout the course of the eighteenth century the corporation parceled out its land to the original patentees, sold and rented land to newcomers, kept large amounts for common use, and held the rest for future generations and sale. The land kept out of circulation could be used or purchased only with the permission of the Board of Trustees.[8]

This corporate character revealed itself in the mutuality of social and eco-nomic interests that wove the residents of valley towns to one another and to their communities. Although not isolated from other communities in the valley, these towns maintained a large degree of autonomy in their social and economic affairs. Farmers, artisans, and shopkeepers depended upon one another for their production and services, both in the local production and trading systems, but also, as was particularly true for a market town like Kingston, in the commer-cially driven Hudson River trade. Mid-valley towns were composed of residents who shared collective economic and social interests, specifically a healthy, thriv-ing community economy, and engaged in mutually dependent economic efforts. As such, although the demands and rewards for residents might vary significantly, the economic and social well-being of valley residents were tied to the success and survival of their community.

The nature and meaning of community life in the mid-valley is demonstrated further in the rights and rewards these towns granted to their residents, or more accurately, to their *members*, and the responsibilities towns demanded. According to the Kingston patent, Kingston was a "commonalty," and only "freeholders" could use the common grazing or pasture lands; take wood, charcoal, stone, or tar from the common forests; fish in corporation creeks; or borrow money from the corporation at a lower rate of interest than non-freeholders. Although people who were not freemen could buy land in Kingston, either from the corporation or from freeholders, this did not automatically grant them "freedom," a status that had to be approved by, and purchased from, the Corporation.[9]

By its very nature, a commonalty was exclusive in the rights and rewards it offered. A commonalty was essentially a chartered corporation and legally a private institution, and residents viewed their membership as comparable to that of shareholders. Freeholders were stockholders who not only invested in a corporate enterprise, but expected and demanded rewards for their investment.[10] One of the most important rewards anticipated by "freemen" was to share in the future parceling of common land holdings. The New Paltz Duzine and the Kingston Corporation granted common land only to freeholders and their families, and they did so on an "application by application" basis. Furthermore, a large amount of corporation land was rented to freeholders. Whether one was hoping for future land distributions, or renting, the control the Corporation maintained over land certainly acted as an incentive for freeholders and inhabitants to follow the town's dictates.[11]

POLITICS IN THE CORPORATE COMMUNITY

One of the most important rewards a freeholder received was political representation and some control over, and voice in, local political, social, and economic decisions. Although office holding in the New Paltz Duzine was restricted to descendants of the original proprietors until the end of the eighteenth century, the franchise was open to all freeholders. Only freeholders could vote in Kingston's elections, or be elected to the Board of Trustees, which determined civil codes, economic policies, land sales, and future land parceling. Although all residents of Kingston were subject to the laws and regulations of the community, to be enforced by the "corporation court," which maintained both civil and criminal jurisdiction, freeholders were the only residents who had an official voice in local politics. Furthermore, the nature of New York's political system extended this beyond town boundaries, since representation at the county level was based entirely upon towns. The Ulster County Board of Supervisors was composed of one representative from each town or precinct. At each level, town, county, and eventually province, one's political power and representation was related to being a freeholder within a community.[12]

However, in return for these privileges, substantial civic responsibilities and duties were demanded. In addition, these privileges were not offered to freeholders as discrete individuals, but as members of communities, whether as children of proprietors or purchasers of "free" status. Although most residents were independent landowners, at every level their social, political, and economic lives were contextualized by the community from which they claimed membership, identity, privileges, and of course, land.

The center of civic life in the eighteenth-century valley was the town government, where freeholders voiced their political opinions and registered their vote. On the first Tuesday in March, Kingston freeholders attended the annual town meeting, where they nominated and elected the twelve trustees for the Town Board, held elections on numerous smaller offices, as well as debated and acted on issues of common concern. Although a town meeting could be called by freeholders at any time, most of the political activities, laws, ordinances, and actions were left to the Board of Trustees. This was true in most other Ulster County communities, as well.[13]

Although New York town governments were not as powerful or active as those of their neighbors in New England, they were nonetheless places of vibrant political activity, recognized community authority, and unifying social institutions within towns. With power over local judicial, political, economic, and social affairs, the various town boards exerted significant influence over their communities, and enjoyed the legitimacy and support of town residents. Although major legislation was implemented by the New York Assembly in accordance with English law, most of the laws of daily significance for rural farmers and artisans were debated, voted, and enacted locally, within towns. Issues of land division and distribution, regulations of economic affairs and social activities, and the adjudication of civil and (through the 1750s) criminal affairs tended to be those of greatest concern and were decided upon locally with the approval and authority of the town's residents.

Much like their New England counterparts, residents of mid-valley communities discussed and debated issues of common concern and importance at the annual town meeting, although legislation itself was enacted primarily by the trustees. Most of the issues discussed and debated at meetings were practical ones for eighteenth-century towns: the need to protect gardens from marauding swine, laying out new roads or building new mills, prohibiting unattended outdoor fires, or setting a uniform height for fences. Equally important, however, were issues of somewhat greater moral and social concern, such as forbidding "riding on the Sabbath day," regulating immigration into the town, or monitoring interest rates and preventing usury. Although the eighteenth-century valley was a hierarchical society, with clear gradations in social and economic status, the town boards that debated these issues were not simply filled by the elite of the towns, as many middling farmers and artisans served as well. Of the 148 freeholders in Kingston in

1728 (roughly three-fourths of the household heads in town), 41 percent served at some point in their lives on the Board of Trustees, a startlingly high figure when compared with New England town boards. However, leading freeholders tended to serve numerous terms, while smaller artisans and farmers one or two terms only. Almost all freeholders served in one or another of the many other unremunerated offices—as fence viewers, assessors, highway commissioners, or constables. Over thirty offices had to be filled each year in Kingston, which meant that a sizeable portion of the freeholding population regularly participated in civic life. The people of Kingston were expected to serve their community, just one of the many responsibilities and duties freeholders owed to the town.[14]

Since one of the most important tasks of the town boards was control over common land, and its distribution within the boundaries of their patents, they were also left with the task of protecting these grants from conflicting legal claims or overlapping jurisdiction. Much of the time and money spent by the Kingston Trustees during the eighteenth century was in litigation in New York City, defending particular individual grants within the town from non-Kingstonians who claimed ownership via a previous or conflicting grant. This legal work was paid for by all freeholders, through common dues and revenue generated from the sale and rental of community land.[15] Legally, all freeholders were protected from an individual suit of this nature by the corporation. Although there were many different individual parts to the town, legally there was only one body.

As might be expected in small agricultural communities with a somewhat closed nature, these towns were wary of "outsiders" and regulated the influx of newcomers. One of the first acts of the new Kingston Corporation in 1688 was to forbid admittance to "strangers from any other town or county," except if "such man shall be bound to take care of himself or his maintenance." This prohibition was codified more fully in 1721, and again in 1786, when it was ordered "that no stranger shall set up his trade, or occupation within the Corporation unless he pay for his freedom."[16]

Outsiders with no visible means of supporting themselves were not welcome in mid-valley communities, as a stranger from Kinderhook discovered when he arrived in Kingston in 1736. Being "Infirm & having Sore Legg The Trustees Have ordered him to be Carried or Rid out of our bounds." When Thomas Chase entered Kingston on November 28, 1788, he was immediately seen as someone "likely to become a chargeable to the poor." Within the week, the trustees appointed a "committee to remove the said Chase out of this town."[17]

This careful control of freehold status and newcomers entering the community was based on several considerations standard to many New York towns in the eighteenth century. First, the limited amount of land each town possessed forced many communities to be restrictive in their land grants, and therefore, restrictive in the number of persons granted freemanship. Furthermore, "freedom" might be denied if there was suspicion that a person would not be able to carry on a livelihood and therefore end up on the town poor rolls. Hudson Valley towns passed annual allotments for the support of their poor, but were less inclined to generate new wards for which they would become responsible. So, even though Peter von Doburgh had resided almost one year in Kingston by 1744, the corporation did not hesitate to "warn" him to "remove w/his family out of the township" when it became apparent he could no longer fully care for them. If he did not comply "by Saturday night, he will be compelled to do it."[18]

Finally, Hudson Valley towns regulated newcomers for social reasons: the desire to maintain the form and spirit of the corporate community. Corporation members received significant benefits and privileges from being freeholders, benefits that demanded reciprocal duties, responsibilities, and subordination to the dictates and desires of the corporation. Therefore, towns were careful about granting freehold status only to those who demonstrated the desire, commitment, and resources to become members of the community.

Nevertheless, while downriver and Long Island communities like Newtown, Hempstead, and others restricted newcomers, mid-valley towns generally welcomed new residents who were capable of supporting themselves. Throughout the course of the eighteenth century, while towns close to New York City witnessed growing population pressures on scarce landholdings and available resources, the populations of mid-valley communities remained relatively small (though growing), land was abundant, and the desire to diversify and build a healthy economic community encouraged a more welcoming attitude.[19]

Other Ulster communities like New Paltz, Rochester, and Marbletown also regulated immigration to the community with respect to land availability, material resources, skills of the newcomers, and economic opportunity. These concerns were primarily social and economic. Unlike New England towns, there is no evidence that ethnic or religious considerations played a role in accepting newcomers to the town or granting freehold status.[20]

Valley communities had relatively few reservations about using their power to protect their corporate standing, whether from outsiders or, more routinely, to maintain the social order within the community. One of the primary roles of the Kingston Board of Trustees and of the other town governments was to protect town land from outside legal suits. The methods by which the corporation carried out its duties in defense of the town varied widely depending upon the perceived threat.

From the 1730s through the early 1760s the Kingston Corporation was engaged in two long-term lawsuits over boundary disputes, one with the enormous Hardenburgh Patent, which bordered Kingston to the west, and the second with the county of Albany, bordering to the north. Boundary disputes of this nature involved real, practical concerns involving access to land resources and disputed claims of ownership, but also symbolically reveal communities attempting to protect their corporate identity from outside threats and encroachment.[21]

Kingston's legal battle with Albany County is of interest, primarily because Albany's lawsuit was against individual householders and landowners in northern Kingston, not against the corporation itself. The Board of Trustees organized and paid for the defense of these land grants, however, recognizing this as a responsibility of the corporation.[22] The questioning of an individual grant essentially questioned the authority, both symbolically and practically, of the *grantor*, which was the Kingston Corporation, New Paltz Duzine, or Marbletown "Twelve Men."

These towns could also act far more dramatically than simply using lawsuits and legal defenses. If anyone from outside the community represented an immediate threat, the trustees responded in kind. In 1727, a group of tenants of the Great Hardenbergh Patent fenced in a section of Kingston's common land for their own use. After unsatisfactory results from written correspondence, the corporation sent out a delegation, which "pulled the fences of some tenants and Discouraged Others by threats."[23]

Most legislation, however, was aimed at regulating behavior within the community. Among people who defined their communities as composed of many individual but interrelated parts, and which demanded subordination of self-interest to the public good, activities that challenged the collective good of the corporation were specifically regulated against and dealt with harshly. Although Kingston freeholders had complete access to the corporation's commons for family and household use, specifically the wood, stone, tar, or charcoal that could be found there, these items could not be "transported or carried out of the corporation" for sale or the transgressor would be fined "5 pounds for every such default, to be levied by the corporation court." In addition, fines were levied against usurers (those who charged higher interest rates than the maximums set by the corporation), and bakers who charged higher than the price cap allowed for bread.[24]

The Board of Trustees also acted against freeholders who reneged in their obligations and duties to the corporation. The response of the board varied from warnings to minor penalties, depending upon the nature of the transgression. With Solomon Freer's 1751 rent for his "lot in town" overdue, the trustees ordered him to pay "on or before the first Day of May or else he may Expect Trouble Forthwith." When Jack Kourning could not "pay His Interest and principalle" to the corporation, the trustees ordered him to "be Imployed" cleaning "up the Rocks out of the Strand Path near Bamakers Fell."[25]

The response of the trustees could be more serious, varying from threats of violence to denying freehold privileges. Jacob Schoonmaker's "inclosure" onto common land in 1757 was "broken down and destroyed" by the trustees who threatened Schoonmaker "not to make any further Improvements on Corporation Land or to Expect trouble." Gideon Ostrander was warned in 1784 to remove a fence he had constructed on Corporation land or "you may depend that Committee of the Trustees will be sent to destroy the fence." Rowland Robertson was put "out of possession" of his common land in 1783 when he refused to respond to trustees' demands for money owed on common duties. Not only were Robertson's rights to the commons lost, but so too were rights to future divisions of corporation land.[26]

Further, the corporation acted against inhabitants who failed to pay rents to other freeholders, evidencing a collective responsibility for its individual parts. In these matters, as in others, the corporation court was not only the judge, but the prosecution as well. In 1734 the Board of Trustees sued Jonathon Wood for failure to pay "three years quit rent" to George Meales, a Kingston freeholder. Although Meales had apparently brought his complaint before the board, it was the trustees who brought the charges. The defendant Wood argued "that he could not expect Justice, by reason of his judges were plaintiffs." After a speedy deliberation, the court ordered Wood to pay the outstanding twenty-one bushels of wheat "and costs of suit."[27]

In the attempt to balance the interests of individual freeholders with the public good and the needs of the community, the corporation sometimes regulated one's control over private property as well. When an outbreak of malaria within the town was blamed on "the Mill Pond lying on the west part of the village of Kingston, in the possession of Benj. Bogardus," the corporation ordered "that the Said Pond be drained within Thirteen days." In this attempt to protect the health and well-being of its citizenry, the town government also revealed the extent of its attempt to reconcile private interests with public needs. The town paid the mill owner for his losses, but only half of what he estimated his damages to be.[28]

A COMMUNITY ECONOMY

Although the Kingston Corporation's charter and Trustees' actions dealt extensively with local lawmaking, land ownership, and judicial responsibilities, one of its primary responsibilities was in the economic sphere. The charters incorporating Hudson Valley towns in the late seventeenth century were issued during the heyday of mercantilist policy within the British empire. As such, the corporate officials were granted the power and responsibility of promoting economic development and encouraging trade. The governors who issued these charters did so explicitly to promote settlement in the rural hinterland, to develop the countryside as a productive region of the colony, and to encourage the town's participation in the Atlantic trading system. The primary role of the various town corporations was to promote the community economy through judicious land grants, careful development of village streets and wharves, regulation of mines, quarries, and other possible profitable enterprises, and the construction of markets and mills to facilitate internal economic development.[29]

However, even if a primary goal of these corporations was to promote profitable economic enterprises, and valley farmers and shopkeepers were active participants in the larger, expanding Atlantic market, their economic activities had to be reconciled with the social needs and demands of the local community. In short, it is impossible to view the economic activities of the farming, mercantile, and artisanal families that lived in the Hudson Valley outside of the context of town government, community, family, and neighbors, which shaped their everyday actions, choices, and economic decisions.[30]

Several significant features characterized the economies of Hudson Valley towns and villages during these early years of market development. First, each community in the mid-valley was primarily an agricultural producer. Even Kingston, with its bustling little port and its historic role in the New York fur trade, was, by the eighteenth century, primarily a farming town. Although a number of artisans, slaves, and shopkeepers serviced the local farming populations, three-fourths of Kingston's residents were members of farm families, and some eighty percent of the smaller back-river towns were. In addition, although Livingston Manor was directly across the river with thousands of farming tenants, the overwhelming majority of families in Ulster County, 76.2 percent in the late eighteenth century, owned their own land. This contrasts sharply with other regions in the mid-Atlantic and the Northeast, such as rural Pennsylvania, where farmers were increasingly dependent on landless wage laborers throughout the eighteenth century.[31]

Second, a healthy household production and community-oriented trade system characterized the local, internal economies of mid-valley towns. Although the export of agricultural goods was an important component of economic activity, particularly in Kingston, also important was the intricate local trading system that linked the various agricultural, service, and mercantile trades in a web of interdependence. Most of the food consumed in Ulster towns, as well as many of the farm tools, manufactured goods, textiles, and household furnishings, were produced locally by farmers and artisans who engaged in complementary systems of small-scale production and local trade. Although by no means isolated from larger markets, before the development of an integrated market system in the early nineteenth century, the economic identities of many mid-valley residents were shaped by, and their livelihoods oriented toward, their dealings within their community.

In a third area, Kingston stood apart from its Ulster neighbors. Although each town engaged in the export of farm produce, Kingston was more closely connected to the New York City market than smaller towns like New Paltz or Marbletown, which lay some seven or eight miles from a river port. A thriving export trade of surplus agricultural goods, especially wheat and flour that contemporaries "reckoned the best in all North America," but also barrel staves and wood fueled the town's economic development.[32] Profits earned from this export trade encouraged local service trades (such as saw- and gristmills), employed day laborers, and generated greater economic activity within the Kingston community. In addition, the marketing of farm products allowed Kingston residents to import a variety of consumer goods produced outside of the valley.

Following the decline of the fur trade, a thriving agricultural trade fueled the economic life of the mid-valley. Roelof Swarthout observed in 1662 that the Kingston area as a "fertile wheatland" where one had "but to spill the grain to get a bountiful crop." This trade was encouraged both locally and at the provincial level.[33] As early as the 1670s, Kingston was being referred to as "the granary of whole New Netherlands, and the adjacent places," and by the mid-eighteenth century Kingston's "wheat flour" had secured the reputation among commentators as being "the best in all North America." Traveler and observer Richard Smith concurred, adding that the Kingston area, the "granary" of the valley, was the greatest supplier of wheat to New York City.[34]

Various measures were proposed by provincial authorities to maintain the quality and promote greater production of valley "flower & bread." Although most of the these attempts at regulation were unsuccessful, the quality of valley grain remained high throughout the colonial period. In 1684 the provincial council put forward a bolting monopoly for New York City, giving the city's millers final authority over gristing and city officials the power over inspection of both flour and grain. This act was repealed during the next decade, however, and further attempts to regulate New York's grain trade did not succeed until the 1760s, when the New York Assembly passed an act calling for the inspection and regulation of flour milled outside of the city. From that point through the early nineteenth century, the long-distance trade of grain, flour, staves, and other commodities was carefully regulated as New York attempted to protect its export market by maintaining certain quality standards.[35]

Although export merchants promoted and supported much of this regulation, Ulster County farmers were less interested in legislation that attempted to regulate their production or add additional costs to their marketing. However, farmers generally supported attempts to promote the export of their surplus grain. As early as 1671, the governor of New York encouraged the "Merchants from the City of New York" to come to Kingston and "Negotiate with the

Farmers." Further, the New York Assembly mandated in 1692 that Ulster County hold "two fairs yearly" with the first to be "kept at Kingston on the Third Thursday in March."[36] Although these public markets benefited consumers by giving them a safe and secure environment to purchase their goods, they also benefited producers by giving them a ready market, and improved quality standards by systematizing the regulatory policies of locally sold grain and flour.

Although provincial authorities engaged in relatively little successful economic regulation throughout the colonial period, local authorities engaged in somewhat more. By focusing more closely on Kingston, the mid-valley's leading port-town, the economic life of a community with both an agrarian character as well as a significant market-producing center is revealed. Throughout the eighteenth century, the "Corporation of the Freeholders" of Kingston provided direction and organization to the town's economy. Although first and foremost a farming community, Kingston was diversified in its social and economic life by the increasing number of storekeepers, artisans, and small manufacturers who made the town their home and demanded greater civic regulation and organization. The corporation attempted to balance these various economic interests through such measures as regulating exchanges on the public market, calculating maximum prices on staple goods, monitoring and limiting interest rates, and controlling the dispersal of common lands.

This local regulation, oriented toward protecting both consumers and the interests of the various economic producers competing within Kingston, did not attempt to cut the town off from outside markets. Indeed, during these years one of the primary tasks of the corporation was to foster economic development within the community and facilitate the marketing of crops and other commodities for commercial profit—profit that would be brought back into the town. In 1736, the corporation constructed new wharves to further encourage and facilitate the growing river trade, regularly allotted money for new streets and roads to promote easy transportation within and around town, and funded and directed the construction of the new public market in 1753.[37]

The corporation also granted land for building grist- and flourmills to encourage agricultural production, and loaned money to private individuals to stimulate new industries, such as sawmills, tanneries, glassworks, and brickyards. Although certain private individuals would clearly gain from being the beneficiaries of particular monopolies or building contracts, such as Cornelius DeLameter, who was granted land to build a flour mill in Kingston in 1739 or Ephraim van Keuren's 1750 grant for "the privilege to Erect a sawmill," the purpose of these grants was to promote economic development and the public welfare of the community as a whole.[38] Kingston was an important market center and the people of the community encouraged this orientation and direction.

The economic policies of the corporation tended to promote economic expansion, which would benefit both the individual proprietor (farmers, miller, shopkeeper, etc.) as well as the corporation as a whole. Although the trustees regulated the sale of goods produced on common land, they did so in the attempt to earn the most profitable return for both the producer and the corporation. Corporation law required residents to petition the trustees for permission to sell outside of the township the wood, shingles, stone, or other products contained on, or produced from, common land. If the "libertye" was permitted, the corporation earned a portion of the profits agreed upon before the sale.[39]

Ideally, a Kingston freeholder petitioned the corporation for permission to sell and transport outside of town. So, in 1785, when Thomas van Steenburgh and Wilhelm Elmrich requested "the liberty to make each 1,000 shingles" for sale outside of town, it was granted by the trustees, under the condition they pay the trustees "at the rate of 12 shillings 6 pence per thousand." If the freeholder failed to inform the corporation, he would, like Johannis Masten, be fined for "cutting and transporting ceader Wood out of said township w/out libertye."[40]

If the trustees discovered an unauthorized sale in process, they might even take possession of the goods from the owner. In March 1786, when word reached the trustees that "a parcel of staves made within the commons were being transported for sale outside of Kingston," the board ordered "said staves" confiscated "and that this committee have the power to sell the same on Hire to the best advantage."[41]

Although one purpose of this regulation was to prevent the export of an item needed within town, such as in 1748 when Barret Lewis was fined for "transporting flour outside the township," its primary purpose was to benefit both the seller and the town. The seller benefited by earning profit on goods produced from the common land. The corporation benefited from the share of the profits they received from the sale. The case of Petrus Witteker clarifies the purpose of this legislation. When Witteker petitioned the trustees in 1789 to sell 4,000 feet of oak plank to John DeWitt of Dutchess County, the corporation sent their representative to inspect the wood to determine their fee. Observing that the wood needed to be used soon because it was close to ruin, the corporation approved the sale. If it had not been sold, the trustees commented, it "would be a Great Loss to Witteker, and also to the Corporation."[42]

Although cooperation over economic policies generally existed in town, Kingston was far from a "utopian community." There were competing economic interests with opposing economic agendas, and differences concerning specific policies routinely occurred within the town. Farmers complained that millers took too large a share of grain for their milling rates, consumers argued that shopkeepers overcharged on necessary items, and merchants found many farmers difficult to bargain with when selling their grain or flour.[43]

Furthermore, the Trustees' records are filled with disputes over land grants, fishing rights, mining privileges, and access to other, limited, natural resources.[44] However, a consensus prevailed that Kingston was first and foremost an agricultural center, and the Board of Trustees' policies reflected this. The various economic interests in town generally supported the trustees' policies because most benefited from this economic orientation and regulation. Farmers exported surplus farm goods that local shopkeepers, millers, coopers, and other artisans processed, packaged, and transported. Both the producing and service trades recognized the benefits of Kingston's agricultural orientation and from living, working, and trading under the regulatory umbrella of the corporation.

Crucial to this cooperation over economic policies and practices within Kingston was the still limited state of market development in the eighteenth-century New York countryside. Although a market economy was developing in the valley, a market society had not. Until the major transportation developments of the early nineteenth century, a thinly populated stretch of the Hudson and Mohawk River Valleys monopolized grain production and trade in New York. Although regional competition existed, this was limited, and without competition from western farmers, not intense.[45]

This limited competition helped to construct a unity of economic interests within Kingston. Although economic differences always existed among various social and economic groups, farmers, local shopkeepers, and the service sector shared common economic goals: the production, processing, and sale of agricultural products to New York City, the importation of consumer goods from the city, and the maintenance of a healthy, vibrant, local trading system. Although it is possible to exaggerate the cooperation between the farming and service sectors, with relatively limited competition from outside Kingston these two groups generally worked together to promote the social and economic interests of their community, which by extension, promoted their own economic positions as well.

The day-to-day workings of this community-based economic system were not left to the vagaries of the free market. Local town governments, as well as New York provincial authorities, enforced formal legislation or exerted informal community pressures that sought to encourage neighborly behavior and discourage any economic actions that might threaten the corporate body of the community. Old medieval injunctions against forestalling—withholding goods from the market in order to drive up prices—and engrossment—the monopolization of products destined for markets—remained on the law books throughout New York, although before the American Revolution they were irregularly enforced.[46]

Over the course of the eighteenth century, valley communities attempted to find the appropriate balance between promoting economic expansion while regulating the local social and economic practices of their residents. Regulation of the local economy relied heavily on the force of community tradition. Where informal means proved insufficient, responsibility for balancing competing economic interests fell to the local governing boards. These policies generally reflected the communities' consensus of the primary importance of fostering a healthy agricultural trade. Nevertheless, local regulations, whether of prices, trading practices, or quality standards, were shaped as much by broad community concerns as by a desire to protect the interests of producers.

The government regulation that began with the original acts of incorporation in the seventeenth century carried into the early nineteenth century. The charter of Kingston called for a public market, eventually located at Hendrick Sleght's, where the weights and measures were inspected, sellers and butchers licenced, financial exchanges supervised, flour and meat routinely inspected, and prices on various goods capped.[47]

The towns of New Paltz and New Windsor set maximum prices on bread and salt, among other goods, and scrutinized wages as well. The regulation of prices and quality of goods continued well into the early nineteenth century in Kingston and Rochester, where the "assize of bread" was regularly posted. The assize listed the price and size of the normal loaf, and set these prices according to the price of local flour. It also ordered that "each loaf shall be marked with the initials of the Christian and surname of the baker."[48]

The corporation also kept wheat on hand in the common store for local use, with limits on the amount one could purchase, a ceiling on prices, and instructions for its use. This wheat, rye, and "Indian corn" was sold at a further reduced rate to poorer residents, so long as it was to be used "for Bread" and not sold.[49] The trustees also regulated interest rates for money put out on loan, with six percent the maximum allowed to be charged within the town. In addition, no more than five percent could be charged to the town's poor or to freeholders, but seven percent could be "Lett out upon Interest out of the Corporation." The trustees also lent money, usually to the poor or freeholders.[50]

Kingstonians' prohibitions against usury and other forms of economic behavior were shaped not only by practical economic concerns, but by religious and moral ones as well. The Dutch Reformed of the mid-Hudson Valley, as Christians in the Calvinist tradition, gained their understanding of usury's immorality from minister's injunctions, and from the Old Testament.[51] Those who were in need and of little means should not be charged high interest. However, the corporation mandated that "such persons as are able to let money out themselves, shall not have it unless they pay 8%."[52]

To what degree this legislation was shaped by religious, economic, or social concerns is hard to determine, and perhaps not even a fully useful distinction. The Corporation of Kingston, like the governments of Hurley, Rochester, and other valley towns, enacted some laws that were strictly shaped by their religious beliefs, such as preventing work and travel on the Sabbath. For example, when Kingstons' Mattheu Blanshan was fined six guilders in 1664 it was because she had continued "churning after the second beating of the drum on the Day of Fasting & Prayer." As late as 1773 travelers who journeyed on the Sabbath through Hurley were arrested, brought back to town, "examined by the justice of the peace," and fined eighteen shillings for "Sabbath-breaking."[53]

Other regulations, such as regulating the use and sale of corporation property or prices on various goods, were primarily economic or social. Finally, regulation of interest rates seem to reveal an intersection between religious and social concerns. Most likely, valley residents would not have fully drawn distinctions between the two, since their understanding of such social and economic matters as money-lending or work on Sundays were shaped by, and connected to, their eighteenth-century Christian background and worldview. Likewise, other economic regulations in the mid-valley, from controlling engrossment and preventing price gouging, whether the result of formal legislation or informal social pressure, have to be viewed as some combination of practical public policy as well as religious belief.

Freeholders of the towns of Kingston, Marlborough, and New Paltz appropriated money annually for the support of the poor. Town governments employed two methods when allotting poor relief. First, the trustees distributed food or "necessaries" to freeholders or inhabitants who needed small amounts of relief, although occasionally a small money allowance might be granted instead. So the Kingston Corporation provided freeholder Petrus Dumond, "a poor man in great want and distress . . . , with 3 skipples wheat and some provisions and a couple of shirts." Jacobus Roosa and his family, "much distressed and in want of the necessaries of life," were allotted some Indian corn, ten pounds pork, and ten pounds hogshead.[54]

The second method, although less common, was for indigent residents who were either homeless or sick and unable to care for themselves to be "taken-in" by Kingston freeholders. The corporation paid the family providing the care and supplied provisions as well. For example, in 1739, Andre van Keuren was asked "to keep Anotie Brafs & to give her Good Sufficient Drink Lodging and Washing for One Year" for £5. In 1783, Eskie Vonk was moved into the house of Sara Osterhoudt for "Lodging and Board at the rate twenty pounds per annum."[55]

Although neither the charter nor any town ordinance required residents to take poor or sick neighbors into their homes, most apparently accepted this as their responsibility as freeholders. Residents who refused requests from the town were treated *harshly*. Evidently, Cornelius Brinck refused to board a local child for the corporation, so the trustees ordered "advertised" that they "Disapprove of [Brinck's] behavior by not complying with their order."[56] In a society where personal reputation was paramount, embarrassing public pronouncements of this sort were intended both to punish and dissuade others from behaving the same way.

Nevertheless, authorities made every attempt to control the number of people receiving relief. First, of course, were the traditional warning-outs, preventing potential wards of the poor from settling within the township. Other methods included making sure male residents took responsibility for children they fathered out of wedlock. When Catharina Reghtmeyer "was lately delivered a Bastard Child and that she has sworn Abraham Snyder is the Father," the trustees notified Snyder to make sure "said Child shall not become Chargeable to the Said Town." Grandparents might even be called upon to care for children that parents refused to recognize. Evert Wynkoop was ordered in 1745 to "Indemnify the Town or Trustees from the Maintenance of a Bastard Child . . . formerly laid to his Son Johannis be Delivered up to him."[57]

Finally, many towns expected the poor to work for their relief—either for the town board or a freeholder. New Paltz ordered the poor to "be compelled to work at the rate of 2 shillings per day for an able bodied man, and a shilling per day for a man of less ability of body."[58] Appropriate rates were also set for women, girls, and boys. Furthermore, it was understood that freeholders who cared for the town's poor in their homes would be allowed to employ the labor of those wards around the farm or shop.[59]

During times of economic crisis, town boards forbade the exportation of staple food products, regulated prices and wages, and confiscated essential goods. Although this practice was uncommon in the valley where foodstuffs were generally plentiful, and was far more common in urban areas such as New York City, occasional examples throughout the eighteenth century reveal the underlying belief that communities could impose such economic restrictions on their inhabitants. For example, a feared flour shortage in 1748 convinced Kingston officials to limit the export of this product from the town. Grain, flour, and salt shortages during the War for Independence brought similar responses in Kingston, New Windsor, and Marbletown. In addition, as in urban areas, popular action in the form of crowd actions, salt and grain riots, and popular seizures of necessities occurred throughout rural Ulster County. Although rare before the American Revolution, the number and intensity of these riots increased dramatically *after* 1775 in response to the economic dislocations and deprivations of the war.[60]

Although this type of legislation and behavior has been interpreted by some scholars as resistance to markets, even anticapitalist behavior, there were few overt signs of an antimarket sentiment among mid-valley residents. Hudson Valley residents were small farmers or artisans who were well aware of, and active participants in, the New York City grain trade. Indeed, this economic legislation was often renegotiated during these years by various interests who were promoting their own economic agendas.[61] In the mid-valley, these laws generally attempted to regulate and organize an embryonic market system and to control unrestricted market development.

A CORPORATE SOCIETY

Small rural towns like Kingston, New Paltz, and Rochester depended upon social harmony and political order in order to maintain economic stability and to prosper. Valley communities relied on a variety of social and political institutions in order to achieve this harmony and order. Town government, the political and social responsibilities demanded of freeholders, and the reciprocal economic relations connecting the town's working people, all ensured a sense of stability and balance for these communities. Equally important for providing order in Ulster County towns were social and religious institutions, the shared ethnic heritage of most Ulster residents, and the customs and traditions that bound many valley residents together.

The majority of the Ulster County residents were of Dutch descent, many of whom maintained Dutch as their first language. Kingston, founded by the Dutch, remained predominantly Dutch throughout the eighteenth century, as did many Ulster County communities. Although few Dutch-born settlers migrated to the mid-valley after the 1720s, the area's Dutch population was reenforced by internal Dutch migration from downriver.[62] Even New Paltz, settled originally by French Huguenots, was culturally "Dutch" by the eighteenth century, with more residents of Dutch descent than French. The New Paltz church records, originally kept in French, were recorded in Dutch through most of the eighteenth century. Right through the American Revolution, only two of the seven towns (New Windsor and Hurley) and precincts that composed Ulster County could claim clear English majorities.[63]

The central social and cultural institution in Ulster County communities through the period of the American Revolution were the Dutch Reformed churches. By the 1730s, Kingston had two Dutch churches, and the towns of Marbletown, Hurley, Rochester, and New Paltz, one each. In addition, New Paltz maintained a French Huguenot church, and a German Reformed congregation was located right outside Kingston. Although these churches were not "official" town churches, the long history the Dutch had in the region, and the fact they formed an overwhelming majority of the population, gave residents few alternatives. Membership was not restricted to people of Dutch descent, however, and many English, Germans, and French were communicants and attended services as well.[64]

The influence of these churches went well beyond religious matters and Sunday worship, however, since these churches helped to reinforce and inculcate a Dutch cultural heritage, fostering a sense of commonality and community among town residents. In addition, the churches often combined with political authorities to administer civil and social functions for all town residents, regardless of ethnic background. The duties of the Kingston Reformed church extended into education, public services, and charitable enterprises, as well as conducting marriages, baptisms, and funerals for people of all religious denominations.[65]

In many of these activities, the church coordinated its activities with the Board of Trustees of the Kingston Corporation, and there was much overlap in membership between the board and the Consistory, the local council that supervised church activities. Indeed, the Dutch church in Kingston, like those in other Ulster communities, enjoyed a quasi-official status: the corporation granted the original 1,000 acres to the Consistory for the church building in 1712, as well as funds for construction, and offered generous land and monetary gifts thereafter.[66]

Not only Dutch communicants, but English authorities recognized the considerable power these churches wielded in their small communities, often making them targets of official attempts to "Anglicize" valley towns. Overt religious or cultural challenges to traditional, local Dutch institutions usually met with stiff resistance from valley farmers, however, and even intensified a greater sense of ethnic identity among Dutch residents, further strengthening the bonds of community.[67]

In 1704, the appointment to Kingston of an Anglican minister by the English governor met with rigid opposition from the town. Governor Cornbury was clear and provocative in his intentions, noting that if the Dutch "churches were supply'd with English ministers that would with English schools be a means to make this Colony an English Colony." Cornbury's appointee lasted less than one year, and before the governor could send a replacement, the Kingston Consistory obtained the services of a Netherlands-born and ordained minister, who, with the support of the local community, refused Cornbury's demand to obtain a civil license to preach. Although there were certainly religious issues at stake here, there were clear *cultural* issues as well, with the Kingston Dutch hoping to retain both control over their own community church, as well as over the religious message that would be preached.[68]

While valley towns resisted these and other official challenges to their traditional cultural institutions, the gradual process of "Anglicization" was slowly, yet inexorably, altering Ulster society. Although a clear majority of Ulster residents were of Dutch background, virtually all were third and fourth generation by the mid-eighteenth century. The continued influx of non-Dutch settlers with their own customs and traditions, along with the intermarriage among these newcomers and established residents, and the growing habit of the valley's youth to reject inherited Dutch culture, speak English, and adopt English customs blurred rigid ethnic distinctions. Although a number of Kingston's inhabitants petitioned the Board of Trustees for an English instructor in 1779, "wherein their children may be taught the English tongue," most of these changes occurred imperceptibly over several generations as ethnic newcomers, still less than one-third of the county's population before the American Revolution, blended into valley towns, adopting Dutch ways while contributing new customs as well.[69]

Community order rested not solely on a shared cultural and ethnic heritage, but on a recognized social hierarchy that gave structure and organization to Ulster towns. Although Edward Countryman is correct in his assertion that the Hudson's west bank was a "society of roughly equal men," a handful of prominent and powerful families exerted considerable social, political, and economic influence. Although this group was in no way comparable to east bank landlords, the highest political offices tended to be held by local elites: large landowners, successful merchants, and substantial yeomen.[70]

More often than not, members of the oldest and most prominent families, such as the Hasbroucks, Hardenbergs, and Ellisons, held the most prestigious appointed political offices in the county, such as sheriff; served in the highest elected offices like county supervisor; or were commanders of the local militias. In this hierarchical, deferential society, these "natural leaders," because of family name, education, wealth, or prestige were repeatedly chosen to represent their communities in the larger political world.

The power of these families extended well beyond the political arena, carrying over to the social sphere as well. The Hardenbergs and Hasbroucks and others of similar rank controlled one of Kingston's most powerful community institutions, the Consistory of Kingston's Dutch Reformed church, which was responsible for its day-to-day workings, as well as the hiring of ministers and dominees. In addition, members of this small elite formed the Board of Trustees of the Kingston Academy, attended almost exclusively by children of the town's leading families. The academy was incorporated by the Kingston Corporation, which also granted the school its land and building.[71]

The power and standing of this social class was regularly reenacted for town residents at various community events. The celebration honoring the coronation of King George is a case in point: a carefully constructed ritual in which the hierarchical social order was demonstrated in rich, symbolic detail through parades, toasts, and cannonade. Militia muster days performed similar roles, with the county's leading gentlemen, such as Johannes Hardenberg and Thomas Ellison, dressed in full military regalia, taking their places as commanders at the head of their troops. Even church services were microcosms of the social order of hierarchy and deference that dictated life in such valley communities. Each Sunday leading families took their seats in family-owned front-row pews reminding the rest of the congregation of their power and station. Public demonstration of this nature was probably all the more essential in Ulster County where the difference between local elite and middling farmer was far less pronounced than across the Hudson where a manorial elite maintained political, judicial, and legal powers over tenants.

The cornerstone of this deferential social order, and the basis for the community stability so necessary for rural towns to grow and prosper, was the household. Much like the larger society of which it was a part, the small households that composed eighteenth-century valley towns were not egalitarian institutions. The head of the family was the father, who exerted almost complete legal, political, and social control over his entire household. The household included not only wives and children, both of whom were politically and legally subordinated to their husbands and fathers, but servants, slaves, and some hired help.[72]

If fathers exerted tremendous authority over their families, they were also responsible for significant obligations and responsibilities, most specifically in ensuring that their families were properly cared for, well-housed, and well-ordered. Community standards and local authorities expected fathers to carry out these duties, since failure to do so might have significant ramifications for community order. Although most Ulster parents seem to have fulfilled their obligations, local records are littered with cases involving squabbling husbands and wives, contentious neighbors, and interfering relatives, all of which challenged the desire for social harmony.

What is most striking about early American communities is not the level of contention among neighbors or within families, but that residents had few reservations about regulating the actions of those households that violated community standards and threatened social harmony.[73] These regulations varied from informal neighborhood or family sanctions against offenders, to more official, and severe, fines, arrest, or occasionally, banishment. Criminal actions against persons or property were prosecuted by county courts, but civil offenses were dealt with locally, within communities.

Not only did Ulster authorities exert their powers to regulate the actions of households and individuals in relation to their impact on the community and other residents, but town officials displayed few reservations about intervening *within* families if circumstances warranted. Family and community were so interdependent that, as historian Helena Wall has observed, the "lines between family and community interests were blurred, when they existed at all." Although the institution of marriage and raising a family were private affairs, they were so only to the degree that they did not disturb community order. Arie Matthisen was arrested and banished from Kingston for one year for abusing his wife and children. However, Ulster authorities, like colonial courts generally, were reluctant to encourage divorce, which was viewed as undermining family order and therefore a threat to community stability. Even when Jeronimous Douwersen claimed that his wife did not love him and refused to "serve him as a wife," the Kingston court refused to sanction a separation.[74]

Although town authorities did not encourage divorce, they were prepared to remove children from households mired in poverty. This action certainly had a practical implication for the town since it attempted to avoid future dependents of the poor wardens. In 1746 Marbletown officials threatened to take custody of children of impoverished families and "put them out until they are of age" if their parents "do not put out such children as aforesaid within two months time." New Paltz authorities took similar action in 1773, ordering children of parents having "no visible way of getting an honest livelihood" to be taken from their families and bound out as an apprentice or to a farm. Kingston's Board of Trustees went "to Benj. Swarts In Order to Bind out Some of his Children" in 1769. Marlborough's Town Board went further still, placing a boy named Liba Heurrington under the care of Urian McKey. McKey was to maintain him until age twenty-one with "Drink, washing and Lodging & Reading, writing, & Cyphering."[75]

Although the measures pertaining to family life seem somewhat more intrusive than the ordinances regulating economic and political affairs, in spirit these various forms of legislation shared much in common. Each form of regulation was attempting to uphold an ideal vision of community: one that demanded residents cooperate, avoid contention, maintain stable households, and subordinate their own private interests when they conflicted with the public good. Valley residents were keenly aware that the social reality often did not conform to this ideal vision, however, and hence the need for regulatory measures. If the social stability and economic health of small communities demanded order, harmony, and neighborliness, these towns were ready to promote this type of behavior, regulate the actions of residents to conform to it, and punish those who strayed from the ideal.

CHANGE AND CONTINUITY: 1750–1775

Patricia Bonomi has observed that a "fervent localism" persisted in New York colony longer than most other North American provinces. Few areas in New York could claim towns with a more intense sense of "localism," a greater desire to remain loyal to inherited traditions and customs, or a greater suspicion of outsiders who might threaten this local order than the mid–Hudson Valley. Most residents were of Dutch background and recognized their minority status in a province that was predominantly English, and hence attempted to protect as much of their cultural inheritance as possible. For example, while New York towns with more equal breakdowns in population had adopted the use of English in political, social, and educational institutions, Kingstonians continued to offer Sunday school lessons in Dutch through the 1750s (although services were offered in both Dutch and English), and court records were kept in both Dutch and English until the eve of the American Revolution. In smaller towns like Rochester, Dutch was spoken more frequently than English through the early nineteenth century.[76]

Valley residents' sensitivity to these issues went beyond the use of language and customs; their concern also extended to what they perceived as outside encroachments into local community matters. Attempts by English governors to "Anglicize" churches and schools in the early eighteenth century is a case in point. As late as the 1750s the people of Ulster were still sensitive to provincial officials' attempts to exert authority in local political and judicial affairs. The "Dutch of Esopus [Kingston]" protested the appointment of Mr. Albertson in 1752 as Ulster Sheriff, claiming he was an outsider (non-Dutch) to the community.[77] Nevertheless, these towns, regardless of their desire for some degree of political and cultural autonomy, did not exist isolated from larger provincial-wide institutions and forces. Indeed, far from being static and unchanging, Ulster communities were growing in size and diversifying ethnically, culturally, and economically throughout the eighteenth century.

Diversity also revealed itself in the social and religious sphere *within* town, as Kingston's central social institution, the Dutch Reformed church, became a battleground between residents who wanted the church to remain subordinate to officials in the Netherlands and those who wanted it to be granted a more independent status. A primary concern was the fear among the most conservative Kingston Dutch that one of the last bastions of Dutch culture and heritage, the town church, was threatened. A protracted, two-year battle resolved itself only when the congregation split into two, with many long-time church members refusing to take communion under the new minister.[78]

The growing diversity revealed itself in the political sphere as well. By the 1760s Kingston was no longer the small homogeneous community of 250 or so Dutch farmers it had been in the seventeenth century, but was a bustling town of 1,200 farmers, shopkeepers, and tradesmen of Dutch, English, and French descent. A sizable minority of these residents were not freeholders in the corporation, and were therefore denied both the political representation and the common rights enjoyed by corporation members. Kingstonians recognized that their trustees lacked several important powers necessary for administering this growing port town. The corporation did not possess the power to tax (its primary income came from the sale and rental of corporation land), and lost jurisdiction in criminal court matters in 1753.[79]

The trustees, supported by the town's freeholders, attempted to strengthen the power and autonomy of their town government by applying to the Provincial Council for a new charter in 1753. The corporation hoped to regain criminal jurisdiction within the town, the power to tax, as well as the authority to make bylaws for the entire community, but their request was denied. The trustees renewed their application for a new charter twice more over the next two decades, the final time in 1773, but still with no success.[80]

Other forces also presented challenges to the autonomy of Ulster communities. Although valley residents' lives tended to be shaped by local political and social forces, Ulster County townspeople were also subjects of the British Crown. By the mid-1760s, the developing crisis between England and her colonies had reached into the valley, offering challenges to the political and social order that had characterized town life for several generations.

Finally, beginning around the mid-eighteenth century, the size and the volume of agricultural production and trade, as well as the growing market for consumer goods, reflect growth in the power of larger commercial markets and reveal that the local economic systems that structured life in valley towns could not continue unaffected by these larger external forces.[81] Although the mid-valley had always been an active participant in the Atlantic economy, first in the fur and later in the grain trade, farmers' participation was structured by a variety of social and community concerns, not solely market ones. An examination of this most important component of eighteenth-century rural life—the market activities of farmers, tradesmen, and shopkeepers—reveals much about the economic behavior of valley residents and the economic culture of rural society in the eighteenth century.

CHAPTER THREE

"A Comfortable Subsistence"

RURAL ECONOMIC CULTURE
IN THE EIGHTEENTH CENTURY

From the first years of settlement in the mid–Hudson Valley, Ulster County residents participated in the developing Atlantic market system. This participation, originally centered around the fur trade, grew stronger when the valley moved into agricultural production by the late seventeenth century. This commercial trade brought prosperity to valley farmers through higher prices for their farm produce and larger and more secure markets. In addition, the export trade promoted diversity within the community, developing a service economy that directed its energies toward both local exporters and internal services. Further, long-distance exporting earned the credits and income needed to purchase imported consumer goods, necessary staples not produced locally, household items, and "luxuries."[1]

Nevertheless, long-distance trade was only one component of a thriving local economy that also emphasized household production, and community-oriented trade with neighbors and storekeepers. This local, community-based trade involved the bartering of goods and services among neighbors, friends, or relatives and relied on regular face-to-face contact among participants. Consequently, relations in the local system lacked the more formal character of the export trade, and displayed a greater emphasis on reciprocity between farmers, artisans, small manufacturers, and storekeepers.[2] Local trade was regulated informally by local neighborhood practices and formally by town and provincial authorities. These regulations, whether of prices, trading practices, or quality standards, were tempered by both community concerns as well as the protection of producers.[3]

An exploration of the complementary relationship among long-distance trade, local exchange, and household production provides a better understanding of the significance of these various economic strategies for farming and artisanal families in Ulster County. In addition, an examination of the people who participated in these production and trading systems and the traditions that governed behavior in each produces a fuller understanding of the economic and social behavior of eighteenth-century households, as well as the ways farmers reconciled new commercial opportunities with traditional family and community considerations. Finally, by focusing on these families and the ways they balanced their economic strategies, a more complete picture of the way community demands, as well as market opportunities, structured the economic choices of its inhabitants and how, in turn, community concerns were textured by the needs of residents emerges.

"A Comfortable Subsistence"
THE FAMILY FARM AND
HOUSEHOLD PRODUCTION

In mid-eighteenth century Ulster County, the basic unit of production was the family farm. Although the Hudson's east bank was dominated by a few large estates populated by thousands of tenants, tenantry was not common on the west bank.[4] The majority of mid-eighteenth-century Ulster households were small, freehold farms averaging a little less than 200 acres in size, with the average tenant holding just under 70 acres. Of this, about one-third of the land was available for tillage and probably one-half of this amount remained fallow.[5]

The farm household was, of course, more than just the home; it was also the location where the family produced many of the daily necessities needed to survive. In a period before industrial mass production and sophisticated transportation and marketing systems, early American families produced the food they ate, much of the clothing they wore, and a myriad of other products (soap, candles, furniture, etc.) consumed or used regularly.

Thesis The primary economic goals of eighteenth-century households were to meet annual subsistence needs, increase the comfort level of daily life, accumulate more land, and transmit these legacies to the household's heirs. Farm families combined and alternated a variety of economic strategies in order to accomplish these tasks: engaging in household production, trading with neighbors and friends, market-oriented commercial export, and acquiring imported consumer goods. Most Hudson Valley farmers would have recognized the complementary nature of these strategies and would regularly combine some, or all, of these practices in order to achieve the long-term security of the family farm, enjoy a comfortable living in their old age, and supply their children with personal and real property.[6]

Eighteenth- and nineteenth-century Americans referred to the goal of the interconnected strategies described here as a "comfortable subsistence" or a "comfortable maintenance."[7] Although what connotes a comfortable subsistence is obviously somewhat relative, dependent upon social circumstance as well as economic context, in the years before the market revolution of the nineteenth century and the resulting availability of inexpensive, mass-produced consumer goods, most Hudson Valley families of middling status (and most valley families were of a middling status) shared common economic goals and strategies to meet these goals.[8]

Although one primary objective of the farm family was to achieve self-sufficiency, this did not mean that the family had to produce everything they wore or ate, an improbable and usually impossible task. However, it did mean being able to use effectively all facets of a family's productive capabilities in order to provide for normal yearly needs. At times this meant producing beef, flour, or homespun for family use. At times it meant trading some of these products with neighbors for goods they manufactured or possessed, or selling them in long-distance markets for some extra cash. At other times, it included employing family labor in the fields or on the looms of neighbors, or dealing with the one person who had more of the materials a farm family needed than any other, the local shopkeeper.[9]

Even if the immediate economic goal of eighteenth-century valley farm households was to meet annual subsistence needs, the ultimate economic *goal* of the farm family was the accumulation of more property and wealth. The strategies employed by farm families to meet subsistence needs and accumulate property varied depending on household size, the extent of land holdings, and a family's location in the household life cycle. Although all families focused their immediate attention on meeting their yearly subsistence, younger families devoted a much larger part of their production to this goal. As a family matured and acquired more land and the necessary hands to work the fields, however, they too devoted more of their production toward sale.[10] Few valley farm families, except the poorest, devoted themselves only to subsistence concerns, since a family unable to earn above basic family needs could not hope to pay taxes, purchase goods from storekeepers, or pass property on to their children.

Few Hudson Valley farmers, however, were entrepreneurial in their endeavor to acquire property, at least in the twentieth-century meaning of the term. Too many adverse repercussions awaited the family that was reckless in production or marketing, or risk takers when issues of family subsistence were at stake. By the same token, few families in the valley were opposed to engaging in commerce, seeing it simply as another strategy to accumulate property and avoid dependence on employers, wage labor, or the vagaries of the commercial market.

Under any circumstances, the objective of acquiring more land for family security and future dispersal was not likely to be achieved in one generation, but rather over several. As farm households increased the size of their holdings, cleared larger amounts of land for production, and increased their production for commercial markets, the real wealth of the family increased. Outside of land speculation and mercantile activities, there were few other opportunities for generating property, except for hard work over many years.[11]

Farming in the eighteenth century was a seasonal affair. The busiest time of the year in the Hudson Valley was from mid-spring through early fall, when both men and women could be found working in the fields. The first major agricultural tasks of the year were preparing the freshly thawed soil for planting. Corn was planted around mid-May; oats were sown soon after. Both crops were used primarily for family livestock, although some families may have produced a surplus for sale or trade to neighbors. By mid-May garden crops such as beans and potatoes would be planted as well. By the end of the month, the first wheat crop (planted the previous fall) would already have sprouted, but much of June would require little labor in the fields. Not until July would the family fully begin the laborious, but all-essential, process of mowing and cradling both the wheat and rye crops.[12]

Much of the heavy labor was the result of the farm tools and the methods employed. Hudson Valley farming practices changed little before the nineteenth century. Wheat was still reaped with a sickle, grass cut with a scythe; both were clumsy tasks, tiring and time-consuming.[13] The most common farm implement was the unwieldy Carey plow, a cumbersome wooden frame with a heavy iron share. It required two men and a four- to six-oxen team (or three horses) to plow one to two acres a day.[14] Such tools, used until the last decades of the eighteenth century, were not conducive to large-scale farm production, even if there had been an available labor force.

By late July the grains were usually fully cut, and the process of collection and bundling began. After the grain harvest was complete, available farm hands cut hay and grass, and by September the cyclical process repeated itself as families sowed winter wheat. Even then activities in the fields were not complete, since many Octobers witnessed farmers cutting down the wheat they had so recently sown, fearful "it will grow too large before winter."[15]

Households in the mid–Hudson Valley produced a variety of crops. Wheat and vegetables were used at home and traded with neighbors. Oats and corn went for animal feed, and grain went to markets.[16] In the mid- to late eighteenth century, west bank farmers cultivated approximately 10 acres of grain per family, and produced 102 bushels of wheat and 67 bushels of rye. Most, perhaps even all, farm families supplied *some* portion of their own diet. Over 35 percent of the inventories brought to probate in the period between 1760 and 1790 recorded grain planted in the ground, as well as a variety of other agricultural products usually referred to collectively as the "garden." This proportion remained about one-third through the late 1820s. The proportion of families growing agricultural produce was certainly much higher, since these inventories often underrepresented the amount of grain produced.[17]

Although valley farmers employed hired hands around the farm in the eighteenth century, they were more likely to rely on family labor and the labor of slaves and neighbors. Although spring was devoted to planting and summer and early fall to harvesting, winter gave farm families the chance to complete unfinished jobs, cut and collect firewood, and engage in small, craft-oriented trades, such as producing staves for barrels, in order to earn some extra credits from the local shopkeeper. Although by the late eighteenth century New Englanders were already engaging in a growing amount of outwork production, this was not common in the mid–Hudson valley.

Work on the farm was a family endeavor, with each member of the farm family participating in some capacity. Although both men and women participated in all aspects of farm work, men were more likely to be responsible for work primarily associated with market production while women were responsible for work centered around the household. For example, field work related to planting, harvesting, or threshing, although at certain times combining the labor of both genders, tended to be the domain of males. Conversely, women often dominated the production of textiles and domestic goods. Nevertheless, some aspects of farm life, such as dairying, were carried on fairly equally by both men and women in the preindustrial Northeast.[18] In addition, at least to a certain age, both boys and girls engaged in household work such as spinning. Finally, the distinction between market and household production was not always firm or clear. Very often the only cash earned by a farm family during the course of the year was the produce of women's labor: butter, cheese, and eggs.[19]

Central to the household economy was the labor of children, around the house in the production of homespun, soap, and other household necessities, as well as in the yard and garden, in dairying and tending vegetables, or finally, in the fields planting, plowing, and harvesting. New York's Governor Henry Moore stated in 1767 that "every house swarms with children who are set to work as soon as they are able to spin and card." Jenny Kiersted of Kingston was spinning at the side of her mother at the age of six, while the two sons of Abraham Bevier were working with the New Paltz farmer in his fields in their teenage years.[20] Not paid wages, but expected to work around the farm felling trees, building fences, threshing grain, carting goods to neighbors and market, the labor of children was an essential component of the household economy.

Although children were not paid formal wages, their labor was an investment in their future. Children of farmers and artisans worked under the authority of their parents, knowing they were securing their future inheritance: money, livestock, personal property, and most important, of course, land. Much of the work children engaged in was not only to meet yearly subsistence demands and buy goods from the local shopkeeper, but to build surpluses that would purchase more real or personal property that would one day become theirs.[21]

Putting children to work at an early age had less to do with attempts to instill good work habits or build character; rather, it was more essential for the daily workings of the household. As such, depending upon the present or future needs of the family, a child's labor could be used around the home or "put out" and traded with neighbors. Ulster families routinely sent their young daughters to the homes of neighbors "to spin and weave woolen" in exchange for goods or the labor of a neighbor's farm boys at harvest or planting time. Ginny Plough, daughter of Teunis, was spinning for neighbors at the age of thirteen. Although the labor was being completed outside the home for neighbors, it was part of an intensive system of exchange primarily oriented toward meeting the needs and demands of the farm household, supplying the particular form of labor needed by the household.[22]

Two other forms of labor were employed on eighteenth-century farms that were not part of the family—"free" and "unfree." Some Ulster households boarded a farm laborer who worked side-by-side with family members in the fields or barn, ate meals at the supper table, and slept within the house. Although these workers usually received a wage, they were just as likely to be paid in room and board. These labor relations varied, with some laborers staying with the family for a few days, sometimes weeks or months, or longer.[23]

Also important to eighteenth-century valley farms was the labor of slaves. The types of work slaves and free laborers engaged in, and the general living arrangements, did not substantially differ. Male and female slaves worked as field hands, plowing, planting, and harvesting; as skilled artisans; or around the house in cooking, weaving, and cleaning. The central differences, of course, revolved around control over their own labor and compensation. Unlike free laborers, slaves were the property of their owners and had no legal power to disagree or diverge from their master's demands. Also, slaves' work went unpaid, and unlike children of farm families, their work was not an investment in a future inheritance. Although some valley slaves were granted their freedom in their owners' will, they were far more often bequeathed to a grantee's child. Those who were freed usually received inconsequential grants of personal property.[24]

The household not only grew crops, feed, and vegetables, but produced most of their own textiles and domestic products. In the rural Hudson Valley, like many areas in the preindustrial Northeast, textile production was centered in the home. One contemporary noted in 1767 that "the custom of making coarse cloths in private families prevails throughout the entire province, and almost in every house a sufficient quantity is manufactured for the use of the family."[25] The regular appearance of textile and dairy implements in the probate inventories supports this observation and points to a thriving home manufacturing system. During the second half of the eighteenth century, almost 80 percent of the Ulster County inventories contained a spinning wheel and over 50 percent record dairy producing implements. In the same period, looms were possessed by about fifty percent of Ulster households (see Table 3.1).

The extent of this household production system can be measured by comparing it to Maine in the same period. Laurel Ulrich's examination of inventories in the Kennebec Valley reveals that 60 percent of inventories recorded spinning wheels, as compared to almost 80 percent in the mid–Hudson Valley. In addition, a mere 25 percent of these New England households possessed a loom, half the proportion in the valley.[26]

Even with this well-developed home manufacturing system, families produced only a portion of these goods for market sale. Although Governor Moore claimed that domestic production thrived in rural New York, he quickly added that valley farm families had no "design of sending any of it to market," or for that matter, importing textiles from outside the local community. Richard Smith

TABLE 3.1

Ownership of Textile-Dairy-Producing Equipment Ulster County, 1760–1791

	1760–1775	1776–1791
Wool	00.0 lbs.	40.9 lbs.
Looms	0%	50.9%
Spinning wheels	44.0%	79.2%
Cows	3.6	5.7
Churns	88.0%	50.9%
Milktubs	55.0%	39.6%
Total inventories	9	53

Source: Probated Inventories of Ulster County, 1760–1791.

saw little evidence of store-bought fabrics on his journey through the valley in 1769, noting that all of the children he saw in the mid–Hudson Valley were "clad in homespun, both linen and woolen." Benjamin Brink argued that the people of his hometown, North Kingston, were "almost entirely clad in garments home-spun and made" through the 1780s.[27] These rural farm families produced surplus homespun primarily to trade with neighbors for goods they needed but did not produce. As late as the 1830s, Ulster County farmers brought their wool and flax to local carding and fulling mills, but their wives and daughters would still spin and weave it in the home.[28]

Even if few of these goods produced by rural farm families were destined for long-distance markets, the high proportion of textile implements reveals the importance of this production. For example, spinning was the most family-oriented of the household tasks since it was often done by all family members, including young children. Families often traded home-produced textiles, or the labor involved in such processes, with neighbors.[29]

About 20 percent of the trading partners of Jacobus Cole engaged in some spinning to earn credits from the Marbletown tailor. For some families, spinning was the only method used to obtain credits. Marbletown's Anthony Crispell entered into twenty-two transactions with Cole, settling his accounts through "spinning flax," "spinning and twisting flax," or simply "spinning." In the eighteenth-century world of New York farmers, families needed to engage in production of this nature in order to maintain their independence in an increasingly competitive economic system.[30]

However, if the ultimate goal of household production was self-sufficiency, other means had to be employed in order to earn the extra money that would allow valley farmers to purchase goods from shopkeepers, pay taxes, and accumulate more real and personal property. An exploration of the various means through which households earned extra money further reveals eighteenth-century economic culture.

MERCHANTS, FARMERS, AND LONG-DISTANCE TRADE

> The Staple Commodity of the Province is Flower and Bread which is sent to all parts of the West Indies. . . . We send likewise a considerable quantity of Pork, Bacon, Hogshead Staves, some Beef Butter and a few Candles to the West Indies . . . we yearly send Wheat and Flower to Boston and Road Island as well as to South Carolina. . . .[31]

As Governor Colden's above report reveals, as early as the first decades of the eighteenth century, New York exported a variety of agricultural products to other areas within the British Empire. What the governor's report does not reveal is that the area most responsible for this production, and central to New York's economic growth, was the rich, fertile farmland of the Hudson River Valley. The thriving export trade in barrel staves, wood, and most especially, surplus wheat and flour, fueled not only the economic development of New York City, which has been well documented, but that of the valley as well. This trade in turn stimulated the emergence of related service industries, creating a demand for day laborers and small manufacturers that contributed to the region's economic diversity. In addition, long-distance exchanges enabled Ulster County residents to acquire a variety of consumer goods and manufactured goods produced outside the valley.

Long-distance trade tended to be commercial trade, conducted through formal arrangements between farmers on the one hand, and shopkeepers or city merchants, or their agents, on the other. For valley farmers, selling their goods downriver usually meant dealing with unknown customers eighty miles away. Therefore, they conducted their affairs in a businesslike manner that emphasized a rational calculation of costs and profits, cash payments, interest charges, and the generally prompt settling of accounts.[32]

This evidence reveals that eighteenth-century New York farmers were, like their Massachusetts and Pennsylvania counterparts, active participants in the Atlantic market system.[33] However, in the late seventeenth and early eighteenth centuries, farmers still shipped only a small portion of the agricultural goods produced in these Hudson Valley farms into long-distance markets.[34] This does not mean that Ulster County lay outside Hudson River transport routes. In fact, merchants in the mid–Hudson River Valley cultivated close ties to powerful New York City merchants such as William Bayard and Oliver DeLancey. These downriver merchants dealt regularly in international markets and supplied the foreign goods and credit Ulster County shopkeepers like Benjamin Snyder and Thomas Ellison needed to carry on their local businesses. In addition, the downriver merchants purchased the agricultural produce that local storekeepers gathered from the farm population.[35]

Still, a number of factors contributed to limiting the extent of economic exchange between Ulster and commercial centers. Although Ulster County was rich in fertile agricultural land and lay on one of the largest natural transportation systems in North America, primitive transportation and communications systems hindered large-scale commercial development. In the mid-eighteenth century, two sloops made voyages back and forth between New York City and Kingston about every other week during the spring and fall, but their runs were irregular and sporadic. Although the wealthy Ellison family of New Windsor owned a sloop and made regular runs downriver to the city, North Kingston sent a sloop to New York City only five times a year during the 1770s.[36] In addition, internal limitations on transporting goods within the valley placed structural restrictions on getting produce to a river port. Poor roads, high costs, and great distance from ports increased difficulties for farm families hoping to bring their goods to market.[37]

Nevertheless, during the course of the eighteenth century, the mid–Hudson Valley became increasingly integrated into the Atlantic trade network. With the cessation of Queen Anne's War in 1713, New York embarked on a period of sustained economic growth. Although furs from New York had always been in demand, it was the rise of a variety of staple products, such as wheat, corn, and lumber, coupled with the growing population within the North American colonies and increasingly bad European harvests that provided incentive to New York merchants to immerse themselves more fully in the transatlantic trade network. Because of New York's unfavorable balance of trade with England, merchants were forced to find other trade outlets and branched off into the coastal trade and the Caribbean market. In addition, secondary items such as flaxseed, potash, and staves turned substantial profits for merchants and the farmers who produced them. Also, war and military expenditures added significantly to the development of the New York economy, as New Yorkers supplied and outfitted several military expeditions and became a veritable breadbasket for British and colonial troops.[38]

New York City merchants sent wheat to New England in exchange for fish and other products that then made their way to the Mediterranean in exchange for bills of credit. More often, though, New Yorkers sent their wheat and flour to the West Indies or the Carolinas in return for sugar, cotton, and rice that was quickly re-exported to England. By the eve of the American Revolution, 40 percent of New York's exports were produced in the colony, up from only 10 percent in the early eighteenth century, revealing both the growth in market production within the colony, and the colony's expanded role in the larger Atlantic market system.[39]

Ulster County was one of the leading grain-producing regions of New York, and this trade promoted increased economic activity within the county's towns. Ulster farmers had several options for marketing their surplus crops to the city. Some dealt with an ambitious group of "lesser merchants" from New York City who combed the countryside buying and contracting grain from farm populations throughout the city's hinterland. Larger, commercial farmers bypassed this method by hiring their own sloops to deal directly with city merchants. Most Kingston farmers, however, could not afford this method, tending to trade surplus produce with local storekeepers who also acted as retailers for the local population.[40]

One of these storekeepers was Benjamin Snyder of North Kingston. Snyder's account books offer a revealing picture of life in the mid–Hudson River Valley in the 1760s and 1770s. Snyder kept a store that served the community and a sloop that transported local produce to New York City and brought consumer goods into town. Snyder's own career reveals the complexity of life in eighteenth-century rural New York. A captain in the militia, a position of considerable respect in this hierarchical, class-conscious society; merchant; and sloop owner, Snyder was also a surveyor, legal consultant, tavern keeper, banker, and seven-term trustee of the Kingston Corporation.[41]

Snyder, who lived for ninety-one years (1742–1833), left three account ledgers detailing the workings of his business in the years 1768 through 1795. One book, the most useful, has a complete account of his transactions for the years 1774 through 1776.[42] In fact, many of these accounts continue into the mid-1790s, when they were settled. Snyder's account book reveals that he transacted business with seventy-one customers during these three years.

In another section of this volume, Snyder kept track of the transactions of his sloop trips. This useful account records the produce he carried out of North Kingston in 1774 and 1775, and what he brought in from New York City in 1774. By supplementing this source with other records Snyder kept, we can reconstruct fairly completely the types and amounts of produce North Kingston farmers sent to New York. Also, we can partially reconstruct what these farmers imported into town via Snyder's sloop. By comparing these two accounts with a third book of Snyder's, an account book covering the period 1768 through 1795, we can determine the amount of goods being sold at his store, what percentage of these were locally produced, and what percentage were imported from a distance.

Snyder carried on a healthy trade between North Kingston and New York City. Although he was more than a shopkeeper, he was something less than a large-scale merchant. He dealt in no international traffic and his business concerns centered primarily around his small hometown. In 1775, he transported £1,400 of wheat and flour out of town destined for the New York City market. In addition, he exported £890 of butter. For a relatively small town, the population of North Kingston was approximately 750, this was a fairly substantial amount of trade and reveals the extensive agricultural production of the Hudson River Valley. A closer reading of this account book, however, focusing on the customers who sold and purchased goods through Snyder, forces us to reexamine certain assumptions about New York farmers and their market orientation.

Catharine Osterhout was involved in eighty-one transactions with Snyder from 1774 through 1777. In 1774, to balance her £15 18s of debits for purchases from the merchant, she sold Snyder some £15 3s worth of wheat and butter. In

1775, with debits of £9, she brought Snyder £10 of wheat. In 1776 she balanced and closed her account with £1 4s in cash. Osterhout's high proportion of agricultural credits was not typical of most of Snyder's customers in 1774, who averaged 60 percent of their credits in the form of agricultural goods. In 1775, this proportion increased to a full two-thirds of the payments Snyder's customers offered in return for salt, sugar, rum, and other items.

In 1774, 25.9 percent of Snyder's credits were in the form of some service for Snyder or a third-party customer who had accounts with Snyder. These third-party transactions fulfilled an important purpose in the small provincial community, as they did in many similar towns in early America. Although all of these transactions were given a monetary value and calculated in cash terms in Snyder's books, there was very little cash actually available or used to make purchases or pay bills. In 1774, only 7.4 percent of the total value of purchases at Snyder's store, a mere £19 7s, were paid in the form of cash (see Table 3.2). Over the next two years this small percentage remained essentially unchanged. However, there was one commodity that these farm and artisan families had plenty of: their own labor. Although labor needs and demands were seasonal and sporadic, they often fulfilled the needs of this cash-starved society. As Fred Anderson has observed for eighteenth-century Massachusetts, the debts and credits that the residents in small rural communities accumulated "often represented work contracts—promises to deliver productive effort at the future point when it would be required."[43]

Adam Short was one of Snyder's regular customers. Short paid for his purchases by occasionally working for Snyder, repairing his boat and helping to "crewe the sloop." In 1775, Short was involved in eleven transactions with Sny-

TABLE 3.2

PROPORTIONS OF SNYDER ACCOUNTS WITH
CREDITS IN VARIOUS CATEGORIES, 1774–1776

TYPE OF CREDIT	1774	1775	1776
Agricultural	64.0%	66.6%	51.6%
Service	25.9	25.0	31.4
Miscellaneous	2.3	0	7.7
Cash payment	7.4	8.3	6.9
Total credits	£256 18s	£251 0s	£70 12s

Source: Snyder Account Book, 1774–1777, NYHS.

der, purchases valued at £7 17s. Over 88 percent (£6 19s) of these were of local items, such as flax, stockings, and cloth. Only 11 percent (18s) were spent on goods that Snyder imported to North Kingston from outside markets, particularly rum and salt.[44] As Snyder's accounts reveal, Short typified his customers. The trade of North Kingston was, as late as the 1770s, primarily local. In 1774, almost 80 percent of the goods purchased by Snyder's customers were locally produced, with the remaining products coming from long-distance markets. The local goods valued £122 5s, compared to the mere £31 1s of long-distance goods. Over the next three years, the amount of local trade grew even larger. Snyder's trade more than doubled in 1775, with locally produced goods supplying the bulk at 80.9 percent. In 1776 and 1777, with wartime restrictions hindering Snyder's business, local goods accounted for over 80 percent of his trade (see Table 3.3).

Snyder's sloop ledger offers evidence of the total amounts of goods produced in the community but exchanged outside of the local market. This ledger, complete only for the year 1775, details Snyder's dealings with twenty-one farmers. These customers were among the seventy-one with whom Snyder conducted business in his regular store account book. This ledger reveals the extent to which North Kingston farmers produced goods for long-distance markets. These farmers produced an average surplus for long-distance exchange of some 15.1 bushels of wheat, 4.4 barrels of flour, and 58.2 pounds of butter (see Table 3.4).

By comparing Snyder's sloop ledger to his store account book, we get some sense of what type of farmers were likely to produce surplus goods for long-distance trade. In 1775, the fifty farmers who did not send goods into the long-distance market averaged £2 9s in credits at Snyder's store. The twenty-one who did make use of Snyder's sloop runs averaged significantly more, some £6 14s per customer. In addition, these twenty-one customers,

TABLE 3.3

PROPORTION OF LOCAL VS. NONLOCAL PURCHASES
IN SNYDER'S ACCOUNTS, 1774–1776

	1774	1775	1776
Local	79.7%	80.9%	84.1%
Nonlocal	20.3	19.1	15.9
Total purchases	£153 6s	£325 1s	£63 13s

Source: Snyder Account Book, 1774–1777, NYHS.

only 29 percent of Snyder's total customers for the year, purchased 77.5 percent of the total value of goods sold at his store that year.

Closer examination of these twenty-one farmers reveals the proportion of their long-distance trade. Looking again at Catharine Osterhout, the accounts show that in 1775 Osterhout sold £87 of wheat (about twenty-five bushels) through Snyder. Twenty-two bushels (£77), fully 88 percent of the wheat Osterhout exchanged that year, was traded via the sloop destined for New York City. Osterhout also exchanged forty-six pounds of butter (some £29 9s) with Snyder. However, none of the butter she produced that year was traded locally through his store: all was shipped on his sloop destined for long-distance markets. Once again, Osterhout, although not typical of the majority of Snyder's customers, was typical of those who traded in long-distance markets. In 1775, Snyder's sloop customers traded £890 4s of butter with him, but only 10 percent of this was marketed through his regular store account book, destined for local markets. Almost £800, 89.2 percent of the total butter they traded, was recorded in his sloop records to be sent to New York City or other destinations. Seventy-one percent of the flour and 92 percent of the wheat these twenty-one farmers produced was shipped to New York City on one of Snyder's five sloop runs that year (see Table 3.4).

By comparing these customers to the fifty who did not use Snyder's ship, we get a better sense of the extent of production for long-distance markets in North Kingston. The twenty-one sloop patrons produced almost 98 percent of the total value of wheat traded through Snyder's store in 1775, and about 97 percent of the flour. Even if we consider only the products traded locally, the long distance market producers clearly dominated, accounting for almost 80 percent of the wheat and 91 percent of the flour (see Table 3.5).

These twenty-one sloop customers directed more productive energy toward the market than did their neighbors. Their aggregate purchases were twice the value of their counterparts, and, of the little cash that changed hands in Snyder's store that year, these twenty-one farmers spent 59.4 percent of it. Although less than 30 percent of Snyder's total customers, these market-oriented farmers produced about 90 percent of all the agricultural goods recorded in Snyder's books, and an overwhelming amount of this was destined for long-distance markets.

By contrast, of course, over 70 percent of Snyder's customers produced no apparent surplus for long distance trade, although they engaged regularly in small-scale, local exchanges. In North Kingston, local market exchanges directed the activities of many farmers. These farmers purchased or traded for goods produced primarily in the community and rarely participated in the more commercially oriented long-distance trade. Although there was a significant amount of long-distance trade, many farm families in North Kingston were able to meet their yearly needs through exchange with neighbors and home production.

TABLE 3.4

Proportion of Produce Destined
for Local vs. Extra-local Trade
Snyder's Sloop Customers, 1775

Product	Local (%)	Extra-local (%)	Total
Wheat	8.2	91.8	£1,207 12s
Flour	29.0	71.0	171 15s
Butter	10.8	89.2	890 4s

Source: Snyder Account Book, 1774–1777, and Snyder Sloop Records.

TABLE 3.5

Local Trade in 1775, Sloop and Regular Customers
Snyder Accounts, Saugerties, New York

Product	Sloop patrons (%)	Local patrons (%)	Total
Wheat	97.9	2.1	£1232 13s
Flour	97.2	2.8	176 11s
Cash	59.4	40.6	20 17s
Service	93.4	6.5	63 0s

Source: Snyder Account Book, 1774–1777, and Snyder Sloop Records, 1775, NYHS.

The mercantile accounts of other valley shopkeepers support this analysis of Snyder's accounts. Consider the case of Jarman Pick. From 1729 until his death in 1741, Pick operated a store in Kingston. From 1762 through 1798, Jarman's son William operated a store of his own, but had by then relocated to Marbletown. Located on the Rondout Creek, an inlet of the Hudson, Marbletown had a population of 1,164 in 1782. The account book begins again in 1826, still in Marbletown, but after two years William once again closed the store.

During the 1760s, more than one-fourth of Pick's credits were in the form of agricultural goods produced by Marbletown farmers. For the most part, the goods traded were wheat, rye, flour, butter, and occasionally apples. In the 1770s, agricultural goods remained a significant portion of the payments Pick's customers offered in return for rum, sugar, indigo, chocolate, and other purchases.

A typical purchase of Marbletown artisans and laborers might include these items and such necessities as flour, eggs, salt, or wood. In the 1760s, about one-third of Pick's credits were in the form of some service for Pick or a third party who had accumulated more credits then debits in Pick's books. Less than half of Marbletown residents' purchases were in the form of cash, and this decreased even further, to less then 40 percent during the first half of the 1770s (see Table 3.6).

Much like their neighbors in North Kingston, Marbletown residents engaged overwhelmingly in local, neighborhood trade. Almost 85 percent of the goods Marbletown residents purchased from William Pick in the 1760s were locally produced, primarily wheat, rye, flour, leather, homespun cloth, yarn, eggs, and butter. During the 1770s, Pick's sales of local goods continued to dominate: less then 20 percent of his customers' purchases were of goods produced outside

TABLE 3.6

PROPORTIONS OF PICK ACCOUNTS
WITH CREDITS IN VARIOUS CATEGORIES
MARBLETOWN, 1762–1775

TYPE OF CREDIT	1762–1769 (n=31)	1770–1775 (n=23)
Agricultural	26.1%	35.8%
Service	32.2	24.7
Cash	41.5	39.2
Total	£44 3s	£15 14s

Source: Account Book of Jarman and William Pick, *1729–1826,*
Marbletown, New York, NYHS.

TABLE 3.7

PROPORTION OF LOCAL VS. NONLOCAL PURCHASES IN PICK ACCOUNTS
MARBLETOWN, 1762–1775

	1762–1769 (n=31)	1770–1775 (n=23)
Local	84.9%	81.3%
Nonlocal	15.0	18.6
Total	£126 8s	£41 17s

Source: Account Book of Jarman and William Pick, *NYHS.*

the area, such as tea, sugar, molasses, earthenware, teapots, and other household items. Unfortunately, because Pick did not systematically record the amounts of produce his customers brought to him (he often bulked together all of the goods in a particular transaction), it is impossible to examine how much of this might have been destined for outside markets.

Thus, while some valley farmers were active participants in commercial trading systems, others oriented their trade primarily toward small-scale, community exchange. However, even the produce of local traders ultimately made its way to larger, commercial markets, since shopkeepers traded many of the goods they accumulated from the myriad of small exchanges downriver to New York City. In this way, small producers were not out of the market as much as indirectly dealing with it, revealing the extent to which market considerations were at work even in the local bartering between shopkeepers and farmers.

For example, New Windsor shopkeeper Thomas Ellison was kept apprised of the shifts in the New York City market through a voluminous correspondence with his son Thomas Jr. The elder Ellison owned a mill and ground the grains of his New Windsor neighbors, which he either purchased from them or exchanged for goods they needed from his store. The shopkeeper held on to this grain until he could get the best market price downriver.

Although Ellison kept a close eye on the city market, it is not clear that many of his customers did. While storekeepers regularly followed the ebb and flow of market prices and the dearness or scarcity of the goods being traded, many valley farmers rarely followed fluctuations in the market, but, as one local shopkeeper lamented, "fixed" their price "by custom."[45] As long as market prices hovered above seasonal ones, however, few problems would result since farmers would receive their customary price, and the merchant could still sell downriver at a profitable market price.[46]

Nevertheless, Ulster shopkeepers had to walk a fine line in these dealings with their customers. On the one hand, shopkeepers dealt with city merchants who were commercially oriented and attempting to get the best produce at the lowest price. On the other hand, valley store owners lived within communities where concerns other than commercial profit were often prominent, and maintaining good relations with their farm neighbors and customers often meant that they could not engage in the same type of entrepreneurial activity that characterized the lives of their city counterparts. Although shopkeepers and farmers might haggle over prices, shipping costs, or quality standards, both groups were enmeshed in a network of reciprocal relations that, especially at the local level, were not exclusively commercial in character.

Shopkeepers who always attempted to get the best deal in their exchanges with their neighbors, or who had a habit of overcharging customers or withholding staple goods from sale in order to raise prices and their profits, were viewed suspiciously and perceived as unneighborly. The Ellisons are once again a case in point. Members of Ulster County's elite, and the leading merchants of New Windsor, this family controlled the export and import market of this small town. However, they were repeatedly the object of accusations of engrossment and price gouging. These accusations grew more pronounced during the 1770s culminating in a series of dramatic food riots and crowd seizures at the merchant's store in 1776.[47]

LOCAL EXCHANGE AND COMMUNITY TRADE SYSTEMS

Even as long-distance trade links grew in importance through the mid-eighteenth century, residents continued to rely on a system of local exchange to meet many of their needs. Household production supplemented the town's export economy and sustained an important community-oriented trading network that linked the various agricultural, service, and mercantile sectors in a web of interdependence. Throughout the eighteenth century, farmers and artisans operating within complementary systems of small-scale production and trade remained the most important source of locally purchased food, farm tools, manufactured goods, textiles, and household furnishings. Thus, despite access to downriver markets, Ulster County residents' economic identities and orientations continued to be shaped by their dealings within their communities.

The long-distance and local exchange networks were not mutually exclusive, many farmers engaged in both types of trade, and each was critical to the economic well-being of the town. Nevertheless, the two systems served distinct functions in the valley's economy. While the export trade provided farmers with access to the profitable New York City market, local trade was an important means of making up deficits with neighbors and shopkeepers, and often, of exchanging seasonal labor. Furthermore, the community-based network enabled families to obtain locally produced goods that they could not furnish for themselves.

Besides serving distinct functions, long-distance trade and local trade involved different sets of economic relations, and the rules governing the behavior of the participants in each of the systems varied accordingly. Long-distance trade was more formal and businesslike than local exchange and usually involved cash payments. Those who sold commercially generally did so to earn higher profits than could be earned locally. By contrast, local exchange satisfied different needs and worked under strikingly different rules of behavior then did long-distance trade.[48] In addition, local trade was regulated by both neighborhood standards and by town authorities. Revolving around exchange with neighbors, local trade systems were tempered by a variety of community concerns and incurred significant social obligations. Practices that were viewed as good business when selling produce to New York City, such as withholding grain from the market if the price was too low, were criticized as forestalling and hoarding if they happened locally between village neighbors.[49]

In addition, attempting to get the best market price for one's produce, essential when dealing in long-distance networks, was viewed as exploitative when dealing with neighbors. Hoping to make a profit when trading with neighbors or relatives made little sense in an economy where one would very likely depend upon these same trading partners for other items or goods in the near future. This type of behavior might gain short-term advantages, but it almost certainly hurt the family's long-term reputation as a trustworthy trading partner. The social repercussions of such behavior could be even worse, such as being shunned by neighbors when attempting to trade in the future. Local economic behavior, unlike long-distance trade, was not conducted in an impersonal market. Thus social settings, personal relations, family and personal reputation, and even economic needs and demands that could not be met through commercial markets, all mitigated against "antisocial" economic behavior.[50]

In small preindustrial communities like Kingston or New Paltz, exchange of goods and services was absolutely essential to supplying all of the needs of the farm family. A few examples of this type of trade will illustrate the kind of exchanges that were common in eighteenth-century rural New York. Some of these transactions can best be described as barter, the exchange of tools, goods, or labor between two parties.

Jacobus Bush traded a skipple of buckwheat with shopkeeper William Pick in 1767 in exchange for a pint of rum. Both items were valued at 4s by Pick, who recorded the transaction in his store book. Petrus Hendricks, a Kingston carpenter, traded one pig "4 wks old" and "1/4 mutton weight" (together valued at 7s) for one bushel of wheat with Daniel Osterhoudt.[51] Pick and Osterhoudt, who entered dozens of exchanges of this nature, were not alone. One Kingston weaver settled 20 percent of his transactions during the 1770s through barter, the exchange of fabric he had woven for goods his customers possessed. Kingston shoemaker John Masten regularly repaired shoes for his customers in exchange for flour or rum.[52] Millowner G. N. Phillips in Phillipsburgh routinely accepted wool or grain in exchange for carding the wool of local farm women.[53]

Like goods, labor, because of its short supply yet vital importance, was exchanged often in eighteenth-century Ulster County. Adam Snyder was involved in eleven transactions with William Pick between the years 1762 and 1798. Snyder paid for his purchases from the Marbletown shopkeeper by performing a variety of day labor jobs, particularly "mowing hay." George Minteny "worked in the field 10 days," while Abraham Newkirk settled his accounts with Pick through "work in the cornfield."[54]

Often, a customer employed a particular skill in the exchange. Kingston shoemaker James Paul paid for his £4 3s of purchases from a local shopkeeper in 1790 by "shoe work."[55] All of the exchanges between Marbletown's Jacobus Cole and Johanis Suyland revolved around their specific skills. Cole, a tailor, mended and sewed for Suyland, a shoemaker, who paid for his services through "making shoes," "mending," and finally, "resoleing [sic]" the shoes. More often, a skill was employed to obtain specific goods. Cole did some tailoring for Jacob Brinck in return for thirteen pounds of sugar, and worked for Cornelius Cole in exchange for "1 bsh Indian corn" and "4 yards cloth."[56] Occasionally, the skill was employed to earn credits for future purposes, as was the case with Maria Hommel, or to pay for past purchases, as was the case of Marytie Rosa, in their dealings with Ben Snyder. Hommel earned £3 4s for "spinning and weaving" for the North Kingston storekeeper in 1775, and Rosa received £20 "For Spinning" in 1783, balancing her ten-year outstanding debits.[57]

Exchanges like those recorded above were essential in agricultural America in order for each household to obtain the goods needed to survive and prosper. Moreover, each of the exchanges recorded above were of goods and services that could not be supplied by any one person. Only through a variety of exchanges could the people of eighteenth-century Ulster County satisfy all of the requirements of daily living. Naturally, this trade, because of the variety of needs involved, grew more complex as it involved a variety of trading partners.

Third-party transactions were common in the Hudson Valley and in fact fill the store ledgers of the county's merchants. Early American farm families could not produce everything they needed, so exchange was essential to the internal economy of the community. In a society where men and women devoted much of their time to maintaining a domestic economy and supplying themselves with goods and services that they could neither produce nor buy with cash, exchanging with a variety of partners made good economic and social sense.

In order to get a sense of the extent of this type of exchange of labor services, it would be useful to examine a series of these exchanges that Marbletown merchant William Pick recorded in his account book. Roeloff Eltinge was involved in thirty-one transactions with Pick between 1767 and 1773. In 1767, Eltinge took his choice of four sheep from Pick, valued at 4s each, and in return, was required to supply "one pound of good wool for each year, the value of 2s" to the merchant. In 1767, Eltinge supplied Pick with the agreed upon one pound of wool. In 1768, over seven separate transactions, Eltinge purchased 7s worth of goods, some leather, wood, and sugar, yet he offered no wool. In 1769 he purchased goods valued at 9s, but still offered no wool. Not until 1770, after thirteen more purchases at the merchant's store, and still no wool from Eltinge, did he and Pick come to a new understanding. Eltinge then worked several days, valued at £1/12s, harvesting for Pick in the fields of Adam Keator, who had built up several pounds of credit in his transactions with Pick. In 1773, Eltinge supplied Pick with £3 in "flax and cash," and in 1774, balanced and closed his account with some 6s of cash.[58]

Local residents not only earned credits in the form of day labor or harvest work, but they also employed their own skill or trade to obtain other goods. Peter Osterhout, for example, entered into forty-six transactions with Pick between 1764 and 1782. Of all his purchases, about 95 percent (£6 3s), were of local goods, mainly flour, butter, firewood, and the like. Only 6s, less than 5 percent of his purchases, were of goods imported from outside the central valley: 1s of rum in 1765 and 5s of tobacco and rum in 1770. Osterhout was a weaver by trade and employed his craft for credits from Pick. In 1765, he wove some fabric for Pick, possibly the fulled and spun wool from Eltinge, and received £1 in credits. In 1766, he did the same for an additional 3s. After another few shillings of credit over the next few years, he wove fabric in 1782 for which he received some £2 in credits. Osterhout's weaving, like Eltinge's labor and Keator's farm products, could probably command the best prices only from Pick, who had a variety of local customers, and therefore skills and products from which to draw.[59]

Most local exchange was for the immediate use of the household or for neighbors. There was little need for cash in many of these exchanges, and indeed, cash rarely appeared in accounts because of deep suspicion of the medium. In an economy where cash was scarce, direct barter or nonfluctuating prices recorded as credits in daybooks were far more understandable and reliable to a family farmer. Indeed, even Kingston Corporation officials preferred goods over cash. Many were like the town clerk Christopher Tappen who, in 1780, "agreed to be paid as last year in wheat." Perhaps a result more than a goal, these local exchanges built stronger community attachments in a society that put high value on generally harmonious relationships among neighbors.[60]

Ultimately an important question needs to be addressed: Were there two types of farmers in the Hudson Valley, acquisitive market producers who participated in long-distance trade, and more communitarian local traders? Although there were certainly some farmers who existed on both ends of this spectrum, most farmers would not have viewed their economic activities in such mutually exclusive terms, since at different points in their economic lives farmers in the mid-valley were likely to engage in both types of activities, and certainly farmers of means routinely engaged in both types of trade.

However, aggressive marketing of farm produce was, much like most forms of marketing in the twentieth century, risky business. There were advantages and disadvantages to consigning farm produce to Ben Snyder, much like there was in simply renting space on his sloop in order to sell to a New York consignment merchant. Some of those who sold on consignment did so to capture the reward of taking the risk involved in selling at New York City instead of locally: They were attempting to get a better price for their goods and were taking a chance in order to do so. Many of those who traded to the New York City market with Ben Snyder were farmers who could take the risks involved in selling and consignment, who had significant amounts of butter and wheat to sell, and as revealed from their purchases at the merchant's store, had extra cash on hand.

On the other hand, the average farmer in North Kingston used half the amount of cash as those who consigned their goods, and were clearly less affluent than those who took certain market risks. The Snyder accounts reveal that these farmers had less to sell, possessed less cash, and could probably not routinely afford to take chances. Although extra cash or credits in Snyder's account book must certainly have been appealing to these farm families, other concerns (such as present family needs, future security, and demands of neighbors) were equally important when contemplating market decisions. In any case, these should not be viewed as mutually exclusive decisions but various parts of larger economic strategies farm families routinely engaged in during the course of the year. The farmer who dealt primarily in local trade with Snyder was making just as much a market decision as one who consigned large amounts of goods. Farmers were aware of the risks and opportunities inherent in both types of trade, and made their decisions accordingly.

The evidence from the mercantile accounts reveals that some farm families were, by the nature of their economic condition, simply unable to participate in commercial trade, were either too poor or economically unstable, had limited resources and even less surplus. By the limited production they engaged in, they were left outside of the commercial networks that developed around them. However, most farming families in the central valley were in economic conditions that allowed them the opportunity to engage in local or long-distance trade. Although many of these families might be occasionally restricted by high carrying costs, limited available transportation, and seasonal constraints, the New York City market was available to them. For them, the commercial market of long-distance trade was simply another, albeit riskier, strategy in the ongoing goal of satisfying familial needs and long-term security demands. It was this very risk, however, that often persuaded farmers to rely on more secure, if less profitable, local markets.

Ultimately, the most persuasive explanation for the economic behavior of Hudson Valley residents is that decisions about production and trade were just as often shaped by practical social and family concerns as by market opportunities. Regardless of the specific channels through which individuals chose to trade their goods, exchanges were made with the goal of earning credits, goods, cash, or labor services that would allow families to subsist, acquire imported consumer goods, accumulate land, and transmit legacies to their children. When farmers made choices about where and how to market their products, they did so with these goals in mind, informed by their perceptions of the potential benefits and liabilities that each trading system held for achieving their desired ends.

Throughout the eighteenth century, even as commercial markets grew in strength, valley residents continued to balance and alternate their commercial trade with household production and exchanges within their communities. The opportunity for realizing profits in the expanding marketplace was merely one consideration, along with community concerns, obligations to neighbors, and household and family demands, that structured and influenced the economic choices and trading practices of valley farm families.

Down the Hudson to West Point, 1861

painting by Charles Herbert Moore
oil on canvas, 19 1/2 by 29 3/4 inches

printed with permission of the Frances Lehman Loeb Art Center
Vassar College, Poughkeepsie, New York
Gift of Matthew Vassar 1864.1.59

Charles Moore's 1861 painting is characteristic of Hudson River school paintings that tended to portray a romanticized vision of the past. Although the paintings routinely pictured a serene, quiet Hudson, they did so *after* commerce and industry began to dominate the river and its valley.

Van Bergen Overmantel

attributed to John Heaten, active circa 1730–1745
oil on cherry wood, secured with white pine battens, circa 1733
printed with permission of the New York State Historical Association, Cooperstown

Although not necessarily a depiction of an "average" mid-Hudson Valley Dutch farm, the Van Bergen homestead reveals the range of agricultural and social activities that characterized an eighteenth century household. Note the Van Bergens, substantial Catskill farmers, overseeing not only family members, but also African American slaves and free white laborers.

Van Bergen Overmantel, detail

Van Bergen Overmantel, detail

Van Bergen Overmantel, detail

High Falls on the Rondout Creek

painting by William Rickarby Miller, 1865
gouache on paper
printed with permission of the Delaware and Hudson Canal Historical Society

William Miller's portrait of Locks 13 and 14 on the Delaware and Hudson Canal in High Falls reveals a bucolic, pastoral countryside. This portion of the canal in High Falls was, from its earliest days, a far more bustling and active place then this sleepy portrait suggests.

CHAPTER FOUR

"We Are Daily Alarmed, and Our Streets Filled with Mobs"

THE REVOLUTION IN THE VALLEY, 1775–1785

The years 1775 through 1783 were marked by warfare, economic deprivation, and political crisis in much of New York. Although the New England colonies were the locale of the war's beginning, and the Southern states its conclusion, New York was the site of continuous military conflict throughout this period.[1] Although limited military action took place in the mid-valley, residents enthusiastically supported the war effort, many Ulster farmers and tradesmen fought in the Continental Army, and the war had significant economic implications for the valley.

Most important, the war strengthened the local social and economic institutions that had structured community life throughout the eighteenth century. Blockaded ports, routine shortages of necessary items, hyperinflation, and an increasingly worthless currency all contributed to economic disorder but also revitalized community trade and exchange networks, strengthening the horizontal linkages and bonds that connected town residents to one another. Furthermore, during periods of rising prices and food shortages, residents of mid-valley towns resurrected traditional economic ideas demanding authorities enforce customary market controls and regulate prices of necessary items, as well as forbid the exportation of locally needed foodstuffs. Generally, local officials performed these tasks, but if their actions proved inadequate, residents participated in popular demonstrations and riots, which had both economic and political meaning.[2]

Nevertheless, even as the war reinvigorated the local community-based economic system, it provided new, lucrative, if temporary, economic opportunities as well. The British blockade of New York City halted the importation of manufactured goods, encouraging increased household production of textiles and other items. In addition, the encampment of the Continental Army in the mid-valley offered farmers a large stationary market for their agricultural produce. Furthermore, war contractors actively sought farm produce, offering a variety of marketing opportunities and supplying a competitive market hitherto unknown to many small farm families in the valley.

The war also provided challenges for the existing political institutions that had structured civic life in these small towns. Wartime Committees of Safety and Observation, followed soon after by new town governments, emerged to meet the political and military demands of the war. Initially welcomed and supported by the local corporations, these new town governments eventually challenged the once privileged role of the governing boards. Although the old corporation boards continued to exist side by side with the new local governments for another thirty years, they did so with declining power and authority, altering the nature of community in these towns.

THE POLITICAL REVOLUTION

The broad effects of the war on Hudson Valley communities are fairly clear. Once war began, a broad-based revolutionary movement quickly seized the reins of power from established authorities. By the end of 1775, the Provincial Assembly had been dismantled and the royal governor could secure his own safety only by residing in a warship in New York Harbor.[3]

Although Ulster County communities remained quiet during the political turmoil of the 1760s, Carl Becker observed that they were "among the most radical communities" during the revolutionary upheaval of the 1770s.[4] In each community, revolutionary committees of Safety, Observation, and Inspection sprung into power, and throughout the war years maintained a strong presence by exerting their influence not only in the political sphere, but also in the regulation of prices, importation of goods, wages, and labor. The actual fighting that occurred in the county itself was limited, since the revolutionary consensus circumvented the civil war that engulfed many other areas of the state. However, the area's strong revolutionary stance received British retribution when an expeditionary force burned significant sections of the town of Kingston in 1777.

The issues that mobilized the farmers and tradesmen of rural mid–Hudson Valley to revolution reflected local social concerns as well as larger imperial issues. For example, one Kingston resident expressed dismay with the Parliamentary attempt to establish "the Romish Religion in America," referring to the 1774

Quebec Act, and was equally shocked by the "avowed design of the ministry to raise a revenue in America."[5] The New Windsor Committee of Observation artic-ulated their fear of Parliament's desire to levy taxes "on us without our consent" and for asserting absolute legislative authority over the colonies. The committee resolved that such powers were "subversive of our natural and legal rights as British subjects, and that we would be deficient in point of duty to our King and the British Constitution were we to yield in tame submission to them."[6]

The various committees elected in the mid–Hudson Valley during the war years were popularly elected and supported. The original committees of corre-spondence were elected at the town meetings of the Kingston Corporation, Mar-bletown "Twelve Men," and the New Paltz Duzine. Although participation in these meetings was not open to all residents—nonfreeholders and women were disenfranchised—all freeholders could participate in the elections.[7]

It was at the March 14, 1775, town meeting that freeholders and "other inhabitants of New Windsor," "legally convened by mutual consent" elected their Committee of Observation.[8] New Paltz and Rochester chose their committees generally the same way—the participation of a majority of male freeholders, where the election was decided by a "plurality of voices." Although the people elected to the committees tended to be chosen from the traditional aristocracy, this reflects the aspirations of a hierarchical and deferential society. Indeed, in many Ulster towns, the people in common voted on most proceedings, such as the Articles of Association, and issued statements concerning them. Even if only a few members were responsible for writing the formal resolves, a majority of the town's men discussed and voted on them.[9]

The various committees enjoyed formidable powers that grew increasingly broad over time. Initially, the committees' role was simply to organize and pro-mote revolutionary support, and to communicate the latest developments in the imperial crisis. With the disintigration of the official provincial government in late 1775, however, the committees became quasi-legal institutions compet-ing with the crumbling remains of the old government for power. This com-petition was not as pronounced in Ulster as it was in other areas because there was close coordination between the committee movement and the local town and county governments.

For example, the members of the New Windsor Committee of Observation in 1775 were all office holders in the official town government. Four of the five members of the New Paltz Committee of Safety in 1775 were former or present town office holders, and five of the seven members of the Kingston's 1775 Com-mittee were present, recent, or future, trustees of the corporation. Marbletown also saw close correlations between the revolutionary committees and the estab-lished town organizations.[10]

However, the powers invested in the Ulster committees were often stronger than those possessed by the town's governing boards. In 1776, the Provincial Congress gave the committees the authority to tax and appoint tax collectors and assessors. Through the course of the war, the committees gradually gained additional powers and became the governing forces of several mid-valley towns. Besides control over local taxation and legislation, the committees also garnered judicial and police powers. Furthermore, committees maintained authority over local militia units, giving these revolutionary groups the necessary support to enforce their rulings.

Usually, the committees did not have to resort to the most menacing features of their power, since they were able to employ community pressures against those suspected of unpatriotic actions or of any activity seen as threatening to the community. These included public denunciations of those who were considered enemies of the cause, symbolic burnings of effigies, or boycotts of shopkeepers or tradesmen who seemed lukewarm to the Revolution. The Kingston committee stated that if anyone was guilty of actions endangering the community, "they should be punished in the publick newspapers as enemies to the liberties and privileges of American subjects," and all residents should abstain from commerce with the guilty offender.[11]

The committees believed one of the greatest threats to community support for the Revolution to be newspaper writers and pamphleters who opposed the revolutionary movement. Ulster committees instructed residents not to buy the publications of these writers because "every shilling of property we put in their hands . . . enables them to purchase the chains to bind us in slavery."[12] One such example was a pamphlet penned by A. W. Farmer entitled *Resolves of the Congress*, a critical assessment of the policies of the Continental Congress. The committees of Kingston and Shawangunk found the pamphlet "replete with falsehoods, artfully calculated to impose upon the illiterate and unthinking." So that there was no confusion about the committees' stance and resolve, the pamphlet was symbolically burned in the Kingston public market.[13]

The committee's assaults were not levied simply at newspaper writers or marginal community members, but at members of the county's oldest and most prominent families as well. In this way, the Revolution offered significant implications for the political and social order that had heretofore shaped life in small valley towns. Leading members of valley towns came under public attack, were dislodged from political office, suffered riots or demonstrations at their homes or places of business, or more ignobly, were arrested and charged as "enemies of the cause." Although some undoubtedly were Tories, others simply exhibited a lack of enthusiasm for the cause, while others engaged in economic activities that residents felt compromised the integrity of the local economies already endangered by the extreme wartime dislocations.

Many of Ulster's old elite found themselves driven from political and military power as the Revolution progressed. Shopkeepers William Ellison and John Hasbrouck, respective commanders of Ulster's two militia regiments at the beginning of the war, and leading members of two of the oldest and most prominent families in the county, found themselves removed from commands they had held for twenty years. Ellison, who was accused of engrossing and price gouging by his neighbors in New Windsor, did not even get enough nominations from his old unit to stand for election, a unit that included many of his neighbors and store customers.[14] William's brother, Thomas, lost his reelection bid to the New Windsor town government, a post he held for six years, while New Paltz's Johannes Hardenberg, Ulster's wealthiest citizen, was ousted from the Committee of Safety in 1775.

The most dramatic assault on Ulster's traditional elite occurred at midnight, June 21, 1776, when the New Windsor Committee of Safety stormed the estate of Cadwallader Colden Jr., Sheriff of Ulster and son of the former governor. Colden was correctly supected of loyalty to the British Crown. The committee searched and ransacked his house, but finding no incriminating evidence, ordered him to appear before their court the next morning. Colden hoped to remain under house arrest, and even offered to pay the guards to stay in his home for the night. The committee refused, and Colden only relented when he was threatened "to be rode upon a rail" to the local jail. Even when shopkeeper William Ellison went before the committee and offered bail, he was refused.[15]

The most significant political outcome of the war was that new town governments were created in Kingston, New Paltz, and Rochester, existing side-by-side with the older governing boards of the corporations. The need for a town government in Kingston with broader political powers than those held by the Kingston Corporation had been recognized for almost two decades, but the exigencies of the war accelerated these demands, and a new government was in place by 1777. Initially, this caused few problems and was even supported by the corporation. The powers enjoyed by each were different, since the new town government's major powers were in taxation and criminal jurisdiction, and there was much overlap between the two in membership and responsibilities. Indeed, the "town government" and the "corporation" conducted their business together at the town meeting until 1788, and the New Paltz Duzine continued to meet with the New Paltz town government until the end of the eighteenth century.[16]

Nevertheless, a dual political structure was created that threatened the existing nature of community order: two political institutions both claiming political jurisdiction, representing slightly different constituencies. Although all corporation freeholders could claim status as town citizens, not all town residents were corporation freeholders. Until the late 1790s, however, these two organizations coexisted peacefully.

WAR AND THE LOCAL ECONOMY

While the traditional political institutions that had governed community life in the central valley were weakening and being replaced with new forms of local government, the community trade and exchange networks, so central in defining the nature of town life and providing for the health and stability of local economies, grew in strength in response to the wartime dislocations and disruptions. In addition, local authorities, in response to popular demands from valley residents, enforced customary economic policies, which asserted community needs over those of individuals, and large numbers of middling farmers and tradesmen either supported, or openly participated in, crowd actions that openly challenged notions of the free market.

For much of the war, the New York City market was closed for trade, exportation and importation. However, local community trade and exchange networks continued to operate. In addition, some long-distance trade via Albany into New England continued relatively uninterrupted. Shopkeeper William Pick's accounts reveal a strenghtening of the local trade networks operating in Marbletown during the war, as families and neighbors became more dependent upon one another for trade, labor, and goods. Pick's customers dealt in agricultural goods and service-related transactions, although they earned a majority of their credits in cash. In this way, they were unrepresentative of most other farmers on the Hudson's west bank.[17] However, the high amount of cash credits, almost sixty percent in the 1780s, can be accounted for by exigencies of the war because of saturation of the local economy with inflated Continental and state currencies.[18]

Most people in colonial New York had infrequent contact with paper money, paying for their purchases in hard specie when it was available, personal notes, or produce.[19] The financial demands of the war years inundated the market with a plethora of paper issues, virtually all of which made their way into the mid–Hudson Valley. The most numerous paper in circulation was the so-called Continental Currency, $200,000,000 of which had been issued by 1779. In 1775, the Provincial Congress ordered the printing and circulation of some $112,000 in paper money, increased regularly throughout the war years.[20] In addition to these, local Committees of Correspondence and the Office of the Quarter Master General issued paper currency and promisory notes.[21]

After cash, agricultural goods continued to form a large part of the credits of Marbletown farmers, a full 40 percent during the first four years of the war.

Many of the prewar trends also continued into the war years, with service-related work settling a significant portion of Pick's accounts. Usually the labor was field work, carried on by the male customer or his sons, but frequently female labor, specifically spinning or weaving, was recorded in Pick's books. These service-related transactions accounted for about 7 percent of credits, and rose to almost 10 percent during the 1780s.

During the war years, local trade dominated Pick's accounts. Ninety-five percent of the value of goods purchased by Pick's customers in the late 1770s were the products of the local exchange system. Almost 85 percent of the purchases at Ben Snyder's Kingston store were of locally produced or manufactured goods. This high proportion should not surprise us when we remember that almost all imports through the port of New York (whether British or outside the

TABLE 4.1

PROPORTIONS OF PICK ACCOUNTS
WITH CREDITS IN VARIOUS CATEGORIES
MARBLETOWN, 1776–1789

TYPE OF CREDIT	1776–1779 (n=23)	1780–1789 (n=11)
Agricultural	40.0%	30.0%
Service	7.1	9.6
Cash	58.8	60.4
Total	£16 10s	£15 11s

Source: Pick Account Books, 1741–1826, NYHS.

TABLE 4.2

PROPORTION OF LOCAL VS. NONLOCAL PURCHASES IN PICK ACCOUNTS
MARBLETOWN, 1776–1789

	1776–1779 (n=23)	1780–1789 (n=11)
Local	95.3%	89.5%
Nonlocal	4.6	10.4
Total	£23 16s	£59 9s

Source: Pick Account Books, NYHS.

Imperial system) were halted with the British occupation of New York City in 1776. Although some trade continued overland via Albany, this was very small in comparison to the prewar trade. Following the end of the war, imports into Marbletown more than doubled, from 4 percent to over 10 percent (see Table 4.2).

The wartime trade of mid-valley shopkeepers like Pick, Ellison, or Ben Snyder was not carried on unregulated, but came under the careful scrutiny of the local Committees of Observation and Inspection. The system of economic controls implemented in mid–Hudson Valley communities to combat the economic dislocations of the Revolutionary War precluded unfettered free market activity. Essentially, this system attempted to subordinate individual economic concerns to the public interests of the community, and to guarantee access to foodstuffs and staple products for the poor during times of economic crisis. These ideas are what underlay the nonimportation agreements, which were enthusiastically supported by Ulster County residents. The nonimportation agreements restrained the right and ability of a merchant or public official to profit excessively from the shortage of British imports. Although this practice of formal regulation was irregularly employed before the 1770s, the dislocations caused by the war resurrected the call for control and gave birth to a powerful movement on both the state and local levels to regulate the social and economic life of New York's citizenry.[22]

Although the Committees of Safety and Inspection that were created in Ulster County, as in much of New York, were primarily political mechanisms, several of the most significant powers held by the committees were in the area of market regulation and control. These powers included price regulation, preventing engrossment and price gouging, and forcing shopkeepers to sell necessary foodstuffs at affordable prices. As early as 1776, local committees had enacted price controls on a variety of staple products, including wheat, flour, and salt. Further, these committees fined shopkeepers and merchants who violated these price maximums, confiscating goods and foodstuffs. Finally, these committees forbade the exportation of certain staple products out of town boundaries.

For the most part, the committees took the lead in economic activities. In 1777, the Ulster Committee met at Andrew Oliver's home on November 11 and forbade the exportation of flour, meal, or grain outside of the county. In 1778, during the height of wartime shortages, the town leaders of Marbletown gave permission to export flour, but "not more than four barrels" per person, and only on the condition that an equal value of salt be brought into the town. By 1779, the situation had grown so desperate in several west bank communities that the export of wheat or its use in distillation was forbidden.[23]

Local committees gained support in market regulation from state authorities who began regulating the prices of various goods in 1777. Each year from 1777 through 1780, price controls were reinstituted at the state level in an attempt to halt hyperinflation. The prices of all grains, plus flour, vegetables, leather, shoes, and a variety of other products were set by the Provincial Congress.[24] In addition, the Congress resumed the task of regulating wages and labor, ordering that "the various kinds of labour of farmers, mechanics and others, be set and affixed, at rates not exceeding seventy-five per centum" over the normal wages for a given locality.[25] However, in 1779 and again in 1782, Ulster authorities requested greater assistance from the state assembly in regulating prices. Specifically, the Ulster County committee requested the assembly to introduce new price controls to regulate the soaring prices of grain and other staples.[26]

Legislation was aimed not only at capping prices and controlling inflation, but toward regulating economic behavior within communities as well. Jacobus Low, one of Kingston's leading shopkeepers, was made the object of a boycott by the Committee of Observation for breaking the nonimportation agreements. With his business in near ruins, Low humbled himself before his accusers, publicly confessing and begging forgiveness for "all the offenses and transgressions where I have offended and injured" the community, after which he was publicly forgiven.[27]

The committees also attempted to punish price gougers and engrossers. Mrs. Jonathan Lawrence was accused by her New Windsor customers of selling tea 2s a pound above the rate set by the committee. Mrs. Lawrence claimed she only charged 6s, "but will not let the purchaser have the tea unless he takes a paper bag to put it in at two shillings." When confronted by the Committee of Inspection, she transported the tea to her husband, Jonathan, the commissary at nearby Fort Constitution. The committee seized the tea, discharged Jonathan from his duties, rebuked the couple, and noted they would keep a careful eye on Mrs. Lawrence in the future.[28] Although the powers possessed by the committees were substantial, even more dramatic was the popular action that occurred throughout Ulster County in the 1770s and 1780s. As early as 1776, residents in Kingston, New Windsor, and Marbletown who felt that their elected officials were not going far enough in regulating the economy and prosecuting engrossers took matters into their own hands. The Ulster Committee reported in 1776 that "we are daily alarmed, and our streets filled with mobs." According to the committee, the situation had grown so desperate in Ulster that if the legislature could not solve the economic woes affecting the central valley, local committees would have to assume authority in the name "of the People at Large."[29]

Indeed, the years 1776 through 1779 witnessed regular boycotts, forced sales of necessary products, and riots on the Hudson's west bank. The first major riot occurred in Kingston in November 1776 when a crowd raided warehouses and stores seizing tea.[30] Two weeks later, one of Ulster's first families, the Ellisons of New Windsor, were the victims of a riot. A large crowd came to William Ellison's store and, after accusing him of price gouging and engrossment, seized all the salt "except one bushel," which they left for the use of his family. Even merchants who lived outside the area were not safe from this form of popular activity. Two Albany merchants who purchased tea in Philadelphia had the misfortune of sending it overland by way of Ulster, through New Windsor. Resting at a local tavern for the night, the transporters were besieged by a crowd of men and women who seized the load, and asserting that it was being marketed at a higher price then the 6s limit set by the local committee, sold it to themselves at that price.[31]

The New Windsor riots reveal that the rioters drew upon the legitimacy of the local committees in order to explain their own activities. The rioters at Ellison's store reminded the shopkeeper of the price cap, which, they argued, he was breaking. The crowd of men and women who confiscated the tea of the Albany merchants did so by specifically invoking the name of the local committee. However, it is important to point out that in each of these activities the rioters went beyond the committee's actions. Neither riot was authorized by the local committee, and indeed, received criticism from at least one committee member.[32]

The activities of the committees in controlling prices and commerce, as well as prosecuting engrossers, are clear indications of a public economic policy that attempted to regulate the workings of the free market and protect the needs and demands of the community. The most radical aspect to these activities were not the policies themselves, since many of the powers of market regulation and price setting were already contained in many community law books, but the mechanisms (committees with questionable legal status) by which they were being enforced.[33]

The actions of the rioters in seizing foodstuffs is another matter. The rioters clearly possessed economic beliefs that denied the role of an unregulated market during times of economic crisis. In addition, the riots legitimized political behavior that went beyond the purview of the local committees, often to the frustration of those committees. Further, these rioters questioned the very essence of the concept of private property when they seized goods, making clear their belief that a shopkeeper was not necessarily the only person who was to decide what to do with his or her merchandise, and that the community had a voice in its distribution as well. What is remarkable is that during the Revolutionary War, these beliefs and activities became associated, even synonomous, with patriotic behavior. Those who participated in the riots claimed that they, because of their actions, were revealing their loyalty to the cause, while their targets, such as William Ellison, were showing signs of Toryism.[34]

Also remarkable is that many of the primary actors in these riots were women. These same women had virtually no public, political role in the mid-valley at this time, since voting, jury duty, even unlimited control over property, were denied to them. However, women often took the lead in Ulster riots, as elsewhere in North America. It was a crowd of women who first confronted Mrs. Lawrence, forcing the committee to act. Furthermore, the crowd that seized tea from the Albany merchants was composed mainly of women. At another New Windsor store, a local observer complained, "the women! in this place have risen in a mob, and are now selling a box of tea of yours [the owner] at 6s per lb."[35]

The action of women in relation to economic controls was not limited only to seizures and crowd action. Women also made it clear that they would use their power as wives and mothers to halt the war effort if certain measures were not taken to regulate the economy. In August 1776, the women of Kingston surrounded the chambers of the Committee of Safety and demanded that if food shortages were not resolved "their husbands and sons shall fight no more."[36] In this way, these riots were not only economic, but also had clear political implications. The site of the women's protest was not the Kingston public market or a shopkeeper's warehouse, but the meetinghouse of the town's political authorities. This was not simply a symbolic location for the women to make a statement, but a place of active public policy with the policy makers meeting inside the building. Finally, these women were not making economic threats of boycotts or disruptions, but promoting a clear political agenda of obstructing the war effort if their demands were not met.

Women, often precluded from public, political activity exerted a public voice around those issues in which the needs of the domestic sphere crossed those of the public sphere. The ability to get salt, tea, or flour at good prices fell firmly within the socially and culturally constructed gender roles of eighteenth-century America. Like their counterparts in the French Revolution, women usually exercised political action around issues of family and domestic concerns, particularly food and supplies.[37]

It is important to note that this movement for increased community regulation of the economy, among both the committees and the public at large, was at odds with a developing strain of thought among other North Americans. By the late 1770s craftsmen, artisans, and intellectuals in New York City, Philadelphia, and Boston, as well as farmers in the rural countryside exhibited doubts about restrictive government regulation of business activity and began to advocate free trade.[38] Free market economics received its biggest boost in New York through the publication of Alexander Hamilton's *Continentalist Papers*, written during his 1782–1783 term in the New York Assembly. Hamilton was neither original nor alone in his thinking; he merely articulated ideas that had been circulating through the colonial intelligencia for several years.

Residents of the Hudson's west bank were divided over the proper policy to follow. As a rule, price controls were rarely needed, usually only in times of economic crisis and only on certain necessities. Furthermore, many farm families had benefited from wartime inflation, since this increased their profits on farm produce. However, others had suffered from depreciated currency and soaring prices at shopkeepers' stores, and by the late 1770s, many Ulster County residents led the battle to implement policies that would halt spiraling inflation. Indeed from 1776 through 1782 calls from Ulster for government regulation of prices, quality, and distribution of various staple products became more pronounced.[39]

The movement for community regulation of prices and wages and the distribution of and access to goods cannot be viewed in isolation from the wartime needs and exigencies that brought it about. Whether in the eighteenth century, or the twentieth, wars engender shortages of goods and demands for personal sacrifice and community-mindedness. Even as the provincial authorities regulated economic affairs, valley communities did so as well. What is remarkable is not these practices per se, but the methods employed to implement them: first, official town authorities who regulated prices, fostered boycotts, and denunciated those who threatened the goals of the Revolution; second, there was the popular action in the form of seizures, public denunciations, and riots that sometimes overlapped, but often were separate from, official action.

Some historians have argued for the existence of a "moral economy" in the eighteenth century—an economy that was not shaped by market forces alone but by community needs and demands. The degree to which this moral economy existed in the mid-valley is difficult to determine. Unlike Europe, most valley residents had access to land and were particpants in the market. In general, the number of "dependent" residents were few. However, it does seem as if that market was seen as only one determinant in the economic process, and the very real needs of neighbors and residents within small, tight-knit communities were another, perhaps as powerful a force as the market.[40] However, if riots and seizures represent the attempt to protect the needs of the community from the profiteering actions of some of it residents, the Revolutionary War also offered opportunities for profit hitherto unknown to many valley residents.

WARTIME OPPORTUNITIES

Even as the exigencies of the war compelled rural residents to strengthen local trade systems and advocate increased regulation of markets, the war also offered certain economic opportunities that were not lost on many enterprising farmers and artisans. The enemy blockade halted the importation of British textiles and encouraged increased domestic production of clothing and other manufactured goods. Perhaps most important for Hudson Valley farmers, the encampment of the Continental Army at New Windsor offered a large stationary market for their agricultural produce.

During the Revolutionary War the people of Ulster County witnessed a situation unique to most Colonial Americans: the existence of a local standing army. From 1779 through 1783, a substantial portion of the Continental Army was encamped in southern Ulster/northern Orange counties. Although most of the troops were stationed in the area around New Windsor, troops were also encamped around Newburgh, Little Britain, and other small communities. The number of the troops changed from year to year (from only a few hundred to several thousand), but there was, almost without interruption, a large body of men and women who needed to be fed, clothed, and regularly supplied.[41]

Although this situation was uncommon, almost all areas of the middle colonies participated in wartime production throughout the war years. For example, even before these troops were encamped in Ulster, the farmers of the county had been brought into a network of production designed to supply the army wherever it was stationed. The Continental Commissary Department built a series of supply routes and depots to follow the army wherever it was moving. This led to a series of essentially permanent depots throughout the northeastern states of New York, Pennsylvania, and Connecticut.[42]

The extent of wartime production in Ulster County can be examined through the *Coenradt Elmendorph Account Book*. Elmendorph was an army commissary, instructed to make purchases for the military throughout Ulster and northern Orange counties. He was a resident of Kingston, a lieutenant-colonel in the Continental Line, and a person of some prestige in the Hudson River Valley. A commissary was a position of power and profit in the Continental Army. Elmendorph directed purchases, hired labor for moving the produce, employed the butchers and bakers servicing the army, and was one of the government's representatives in determining the prices of goods for a given locality. Elmendorph received a commission on his purchases, and also forged a variety of important political friendships that would be of import to him later in his career.[43]

Elmendorph's *Invoice of Supplies, 1778–1779* runs from April 1778 through November 1779. This account book records in detail the types of goods he purchased, the quantity, plus the unit cost and total price. His book also lists the farmers he purchased goods from, their hometowns, the date of the purchase, and the payment his customers were to receive. This ledger reveals the opportunities open to Ulster farmers to participate in war-created markets and the extent to which they took advantage of the opportunities.

Altogether, Elmendorph transacted business with 440 customers. The majority of his customers were from Kingston, New Paltz, New Windsor, and Shawangunk. Interestingly, alcohol, primarily in the form of locally distilled grain whisky and rum, earned the highest profits for local farmers in their dealings with Elmendorph. Although only 40 of the 440 local farmers produced this good, it accounted for nearly 40 percent of local earnings. Meat products, primarily beef and pork, accounted for about 35 percent of Elmendorph's purchases. Agricultural goods, in the form of wheat and flour, formed about 25 percent of farmers' earnings. However, far more farmers engaged in the production of beef or grains than in whisky. Altogether, 183 farmers produced meat products, and 266 farmers produced wheat and flour.

For the most part the farmers who dealt with Elmendorph produced only one item, or at least sold him only one type of good. Only thirty farmers sold both agricultural and meat products, and only three sold goods from all three categories. It seems that, for the war years at least, Ulster farmers engaged in a certain degree of specialization (see Table 4.3).

It is hard to estimate the earnings of Ulster farmers engaged in trade with the army, since the payments recorded in Elmendorph's book (recorded in pounds sterling) were made in inflated Continental dollars or wheat certificates. For example, Lawrence Alsdorph sold six bushels of wheat to Elmendorph and earned £48, about £8 per bushel. This is fully three times the price Alsdorph could have earned a year and a half earlier, in 1776. Therefore, the most accurate estimates of surplus production must be made from the amounts of wheat or beef these farmers sold to Elmendorph, not the monetary values assigned to them.

By comparing the amounts of produce local farmers sold to Elmendorph to the amount recorded in the probate inventories and accounts, we can get some sense of the proportions of surplus production engaged in by Ulster farmers dur-

TABLE 4.3

PROPORTIONS OF VALUES OF VARIOUS CREDITS
RECORDED IN ELMENDORPH ACCOUNTS, 1778–1779

TYPE OF CREDIT	(%)
Whisky/rum	39.2
Beef/pork	35.9
Agricultural	24.8
Total	£1,426 3s
Total cases	440

Source: Coenradt Elmendorph Account Book, *1778–1779,*
New York State Library, Albany, New York.

ing the war years. Although the probate inventories do not reveal actual production levels (since they vary by the time of year the estate was inventoried and the age of the decedent, among other variables), they are still an important source for understanding farm life in Revolutionary New York.

During the war years, inventories reveal that Ulster farmers owned about seven cows' worth of beef and four pigs. In this age of prerefrigeration heightened by the wartime salt shortage, there were few possible methods of food preservation, so much of this meat was still on the hoof. When selling beef or pork, most farmers simply kept the herd well fed and marched it to the local market. It is important to remember, therefore, that much of the livestock recorded in the inventories was not necessarily sold, or consumed, that year.[44]

Elmendorph's west bank customers sold, on average, three steers to the commissary over the eighteen-month period. In addition, Elmendorph purchased about 14 pounds of beef per person and about 3.3 pounds of pork. By comparing these figures to those generated above, west bank farmers, in a twelve-month period, sold on average about 29 percent of the average beef herds recorded in the probate inventories for this period. However, they sold less than 1 percent of the pork recorded in the inventories for the period 1776–1791. It should be made clear that the records of the 440 farmers Elmendorph dealt with are being compared with the 53 probated inventories and accounts that survive for Ulster County during this time.

Elmendorph also purchased grain from local farmers. Farmers sold, on average, 60 bushels of grain to Elmendorph. Wheat sales, too, can be compared to the amount of wheat production recorded in the probate inventories. During the

TABLE 4.4

AMOUNTS OF VARIOUS PRODUCTS
RECORDED IN ELMENDORPH ACCOUNTS, 1778–1779

TYPE OF CREDIT	VALUE	ADJUSTED (12 months)
Beef cows	3.0	2.0
Beef (lbs.)	14.8 lbs.	9.8 lbs.
Pork	3.3 lbs.	2.6 lbs.
Flour	15.0 barrels	10.0 barrels
Wheat	.9 bshs.	.6 bshs.
Total cases	440	

Source: Coenradt Elmendorph Account Book, *1778–1779,*
New York State Library, Albany, New York.

war, Ulster appraisers recorded about 106 bushels of wheat per inventory. Since wheat, unlike beef, is a cyclical crop and not a capital investment, it can be more accurately compared to the grain yields recorded in the probate inventories. West bank farmers sold about 38 percent of their yearly grain yields to Elmendorph.

In sum, the Elmendorph account book reveals that many farmers in Ulster and Orange counties marketed a large proportion of their grain and livestock, between 25 and 38 percent. Although patriotism and devotion to the cause cannot be discounted as possible motivation, an army supplier with ready cash most certainly induced many to sell. In addition, if farmers did not sell, the army would simply have requisitioned whatever they needed anyway, leaving the farmer in no position to decide what could or could not be sold. The most significant aspect of this production, however, is the way it was marketed. Almost all of the produce was sold to an army agent who paid in cash. This was new to many west bank farmers. In the period before the war, cash was used infrequently by small farmers, since most Ulster farmers exchanged produce with neighbors or to obtain credits from local merchants like Pick and Snyder.

The use of paper money, which routinely fluctuated in value, compelled farm families to become more aware of, and expert in, commercial transactions, since they had to be certain of the value of the currency they were receiving relative to the value of the goods they were selling. In addition to this, their education in the use of paper currency had to be obtained during a period of hyperinflation. As James Henretta has commented, the war years "forced nearly every family to look out more carefully and more persistently for its economic self-interest."[45]

WAR AND THE HOUSEHOLD

Important in this developing shift in trade and production was domestic textile manufacturing. In the years before the Revolution, the North American colonies imported more than 10 million yards of linen and other cloth from England annually.[46] Domestic manufacturing received its greatest impetus from the revolutionary movement and the virtual halt of these English textiles. Not only did the farmers of Ulster communities agree not to import British manufactures (a position clothed in symbolic stances of the unnecessary luxury supplied by British goods), but they encouraged the wearing of homespun and explicitly encouraged domestic manufacturing. In order to achieve a greater wool crop the Ulster County Committee of Safety voted to "improve the breed, and increase the number of sheep," and wanted to secure a pledge from local yeoman not to kill any "sheep under four years old, or procure them to be killed by others; neither will we sell the best of our sheep to butchers, or others employed by them to purchase, whereby the breed of our sheep is so much injured."[47] Anyone who sold or ate lambs or ewes were denounced as enemies of the American cause.[48]

During this period many people began to invest more fully in domestic manufacturing. In 1793, Cornelius Wynkoop of Hurley owned six spinning wheels, twenty pounds of wool, eight slaves to work the wheels and some twenty-seven sheep to keep the wheels supplied. When New Windsor's James McClaughry died in 1790, he owned fifty yards of yarn, fifty pounds of wool prepared for carding, and maintained a herd of some fifty sheep. McClaughry's seven children, along with two slaves, did much of the spinning and weaving on his wheel and loom. In 1795, Roeloff Eltinge of New Paltz ran two looms and two wheels, owned fifty-six sheep, fifty-one pounds of wool cloth, and fifty bushels of hackled flax ready for spinning by his three slaves.[49]

These three farmers were not alone. During the war years, their neighbors throughout Ulster County increased their investments in implements to produce domestic textiles. In the period 1776–1791, over 90 percent of Kingston households contained at least one spinning wheel and 74.4 percent of back-river towns' households contained at least one wheel. A further breakdown of the households reveals the importance of home textile production. In Kingston, 50 percent of the decedents owned two wheels, 21.4 percent as many as four and more than 7 percent had six wheels. The smaller towns reveal similar findings, with 51.3 percent owning at least two wheels and almost 8 percent of the households containing four spinning wheels or more. In the same period, looms were possessed by two-thirds of the Kingston decedents, and almost one-half of the residents of the back-river towns owned at least one (see Table 4.5).

Clearly, a spinning wheel was deemed essential by an overwhelming majority of Ulster residents, which might reveal an orientation toward outwork spinning. Equally important is the large proportion of households with looms. A loom was a far greater investment than a wheel (sometimes costing as much as four times the price of a wheel) and, even more than the ownership of a wheel, reveals the extent of the home manufacturing system. Not only were these people filling the needs of their own households, but it is also quite possible that the finished products of Ulster looms were available on the local exchange networks, which may reveal that many of the Ulster families who owned these looms engaged in a significant amount of weaving.

However, even with these developments, many of the traditional methods of producing textiles persisted. Frederick Westbrook, a Kingston weaver, still wove his neighbor's cotton and wool thread. Although his customers usually paid him in cash, they often gave him a certain portion of the linen he wove in exchange for his services. In fact, Westbrook settled forty percent of his transactions during the years 1779 through 1782 by accepting a certain portion of the goods he produced.[50]

TABLE 4.5

OWNERSHIP OF TEXTILE AND DAIRY-PRODUCING EQUIPMENT
IN ULSTER COUNTY, 1776–1791

TEXTILE PRODUCTION

	KINGSTON	RURAL TOWNS
Sheep	12.0	15.2
Wool	36.0 lbs.	42.6 lbs.
Looms	64.3%	46.2%
Spinning wheels	92.9%	74.4%
Total	14	39

DAIRY PRODUCTION

	KINGSTON	RURAL TOWNS
Cows	6.8	5.3
Churns	57.1%	48.8%
Milk tubs	50.0%	35.9%
Firkins	7.1%	10.2%
Total	14	39

Source: Probated Inventories of Ulster County, 1776–1791,
Ulster County Clerk's Office, Kingston, New York.

A strong correlation existed between home textile production and other aspects of the domestic economy, particularly dairying. As long as the goal of production was subsistence and local trade with neighbors, the two processes could be carried on simultaneously. However, specialization in some facet of dairy production (in this case butter making, which occurred in the early nineteenth century) came at the cost of a decrease in the home production of textiles.[51] Measuring the extent of home manufacturing illuminates both the household system of production and the workings of the informal, female-controlled system of trade and exchange.

In Ulster, during the period 1760–1791, 39.6 percent of the inventories put to probate contained milk tubs, which were used in cream separation. Over 50 percent of the inventories include churns, the most important implement in butter production. Firkins (approximately one-quarter of a barrel or 112 pounds of butter), used for storing large amounts of butter for transport and trade, turned up in far fewer inventories; only 9.4 percent of Ulster inventories include a firkin.

Clearly butter making (and, no doubt, some cheese making) was carried on in about half of the households in west bank communities. Production of butter in large amounts, however, was confined to a small number of Ulster families. It appears that about half of Ulster households supplied their own families and, probably through local trade, their neighbor's families with dairy products. Almost 10 percent of Ulster households, however, engaged in a somewhat greater production, most probably for trade and some profit.

With this increase in dairy and textile equipment, and the demands of the war period, the communities of Ulster County seemed to develop the beginnings of a small putting-out system. During the war, the Committee of Safety employed hundreds of Ulster women to sew stockings and blankets, and to weave the fabric needed for uniforms for the troops. The state government assessed local towns a quota of shirts, shoes, and other products, and sent to the towns the wool, cloth or other raw products for producing these goods. The local committees distributed the materials to local farm families who spun and wove the finished products, which were then collected by the committees and sent to the army supplier. For example, in April 1777, the Provincial Congress paid £600 to the Ulster Committee for stockings and blankets. The committee distributed the cloth and yarn to local farm families for production. Ulster also became a focal point for shoe manufacturing for the Continental Army, as the various county committees collected and then sent hides to Marbletown where the hides were tanned and then put-out to local cordwainers to manufacture shoes at 18 to 20 shillings a pair.[52]

Even with these changes, the mid-valley did not develop extensive manufacturing. It failed to occur at this time for several reasons. The market for finished products was still small and dispersed, and those urban areas that did have the demand could, after the war, get their goods more cheaply from British producers. In addition, local merchants in Ulster and elsewhere invested in bonds and certificates, bought real estate, and invested their money in a variety of areas, but not into developing a rural outwork system. These other mediums were much more profitable than developing a large-scale network of outwork production in the years following the war.[53]

However, mid-valley farmers' connection to more commercial markets received a boost from the war, as military contractors and merchants actively sought the farmers' goods, offering a variety of opportunities and supplying a competitive market hitherto unknown to many yeoman farm families. Speculators from New York City, recognizing the possibilities that lay in developing the Hudson Valley into a sophisticated wartime production region made their way north to implement their ideas. Daniel Parker and William Duer had contracts to supply French forces and opened a series of stores in Ulster and Orange to purchase

local grain. Melancton Smith, one of New York's leading anti-federalists, opened
a store in 1783 near the main army camp in New Windsor with the plan of promoting a continued high level of market production in the area, now that the end
of the war and the removal of the army seemed to imply a cessation of production. In this way, the war increasingly compelled farmers to view their production
and trade in market terms.[54]

Even with this failure to develop a unified merchant class or a rural domestic manufacturing system, the Revolutionary War had profound effects on the
Ulster County economy. First, the mid–Hudson Valley, like much of the Northeast, was flooded with a variety of paper currencies. Some small farmers had
never used cash in any form before, and certainly most had never used it with
such regularity. In the decade before the war, merchant William Pick's customers
obtained less than 40 percent of their credits in cash, while the farmers who dealt
with Benjamin Snyder obtained about 8 percent of their credits in cash. During
the war, this changed dramatically. With the flood of paper currencies, local
farmers exchanging goods with Pick now settled about 60 percent of their transactions in paper money.

The war, therefore, helped produce a farm population far more astute in
commercial matters. Before the war many farmers had dealt only with neighbors
or their local shopkeeper, and this was primarily for obtaining goods—the farm
produce they exchanged was a tool to help obtain the goods they needed. Now,
however, there were developing changes in the distribution system, as public contractors like Elmendorph and private speculators like Melancton Smith increasingly offered paper currency, not other merchandise, in exchange for the produce
of farm families. In this way, the war increasingly compelled farmers to focus
their production toward commercial markets.

The war also paved the way for an increase in the system of domestic production. The probate inventories reveal that both textile and dairy production
increased during the war years, most probably as a result of the halt of British
goods into New York, and the increased demands of wartime production.
Although this production system did not develop rapidly following the war, the
beginnings of a scattered rural outwork system was taking form.

However, it is important to note that while many farm families were increasing production of both agricultural goods and textiles and were participating in
more commercial trade, the war years also witnessed a strengthening of the local,
community-based productive and trade systems. Further, Ulster County, like
much of the Northeast, implemented a variety of price and wage controls during
the war, rationed goods, rioted against price-gouging merchants, and promoted
a variety of policies that significantly restricted the workings of the free market.
The war seems, therefore, to have brought about a series of contradictions. On

the one hand, farmers increasingly took part in commercial exchanges, used paper money far more than they ever had, and increased domestic production to fill wartime needs. On the other hand, local farmers' understanding of the market and of commerce was shaped by traditional ideas of political economy that did not give market expansion free reign.

Nevertheless, an important question remains: Were these new wartime developments in the Hudson Valley economy—increased long-distance sale, greater use of cash, and intensification of textile and dairy production—a major first step in the process of economic change, or an aberration caused by the war? Although these developments were significant for the war period, it would seem that each was an aberration, since the increased production of agricultural goods and textiles was not sustained in the years following the war. Essentially, this enlarged production, much like the increased use of cash, was a response to immediate wartime needs. The relatively limited market for manufactured goods, as well as the existence of alternative, and more profitable, investments for those with capital, restrained, at least temporarily, long-term economic development.

CHAPTER FIVE

"The Farmer Now Sells for Money"

Hudson Valley Farmers
and the Market Revolution,
1785–1820

Although the Revolutionary War facilitated some change in the economy of the mid–Hudson Valley, there was still much continuity with the past, and few significant differences emerged in the postwar economy. However, the decades following the war witnessed the beginning of the so-called market revolution. This period of wide-scale social and economic change transformed the northern United States. Improved transportation was the mechanism, with superior roads, turnpikes, and canals linking together formerly isolated regions of the nation into a increasingly complex national market system. It was the actions of political officials, financiers, manufacturers, merchants, and thousands of shopkeepers, tradesmen, and farmers that were the catalysts for these changes.

This market revolution had substantial implications for the Hudson Valley. Many prosperous farmers enthusiastically responded to the growing demand for agricultural goods and increased their production, and made the switch from farmer to businessman. Many others, however, unable to produce at the level necessary to succeed in the new commercial environment, altered their production and began producing specialized market-oriented agricultural crops or manufactured goods in order to make ends meet. Eventually, all were affected by this transformation—small and large producers alike—although somewhat differently.

With the rumblings of industrialization emanating from New England, and to a lesser degree the valley itself, large amounts of inexpensive, mass-produced manufactured goods were making their way into valley shops. As families purchased more items from shopkeepers, they bartered less with neighbors, decreasing the importance of the local trade systems that had once tied neighboring households into intricate webs of economic exchange. The demand for "ready-made" and "store-bought" products increased the need for cash among households, further requiring them to earn money for their produce as opposed to bartering with neighbors. As the old neighborhood trade systems declined in importance and households increasingly oriented their economic production outside of their communities and toward distant markets, challenges emerged for the "corporate" economic communities of the mid-valley.

THE FARM HOUSEHOLD IN THE
LATE EIGHTEENTH CENTURY

In the last decade of the eighteenth century, economic activity in the Hudson Valley was much like it was in the first decade of the century. The majority of farm households in Kingston, New Paltz, Marbletown, and other small towns and villages were farmers who supplied their own needs first, traded goods with neighbors and shopkeepers for items they did not produce, and sold small amounts of surplus grain, flour, or wood downriver to New York City. The number of farm households engaged in commercial sale was still very small. In 1799, only 12 percent of Abraham Hasbrouck's customers sold goods to New York City, while more than four-fifths of his customers bartered and traded for other goods at his store. Although one-third of William Van Gaasbeck's customers purchased goods in cash, the rest bartered "country produce" or "marketable goods." Over eighty percent of Van Gaasbeck's customers' purchases were of locally produced items.

During the last decade of the eighteenth century, Ulster farmers cultivated about 12 acres of grain, produced 145 bushels of wheat and another 100 of rye, numbers that give evidence of an increase over output during the colonial period. Further, although more farm families used sophisticated iron tools than in earlier years, most families used the machinery, tools, and techniques used by their grandparents. Most farms still used scythes and sickles for cutting grass and reaping wheat, as well as wooden plows and harrows. Less than 20 percent of probate inventories from the 1790s record iron tools.[1]

Most farm households continued to produce their own household items, manufacture their own textiles, and keep their own dairy and gardens. Almost 73 percent of Ulster families possessed spinning wheels, 40 percent looms, and the average farm household maintained a flock of fifteen sheep. Home spinning continued well into the nineteenth century, as thirty-three percent of Daniel Osterhoudt's customers in the 1820s settled some portion of their accounts with the Kingston farmer through spinning. About 20 percent of the accounts of Jacobus Cole, a Marbletown tailor from 1789 through 1831, contained some spinning.[2] As late as the second decade of the nineteenth century, one New Windsor resident claimed, "Our clothing was all manufactured from flax and wool grown on the farm. There were young women who went from farm to farm to spin and weave woolen, but the flax was spun by the women of the house."[3]

Further, 58 percent of inventories record butter churns, 50 percent milk tubs, and 23 percent firkins, which were used to store or transport large amounts of butter. Further analysis reveals that a significant number of Ulster households produced enough dairy and textiles to meet their own needs. Forty-six percent of probate inventories at the end of the eighteenth century record both spinning wheels and dairy producing implements, revealing that these households probably practiced both textile manufacturing and dairying at the same time, specializing in neither.[4] As long as the goal of production was to maintain a "comfortable subsistence," both could be carried on simultaneously.

THE EXPANSION OF COMMERCIAL TRADE

In order to measure the changes the market revolution brought about, it would be worthwhile to explore the economic activities of ordinary farm households during these early years of economic change. The account books of shopkeeper Abraham Hasbrouck Jr. allow us to explore changes in production, trade, and consumption in the port town of Kingston. Hasbrouck opened his store at Kingston Landing in 1797, and quickly emerged as the leading shopkeeper and export merchant in the region in the late eighteenth and early nineteenth centuries.[5] Hasbrouck either consigned his customers' products to New York City merchants or marketed under his own account produce he stockpiled from exchanges with customers. His store's rich, forty-three volumes of account books open up the economic activities of thousands of Kingstonians during the years 1797 through 1843.

Often, historical studies of economic behavior of farm households have been based on information culled from farm daybooks, records that tend to be disproportionately representative of larger commercial producers, or in the words of Gloria Main, the "records of busy, successful men."[6] The behavior and perspective of the multitude of smaller farmers, who traded locally and sold on regional markets, remain largely unexplored. Hasbrouck's account books reveal the shopkeeper's extensive dealings with both large and smaller farmers, allowing for an exploration of farmers' behavior as both producers and consumers, and provide insight into the factors that guided their choices when producing, trading, selling, and buying during a period of heightened market development.

Storekeepers like Hasbrouck performed several important services for valley residents. First, they functioned as export agents, consigning grain and barrel staves for their customers, as well as marketing their own stocks acquired through daily exchanges in the local trade network. Second, storekeepers were the primary source of consumer goods produced outside the valley. Finally, they frequently acted as bankers, carrying debts and delaying settlement of customer accounts for months, and more often, years.[7]

Three years of Hasbrouck's account books have been selected for detailed examination: 1799, 1820, and 1839.[8] By systematically examining Hasbrouck's accounts, we can analyze what types of goods his customers produced and the volume of their production. By linking these records to census and tax returns, we can answer important questions concerning the social and economic status of those families who dealt with Hasbrouck, the family composition of the producers, and gender distinctions in production and trade.

Hasbrouck carried on an import-export trade in grain and agricultural goods, home-produced textiles, barrel staves, and lumber, and supplied the community with a variety of manufactured and dry goods, as well as food products.[9] In return, Kingston residents sold Hasbrouck oak wood, wheat, flour, and butter, along with a variety of other agricultural goods. Kingston residents supplied Hasbrouck with very few textile or manufactured goods—the only manufactured product exchanged in any amount was barrel staves.

In 1799, Hasbrouck recorded 600 business transactions with 186 customers. Hasbrouck carefully recorded all of his exchanges in his daybooks, which list the goods purchased by his customers under the debit column and the credits he recorded in customers' accounts for the staves and farm products they brought him. The most common credits recorded in Hasbrouck's ledgers were agricultural credits, found in about 25 percent of accounts in both 1799 and 1820. Textiles, clothing, and other home-manufactured products made up a very small percentage of the trade of Kingston's residents. In 1799, less then 5 percent of Hasbrouck's customers recorded credits in the form of products and goods manufactured at home, and this decreased even further, to less then 3 percent, in 1820.

Cash was used in 18.2 percent of 1799 accounts, and this changed very little during the next twenty-one years: in 1820 the proportion of accounts with any cash credits increased to only 20.4 percent. This situation deserves some attention. The amount of cash and currency in circulation had increased dramatically during the Revolutionary War as the national, state, and local governments issued large amounts of securities and paper money.[10] Although much of this currency was eventually retired, residents of the Hudson Valley had far greater access to paper money in the years after the war than at any time before

TABLE 5.1

Proportions of Hasbrouck Accounts with
Credits in Various Categories, 1799 and 1820

Type of Credits	1799 (%)	1820 (%)
Agricultural goods	24.1	26.1
Barrel staves/oak wood	21.5	53.4
Textiles, clothing	5.3	2.6
Service	1.0	1.4
Cash payments	18.2	20.4
Total cases	186	601

Source: Abraham Hasbrouck Account Books, *New York Historical Society.*

it. However, few of Hasbrouck's customers used cash at his store, as less than one-fifth of all accounts involved the use of cash.

A variety of circumstances contributed to this relatively high level of non-cash exchanges, including the inability of some residents to obtain cash, a reluctance to use the medium, and finally, merchants' willingness to accept produce and goods that were more widely available to the local producer than was cash. All three explanations deserve consideration. Although cash circulated in Kingston throughout the period under discussion, certain groups had more use for, and access to, cash than others. Poorer farmers had less contact with paper currency, and the process reinforced itself since they were consequently more likely to exchange their goods using noncash means.

Beginning with the American Revolution, and continuing for many years thereafter, cash was either scarce and overvalued specie, or, as during the 1780s, came in various and often unreliable forms. Under such circumstances, farmers were well-advised to take payment in some form of credit. To accept cash was to accept risk, and it made good economic sense for people to rely on more traditional ways of dealing with the local merchant—exchanging goods and services that were recorded in the merchant's ledger with an equivalent cash value.

Finally, many rural transactions, whether with fellow farmers or with a merchant like Hasbrouck, simply did not need cash since almost all of the products needed by farmers could be acquired without cash simply by trading goods or services with other farmers or shopkeepers. Furthermore, exchanging goods and services over time allowed community members to prove their ability to meet obligations in ways that were necessary to other farmers. The credits built up through this system became a more important determinant of a farmer's ability to borrow than the use of cash.[11] Although cash was occasionally exchanged among farmers or between merchants and customers, Hasbrouck's accounts reveal this to be the exception, rather than the usual form of payment.

Many farm families found it more convenient to settle accounts with goods, such as barrel staves. During the winter months, farm families rived barrel staves from the oak wood they cut on their property. In 1799, staves appeared in over 21 percent of patron's accounts, only slightly less often than agricultural credits. Apparently, staves were used as a substitute for cash—what scholars have described as "commodity money." Although staves rarely appeared in exchanges between farmers, they were often used to "buy" products in much the same manner as cash. With cash in short supply, staves could have satisfied many of the same demands and requirements of cash, with fewer of the risks associated with depreciation or discounting.[12]

Hasbrouck's customers used two options when trading goods at his store: exchanging through Hasbrouck's local accounts or consigning goods for long-distance trade. The former was the preferred method, as reflected in the fact that 81 percent of the 3,848 transactions recorded in Hasbrouck's 1820 accounts were exchanges of this nature. In 649 transactions, customers consigned their goods to Hasbrouck. This system was somewhat more complicated, although it was usually more profitable for both the customer and for the shopkeeper. Farmers who chose this path of sale did so because city prices for grain and barrel staves were routinely higher than the prices offered by Hasbrouck in Kingston.

Although long-distance sale was open to anyone who chose to sell on commercial markets, farm families who actively engaged in this trade were a minority in Kingston, and they were different from local traders in a variety of significant ways. In 1799, local customers averaged about £10 in agricultural credits, about half the £19 earned by those who used Hasbrouck's sloop. Local traders averaged £4 5s of barrel staves, much less than the £12 9s earned by Hasbrouck's sloop customers.

Hasbrouck's sloop ledger, contained within the account book, reveals the amounts of goods produced in Kingston, but sent into long-distance markets. In 1799, twenty-three Hasbrouck customers sent through produce to New York City via his sloops, with agricultural goods comprising almost 60 percent of the value of their exports. No textiles for trade were recorded in his sloop accounts, but barrel staves and oak wood were. About 40 percent of Hasbrouck's exports were of these items.

By comparing sloop customers to customers who did not send their goods to New York City, we get a better sense of the extent of market production

TABLE 5.2

Values of Various Credits Recorded in Hasbrouck Accounts, 1799 and 1820

	1799	1820
Agricultural goods	£2 18s	£5 6s
Barrel staves	£1 4s	£3 8s
Textiles	1s	5s
Service	1s	1s
Cash payments	16s	£2 14s
Total credits	£5 0s	£11 14s
Total cases	186	601

Source: Hasbrouck Account Books, *New York Historical Society.*

TABLE 5.3

Average Credits for Sloop and Nonsloop customers, Hasbrouck Accounts, 1799

Product	Sloop customer	Nonsloop customer
Agricultural	£19 19s (13)	£10 15s (30)
Textile	0	0
Staves	£12 9s (15)	£4 5s (29)
Service	0	0
Cash	(7)	(14)
Total cases	23	163

Source: Hasbrouck Account Books, *New York Historical Society.*

among both types of customers. Since any of Hasbrouck's customers could use the merchant's sloop, it is important to distinguish the local from the long-distance traders. Hasbrouck transported goods to New York City for any farmer who chose to employ his service. There was, apparently, no minimum size requirement on the amount of goods Hasbrouck would transport, although his carrying cost would make it unprofitable to exchange small amounts of goods.

In 1799, Henry Graham was one of Hasbrouck's regular customers. Over the course of the year, Graham and Hasbrouck completed twelve transactions. Graham exchanged £10 16s worth of agricultural goods, all of it destined for the local market. Graham was typical of most of Hasbrouck's customers. The average customer who did not trade on Hasbrouck's ship averaged about £10 in agricultural credits, about half the £19 earned by those who used Hasbrouck's sloop. Local traders like Graham averaged £4 5s of barrel staves, much less than the £12 9s earned by Hasbrouck's sloop customers (see Table 5.3).

In 1799, those who dealt on Hasbrouck's sloop produced and exchanged many more goods than did those who exchanged exclusively on local markets. Twenty-three Hasbrouck customers—12 percent of all customers—exchanged 75 percent of the agricultural products that passed through his store that year. In addition, they exchanged about 70 percent of the barrel staves.

For the twenty-three sloop patrons in 1799, long-distance, commercial trade dominated. Although a minority of Hasbrouck's customers, those who were regularly involved in exchange on long-distance markets, made up a much larger share of the merchant's trade and tended to use cash far more often then those who were not involved in extra-local exchange. For these farmers, at least, the developing market system offered attractive opportunities for profits (See Table 5.4).

In 1799, 180 men and 6 women traded agricultural goods, home manufactures, and staves with Hasbrouck in exchange for salt, sugar, rum, and manufactured goods. If a Hasbrouck customer used cash, he or she was unlikely to exchange much agricultural produce or barrel staves at the store. A few figures are revealing. Of the 34 people who paid cash at Hasbrouck's store in 1799, only 8 also traded agricultural goods and a mere three exchanged barrel staves. A Hasbrouck customer who earned agricultural credits (some 45 did), was unlikely to use much cash, but did exchange barrel staves. Only 8 of these 45 ever used cash, but 14 regularly exchanged staves. Finally, of the 40 customers

TABLE 5.4

PROPORTION OF PRODUCE DESTINED FOR LOCAL VS. LONG-DISTANCE
TRADE, HASBROUCK'S SLOOP CUSTOMERS, KINGSTON, 1799

Product	Local	Extra-local	Total
Agricultural	24.2%	75.7%	£265 15s
Textiles	—	—	—
Staves/lumber	28.5	71.4	£197 9s

Source: Hasbrouck Account Books, *New York Historical Society.*

who earned primarily stave credits, 14 also exchanged agricultural goods with Hasbrouck, but only 3 paid any cash to him.

The values of the credits earned by these farmers lend support to the above findings. Those farmers who paid cash averaged £5 10s of agricultural credits, significantly higher than the £2 18s overall average of Hasbrouck's customers. The Kingston residents who earned agricultural credits also earned £1 16s of stave credits, but used only £1 2s worth of cash. The farmers who regularly brought in staves earned a significant amount of agricultural credits from Hasbrouck, some £6 2s, but only a mere 4s in cash credits. Customers who earned cash credits rarely exchanged agricultural goods or staves, but when they did, they did so in amounts much higher than the average. Conversely, farmers who brought in either agricultural goods or barrel staves to Hasbrouck's store were just as likely to use either for credits, but rarely exchanged cash.

Linking these 186 customers to the 1798 Kingston Tax Assessment answers questions regarding the social and economic standing of Hasbrouck's customers, and what types of people, wealthy, middling, or poor, were likely to use cash, deal in agricultural products, or trade staves. The 1798 Tax Assessment recorded the real and personal property of the residents of Kingston, Marbletown, and Hurley. Altogether, 638 families were assessed. One hundred twenty-seven of Hasbrouck's customers appeared on the 1798 tax assessment. The mean assessment of Hasbrouck's customers was £194 13s, but this included a great disparity between the lowest assessed, John Roberson, at £61 1s, and the highest, James Hasbrouck, at £960. The mean assessment of those Hasbrouck customers who regularly exchanged agricultural goods was £161 8s. Farmers who earned stave credits were assessed £169 8s. Not surprisingly, Hasbrouck customers who used cash at his store were assessed the highest, some £297 1s.

Further analysis supports these findings. Hasbrouck customers in the bottom quarter on the tax list (assessed less than £114) had primarily agricultural and stave credits, valued at £4 13s and £7 5s, respectively. Farmers in the middle of the tax list (twenty-fifth to seventy-fifth percentiles) also earned primarily agricultural and stave credits, although valued substantially higher than their poorer neighbors. This group of Hasbrouck customers averaged £18 in agricultural credits and £5 16s in stave credits. Neither group, the poor or the middling, tended to use much cash. Those in the middle percentile of the tax assessment used only £3 16s in cash. Only two of thirty-two farmers in the lowest quartile earned any cash credits. Those in the top 25 percent of the tax assessment were less likely to exchange agricultural goods at Hasbrouck's store, but the five farmers who did earned £19 13s in credits for these goods. In sum, poor or middling farmers were more likely to settle their accounts with agricultural and stave credits, and, very infrequently, cash credits. Conversely, the more affluent residents of Kingston rarely exchanged goods at the merchant's store, but used a significantly higher amount of cash (about £17 each) than the 1799 average of 16s. Quite simply, the wealthier customers of Hasbrouck settled accounts in cash, and the poorer in goods.

What were the differences between a "commercial" farmer who consigned goods on Hasbrouck's sloop and a farmer who traded locally? Some differences were the amount of capital resources and land one possessed. Take the case of

TABLE 5.5

REAL PROPERTY OF KINGSTON RESIDENTS BY TYPES OF CREDITS, 1799

CREDITS EARNED	VALUE OF REAL PROPERTY
Agricultural	£161 8s (35)
Staves	£169 8s (24)
Cash	£297 1s (14)
Service	—
Textiles	—
Missing cases	54

Source: Hasbrouck Account Books, *New York Historical Society;*
1798 Kingston Tax Assessment, Kingston Senate House Museum.

TABLE 5.6

VALUE OF VARIOUS CREDITS BY REAL PROPERTY HOLDINGS, 1799

PRODUCT	LOWEST 25%[a]	25–75%[b]	TOP 25%[c]
Agricultural	£4 13s (12)	£18 0s (18)	£19 13s (5)
Staves	£7 5s (6)	£5 16s (13)	£2 1s (5)
Cash	£8 16s (2)	£3 16s (9)	£17 7s (5)
Service	0 (0)	£4 16s (1)	0 (0)
Manufacturing	1s (2)	£5 13s (1)	£6 5s (3)

(a) Assessed less than or equal to £114
(b) Assessed £115 to £240
(c) Assessed £714 or more

Source: Hasbrouck Account Books, *New York Historical Society;*
1798 Kingston Tax Assessment.

Nicholas Hardenbergh, a commercial farmer who traded regularly with Hasbrouck. Hardenbergh owned 272 acres (almost 100 more than the average Kingston farmer), 12 cows, 17 sheep, 2 spinning wheels, a loom, as well as a substantial amount of dairying equipment. With the help of his wife, four children, and two slaves, Hardenbergh produced food and textiles for home use, and grain, flour, and barrel staves for trade and sale. Hardenbergh regularly did business at Hasbrouck's store, trading both locally and consigning produce on his sloop. Assessed £292 (which placed him in the top 25 percent of Kingstonians in 1799), somewhat above the £222 average for a sloop customer, Hardenbergh routinely paid Hasbrouck in cash for purchases. In 1799 he sold almost three times the amount of produce and staves of smaller local traders.

Wilhelm DuBois and Peter Burhans also traded with Hasbrouck, but in significantly smaller amounts than their more affluent neighbor, Hardenbergh. DuBois or Burhans were assessed roughly the £171 average of Hasbrouck's local traders, and owned 152 acres and 139 acres, respectively. DuBois owned a slave, who, along with DuBois's wife and three children, labored in the fields, tended 4 cows and 7 sheep, and worked a spinning wheel. Burhans, his wife, and four children (no slaves), owned 5 cows, a spinning wheel, but no sheep. Both farmers traded goods at the Hasbrouck store, but all their transactions were local; neither consigned produce on Hasbrouck's sloop. Burhans never paid cash in any of the seven years he traded with Hasbrouck (1798–1804), nor did he trade barrel staves, although DuBois did.[13]

Although it is not possible to determine the personal and real property of each of Hasbrouck's customers (local tax records do not record acreage or personal property, simply an assessed value), the available evidence clarifies patterns of who sold commercially and who did not. Families who sold commercially on Hasbrouck's sloop produced and traded substantially more grain and flour than local traders, tended to possess larger than average amounts of property, were assessed on average £222 (about £35 higher than the average Kingstonian) and owned five slaves. Although these commercial farmers also engaged in local trade with Hasbrouck and smaller farmers, they oriented large portions of their production and sale toward the city market. Further, unlike most local traders, they used cash at his store.

On the other hand, farmers who traded only locally with Hasbrouck possessed smaller farms, had an average assessment of £171, fulfilled their own needs first and traded surplus with neighbors or shopkeepers, and rarely used cash in these exchanges. Although most local traders did not own slaves, those who did averaged three per family. Family size and gender composition had little effect on Kingstonians' choice of produce for credits or their economic standing within the community.[14]

While Kingstonians were engaged in the marketing of surplus agricultural produce outside of the area, they were also consumers of goods purchased from Hasbrouck. Kingston farms generally produced enough staple products to supply the local population, but a variety of other commodities had to be imported from outside the region.[15] Food products accounted for slightly more than 60 percent of the value of store purchases in 1799.[16] On average customers annually consumed £6 6s in agricultural goods. Sugar, salt, tobacco, and rum were the most common purchases, occasionally supplemented by tea, honey, beef, flour, fish, and molasses.

Hasbrouck patrons averaged £2 13s a year in purchases of household items, such as wooden bowls, earthenware, and "smoothing irons." On occasion, a Hasbrouck customer might buy more refined items, such as "6 pewter plaits at 8s" or "2 rugs." Keeping in mind that most of the household items that Hasbrouck sold were inexpensive ("common chairs" were offered at 1s each, a set of twelve teacups and saucers sold for 2s), customers could accumulate a healthy stock of goods over the course of the year for a relatively small amount of money.

Most customers made their purchases during the period from February to May. Indeed, 52 percent of the purchases made at Hasbrouck's store in 1799 were made in these four months, with fully 18 percent of the total annual sales completed in May. This pattern was repeated in 1820, where 59 percent of the 3,162 purchases occurred during this same four month period. Although the account ledger reveals that Hasbrouck's store was open year-round, some months, like December, had very little business at the shopkeeper's store. Only 43 purchases, or 5 percent of the total sales for 1799, were completed in December, and even fewer, 3 percent were completed during December 1820.

When customers made purchases was related to their selling habits. Sixty-eight percent of sales to Hasbrouck occurred during the first half of the year, January to June. Indeed, a full 23 percent of customers' sales (primarily of staves and lumber) to the storekeeper were concluded in February. Customer's consuming habits followed their selling practices. When at the store selling a bushel of grain or a load of wood, customers also purchased or traded for items they needed.

Although close to 19 percent of the value of store purchases were of household items, "sundries," or manufactured tools and the like, this was, on balance, a relatively small portion of the merchant's total sales, pointing to a limited consumer market for manufactured products in the late-eighteenth-century valley. Through 1800, consumption remained centered around agricultural items and unfinished cloth, rather than durables. Table 5.7 details the distribution of purchases across the various items Hasbrouck sold.

In sum, the economic activities and practices of farm families in the late eighteenth century reveals much in common with the colonial and revolutionary

TABLE 5.7

Types of Purchases Made by Hasbrouck Customers, 1799

Type of purchase	Proportion
Food	60.8%
Unfinished cloth	19.9
Agricultural implements	8.1
Household item	6.2
Sundries	4.3
Total accounts sampled	49

Source: Hasbrouck Accounts, *1799, New York Historical Society.*

periods. Although marketing opportunities were increasing, and there was grow-ing demand for valley produce, methods of production and trade were conducted much like they had been for decades. Traditional local and long-distance trading systems continued to coexist, indeed, at times they blended imperceptibly. Although a small proportion of Hasbrouck customers were market producers, this was only about 12 percent in 1799. These farm families tended to own more property, possess larger productive capacities and more farm laborers, often slaves, than their local-trading neighbors. Further, they produced over 70 percent of the goods sold to Hasbrouck.

THE MARKET REVOLUTION

The first several decades of the nineteenth century witnessed the growth of larger markets, offering greater economic opportunities for some valley farmers, but challenges for others. This is the period of the "market revolution." Formerly iso-lated towns and villages throughout the northeastern United States were brought into an increasingly complex market system through the construction of turn-pikes and canals. Between 1790 and 1820, 278 turnpike companies had built over 4,000 miles of road in New York and pulled fertile farmland from the rural interior into direct market competition with what were formerly privileged pro-ducing regions like the Hudson Valley. Within the decade, both the Erie Canal, and even more significant for mid–Hudson Valley farmers, the Delaware and Hudson Canal, had opened up the rich, grain-producing western hinterland of the state to the New York City market, in direct competition with valley farm families.[17] The implications of these developments were profound.

Before this period, with limited competition from western producers, valley farmers paid little attention to the way they cultivated their crops. Farmers failed to rotate their crops in any systematic fashion and failed to regularly manure the soil (which would have maintained the humus content), therefore contributing to the growing exhaustion of their lands. Constant cropping, winterkill, and various pest infestations reduced grain yields throughout the Hudson Valley.[18] By the 1820s, after generations of neglectful farming methods and general soil exhaustion, wheat yields in the mid-valley had decreased from a high of fifteen to twenty bushels per acre in the eighteenth century, to about ten bushels. In contrast, yields in western New York counties now entering the New York City market climbed to some twenty bushels an acre.[19]

Farmers attempted to offset these losses in productivity and remain competitive with western producers by putting all available land under cultivation, some of it inferior land that had been previously depleted through agricultural production. Although Kingston farmers cultivated roughly the same amount of land throughout the period, almost twelve acres, farmers throughout Ulster County increased the land under cultivation by almost 50 percent, from nine acres in the 1780s to thirteen acres by the 1820s.[20] However, this was probably the maximum amount of land farmers could hope to cultivate, and with production per acre roughly half that of western producers, many valley farmers could no longer compete effectively in the grain trade.

The increased competitive marketplace offered by the transportation revolution encouraged alterations in the way many farm families in the mid-valley produced and marketed their goods. Valley farmers, under strain from western competition and declining grain yields, invested in more sophisticated farming equipment, such as the iron-toothed harrow and the iron plow. They put more land under cultivation in order to make up for declining yields per acre. *More significantly*, larger numbers of farmers in the mid-valley began specializing in single cash-crop production and selling their produce commercially.

Once again, the rich Hasbrouck account books reveal the economic activities of hundreds of families in the Kingston area during this important period of market development. Hasbrouck's business had grown significantly during the first twenty years of the nineteenth century, as he dealt with 601 customers that year. Further, the percentage of Hasbrouck customers who sold their produce to New York City had more than doubled since the late eighteenth century—from 12 percent (23 of 186 customers) in 1799 to 27 percent (165 of 601 customers) in 1820.

Kingston was still an agricultural area, with farm goods (primarily grain and flour) comprising almost 65 percent of the exports on Hasbrouck's sloops. Barrel staves and shingles comprised almost 35 percent of all exports, while the products of home manufacture constituted 1 percent.

TABLE 5.8

Average Production of Grain in Ulster County, 1776–1820

PRODUCTION OF WHEAT

	Kingston BUSHELS	Rural towns BUSHELS
1776–1790	86.4 (5)	106.2 (23)
1791–1805	125.5 (9)	154.9 (39)
1806–1820	110.0 (8)	147.3 (41)
Missing	54	103

PRODUCTION OF RYE

	Kingston BUSHELS	Rural towns BUSHELS
1776–1790	97.7 (4)	51.7 (8)
1791–1805	47.2 (4)	127.8 (25)
1806–1820	20.0 (2)	75.1 (25)
Missing	66	149

AVERAGE ACRES OF GRAIN UNDER CULTIVATION,
ULSTER COUNTY, 1776–1825

	Kingston	Rural towns
1776–1790	11.1 (6)	9.1 (13)
1791–1805	10.6 (5)	17.3 (26)
1806–1820	11.3 (6)	13.3 (30)
Missing	60	138

Source: Ulster County Probate Inventories, 1776–1820, Ulster County Clerk's Office.

However, by 1820, some of the differences between local and long-distance traders had become more pronounced. The 165 long-distance traders in that year earned seven times more agricultural credits than their local-market neighbors, and five times the number of stave credits. In addition, customers who used Hasbrouck's sloop in 1820 used three times as much cash, and earned only one-third as many service-related credits as their local-market neighbors. Although more families traded textiles at Hasbrouck's store in 1820 than twenty years earlier, the increases were modest. Textiles were traded by only thirteen local customers in 1820, valued at £9 7s, about the same amount earned by Hasbrouck's sloop customers (see Table 5.9).

However, much like twenty years earlier, few customers used cash at the shop-keeper's store but tended to barter and trade products they grew or manufactured for goods sold by Hasbrouck. Unlike the eighteenth century, far more cash was in circulation throughout New York by the 1820s. However, the contraction of circulating currency resulting from the 1819 financial crisis was still being felt in the valley in 1820, so less cash was available in Kingston, as throughout the United States, and this probably affected its use at Hasbrouck's store for that year. Customers did use less cash at the store in 1820 than in 1815 or 1825. However, the proportion of customers using cash, roughly 20 to 25 percent, was consistent from the late eighteenth through the mid-nineteenth century. In the mid-valley, the crisis affected how much those who already used cash relied on the medium, not how many people used cash.[21]

TABLE 5.9

Average Credits for Sloop and Local Customers, Hasbrouck Accounts, 1820

Product	Sloop customer	Nonsloop customer
Agricultural	£21 4s (137)	£3 5s (88)
Textile	£9 5s (13)	£9 7s (13)
Staves	£15 16s (90)	£2 15s (230)
Service	£1 10s (2)	£3 17s (8)
Cash	£22 9s (51)	£7 2s (68)
Total cases	165	436

Source: Hasbrouck Account Books, New York Historical Society.

TABLE 5.10

Proportion of Produce Destined for Local vs. Long-Distance Trade Hasbrouck's Sloop Customers, Kingston, 1820

Product	Local	Extra-local	Total
Agricultural	10.2%	89.7%	£2,906 11s
Textiles	32.3	67.5	£27 16s
Staves/lumber	23.6	76.3	£1,424 5s

Source: Hasbrouck Account Books, New York Historical Society.

By 1820, the proportion of trade dominated by Hasbrouck's sloop customers had increased even further. His long-distance traders—27 percent of Hasbrouck's customers—now produced about 90 percent of the agricultural exports and over 75 percent of the stave trade. In addition, of the £1,627 worth of cash used for purchases at Hasbrouck's store, these 165 customers spent 70 percent of it. Most of the goods produced by these residents were destined for long-distance trade. Cornelius Cole was one of those Kingston residents who used Hasbrouck's sloop. Cole earned £8 of agricultural credits and over £5 in stave credits through the local account book. However, he earned some £15 10s in agricultural credits in Hasbrouck's sloop account book. Cole is representative of many of Hasbrouck's sloop customers. A mere £4 6s of agricultural goods were traded per sloop customer on local markets, and only £3 15s worth of barrel staves. This was only a small portion of their trade, however, since they averaged £19 1s of produce and £24 3s of staves on Hasbrouck's sloop.

The developing commercial market, added to the new western competition, was influencing the size of farmers' production, as some households responded to new competitive demands by producing and trading more grain and flour. During the first two decades of the nineteenth century, the proportion of farm families who produced for commercial markets more than doubled in Kingston, and farm households brought more land under cultivation to stay competitve with growing western competition. Clearly, these farmers were active commercial producers who benefited from the economic changes taking place during these years.

This is consistent with other regions of the Northeast. Studies of Massachusetts' farmers reveal the extraordinary distances farmers traveled to receive the most profitable returns for the sale of their produce.[22] Pennsylvania farmers responded enthusiastically to the thriving market economy and to the expanding rural industry that offered them opportunities for profit. Indeed, Paul Clemens and Lucy Simler have argued that one of the most distinctive characteristics of the Pennsylvania economy was the "prominence of market agriculture in the lives of most residents."[23] Clearly, many farmers, whether in Pennsylvania, New England, or the Hudson River Valley, responded positively to the opportunities offered by the expanded marketplace, and shared its benefits.

However, those families who became extensively involved in commercial markets were, for the most part, larger landowners with greater productive capacities who had significant surplus agricultural goods to sell. Hasbrouck's accounts reveal that "ordinary" farm families did not increase their production or sale of farm produce. Nevertheless, even smaller producers who could not increase their agricultural production were affected by this developing market revolution. As many farmers found it difficult to compete with western farmers in the grain trade, they diversified their production in order to meet market demands and maintain their standard of living.

Some households increased their textile production for market sale. Ulster County families increased the *amount* of home-produced cloth, as production rose from 5.78 yards of wool per capita in 1810, to 6.08 yards in 1820, to 8.6 yards in 1825.[24] By 1820, Ulster contained close to forty carding machines, thirty fulling mills, and 188,168 yards of cloth were manufactured in the home. This increased production primarily reveals an intensification of production within households, since there was little change in the proportion of households involved in textile manufacturing. During the last decades of the eighteenth century, probate inventories record that 76 percent of Ulster County homes owned at least one spinning wheel, and about 40 percent owned a loom. Through the 1820s, these proportions remained virtually the same, although the amount of home-produced cloth increased substantially (see Table 5.11).

Other mid-valley families became involved in the commercial textile industry by increasing sheep raising and wool production, while others still increased their production of dairy and livestock.[25] Beginning in the first decade of the nineteenth century, New England manufacturers sent agents to purchase wool in the mid–Hudson Valley. These agents, working under commission, visited farms in Ulster and Orange, buying the surplus wool of farm households. Although families in the Kingston area enlarged the size of their sheep herds, with the size of flocks increasing from about eleven per household in the late eighteenth century to about fifteen in the second decade of the nineteenth century, the size of sheep herds in the county as a whole remained steady (see Table 5.11).

TABLE 5.11

PROPORTION OF PROBATES WITH TEXTILE-PRODUCING EQUIPMENT,
ULSTER COUNTY, 1791–1820

	1791–1805	1806–1820
Sheep	15.5	14.9
Looms	40.0%	43.3%
Spinning wheels	72.2%	76.6%
Wool (pounds)	46.5	43.8
Total	90	90

Source: Probate Inventories of Ulster County, 1791–1820, Ulster County Clerk's Office.

Ulster also witnessed the development of several small textile mills. Although only a minor portion of the local economy, and insignificant compared to New England's mills, local mills employed weavers at the looms, and put out spinning to farm families in the mid-valley. In 1815, John Buckley, who had worked for several years for Almy and Brown in Providence, Rhode Island, purchased a farm and opened a mill in Marlborough, carding and spinning wool for farmers in southern Ulster and northern Orange counties. Buckley added several looms and by 1822, the Marlborough Woolens Factory was weaving cloth and distributing yarn to local families for spinning. Although a relatively small operation, Buckley remained in business through 1855, employing several operatives and a network of local spinners.[26]

As historians of the textile industry have demonstrated, rural outwork production offered many farm families their first exposure to cash wages.[27] In addition, through this work and the wages earned, valley families were able to increase their purchases of manufactured goods being sold in local stores. This process increased market ties and is pivotal in the process of turning valley farm families into consumers. Finally, it offered farm families in economic difficulty an opportunity to gain side employment.

Nevertheless, textile manufacturing and wool production remained a relatively small part of the Ulster County economy, and although undoubtedly important to the economic success and survival of those households that participated in it, the number of Hasbrouck customers involved in the marketing of these goods was relatively small. Although shopkeepers exported more textiles in the 1820s than they had earlier, the increases were modest. Most domestic manufactures were still consumed at home or traded locally among neighbors. However, for those families who did increase production, they were reorienting household labor, time, and energy away from traditional agricultural pursuits toward domestic manufacturing.

If most Ulster County households did not respond to market changes by producing more agricultural goods or textiles, how did they settle accounts with their shopkeepers, obtain extra cash, or purchase consumer goods? As late as 1820 only one in five Hasbrouck customers used cash at his store, and this was little more than the proportion of customers who used cash twenty years earlier. Other Ulster County shopkeepers' accounts support the still limited state of a cash economy in the mid-valley through the 1820s.[28] Further, the same proportion of customers sold or traded agricultural goods in 1799 and 1820, and even if some Hasbrouck customers increased their production and commercial sale, most did not. How were ordinary farm families affected by the demands and opportunities of the growing market economy?

Consider the case of John van Keuren, a Kingston farmer who traded with Abraham Hasbrouck from 1811 through 1827. Van Keuren traded small amounts of grain, flour, and eggs in exchange for consumer goods, averaging £2 18s in credits per year. On occasion, though not every year, he sold Hasbrouck some barrel staves. From 1816 through 1827 he brought an increasing number of staves to the shopkeeper each year. Although he never stopped selling farm produce, barrel staves comprised a growing portion of his credits.[29] Van Keuren was not alone. In the late eighteenth century only 20 percent of Hasbrouck's customers traded staves, while 25 percent traded farm goods. During the first two decades of the nineteenth century, while the percentage of customers exchanging farm goods remained the same, the proportion of families producing and trading staves increased dramatically. By 1820 over 50 percent of his customers traded or sold barrel staves. Further, not only were more customers trading staves, but staves were forming a larger portion of customers' accounts. Staves accounted for only 25 percent of the *value* of farmers' accounts in 1799, while agricultural produce was 60 percent. By 1820, as agricultural produce declined to 45 percent of the value of farmers' accounts, staves had climbed to over 30 percent.

Increasing the production of wooden staves was an attempt by households in this long-settled farming community to respond to the challenges of sharpened market competition of the early nineteenth century. Families in tenuous economic positions throughout rural New England and the mid-Atlantic states were faced with similar circumstances. In those regions, families took part in the outwork production of a variety of products, including shoes, textiles, and palm-leaf hats.[30] With less land to offer children and an inability to satisfy basic needs through agricultural production, farm families devoted increased energy into nonagricultural pursuits, part-time trades, and outwork production, or, in the case of Kingston-area farmers, the production of barrel staves.

Manufacturing barrel staves, which valley farmers had done since the mid-seventeenth century, fit the seasonal nature of farm life perfectly. During the winter months, farm families rived barrel staves from the oak wood they cut on their property, allowing them to do their work in the fields and use slack times for the construction of a marketable product. Stave production required very little investment of capital, since the materials were the oak wood that was being cut down anyway, and further, the tools needed for production were modest and unsophisticated. Barrel stave construction needed no factory, and throughout its heyday in the valley remained centered in the household. Kingston farmers produced and traded red oak staves—weaker, cruder staves used primarily for grain and flour barrels—not the white oak staves used for "wet" barrels or kegs.[31]

Constructing and trading barrel staves, although a manufactured item, was significantly different from braiding palm-leaf hats, weaving cloth, or binding shoes. These latter forms of home industry often witnessed farm families working for rural manufacturers who owned the materials, controlled the production, and paid the wages. Even if there was more freedom for "outworkers" than factory employees, one was essentially working for someone else. Although many families succeeded in integrating production into the household economy, scholars of these industries have observed that merchant-controlled outwork was one of the first crucial steps toward capitalist productive relations in the countryside.[32]

Manufacturing staves was another matter, akin more to agricultural by-industries like cheese and butter production.[33] Like these other home industries, stave manufacturing enabled producers to maintain a significant degree of freedom and control in their production. The wood traded grew on the farmer's land, the work was done according to the farm families' schedule, and the profit earned from sale or trade was primarily theirs. Stave producers not only maintained control over this production, but whether by choice or by circumstance, they were able to avoid dependence on employers and laboring for wages. Further, farm families traded staves with shopkeepers like Hasbrouck much like they had flour or grain, earning cash or credits in shopkeepers' accounts, so no new methods of marketing had to be employed.

Nevertheless, even as stave manufacturing allowed farm families to maintain the integrity of the household productive system, it also increased farm households' relationship to the market. These staves were not simply the surplus farm produce of earlier years, used to balance accounts, but also a commodity, sometimes produced for bartering with neighbors, often for market sale. Even if the methods families employed to produce staves did not change, the size of the trade reveal families were spending more than just their "slack" time constructing these items. As scholars have noted for other forms of home industry, stave production was reorienting the internal workings of the household productive system. As farm families devoted more attention and time to stave production, or other nonagricultural pursuits, they were devoting more of the households' productive energies toward market involvement.[34]

Further, the increasing reliance on stave manufacturing and other nonagricultural industries reveals changes not only within households, but in the character of the mid-valley's economy and its relationship to the developing national market. A maturing market system now linked formerly separate regions of the northern countryside into an interconnected and increasingly complex commercial network. Hudson Valley staves were not only manufactured to package valley grain, but also for western produce as well. Although agriculture continued to play an important role in the local economy, the market revolution ushered in a new stage in the town's development as a servicing and shipping community closely connected to, and interdependent with, other economic regions.

THE IMPLICATIONS
OF THE MARKET REVOLUTION

Between the years 1790 and 1820, mid–Hudson Valley farmers altered their agricultural practices in order to meet the needs and demands of the growing national market. Although the market revolution encouraged commercially oriented agricultural production and increased reliance on capitalist-controlled forms of outwork in New England and other mid-Atlantic regions, evidence from the mid–Hudson Valley reveals a somewhat different pattern. Some farmers increased agricultural production, but this group remained a minority of the Ulster County population. Many families, because of insufficient or inadequate landholdings, could not compete in the new, more competitive agricultural market. For the most part, it was larger producers, like Nicholas Hardenbergh, who owned substantial amounts of property, farm animals, and equipment who became large market producers. Extensive market involvement, whether in the mid–Hudson Valley or other parts of the rural Northeast, tended to be the province of larger producers.

However, this does not mean that ordinary farm families were not affected by market changes. As these families sought to maintain or raise their standard of living, they turned to "specialized," nonagricultural market activities. Some households increased home-textile production, but most were like John van Keuren, who turned to various forms of rural manufacturing, particularly barrel-stave production, to make ends meet. So, even if not producing agricultural goods, these smaller producers were aiming more of their production toward commercial markets.

Nevertheless, stave production in the valley was different from the rural manufacturing systems taking shape throughout New England. There, production was controlled by manufacturers who employed farm families in increasingly complex putting-out systems. Although woolens were put-out for spinning by mill owners like John Buckley, this was a small part of the valley's economic life. In Ulster and Orange counties, farm families produced staves, maintained control over production, and earned the profit from its sale.

However, even as the market revolution restructured economic life, certain patterns of trade and production persisted in the mid–Hudson Valley. Many families continued to structure their production around the home, maintaining control over what was produced and the methods employed. Most families still traded locally through the 1820s and did not ship large amounts of produce or staves to New York City, although much of their produce ended there eventually. Indeed, a vibrant local trading system, centered around household production and barter with neighbors and storekeepers, continued to exist along with the more commercially driven New York City trade.

Nevertheless, mid-valley farm families were changing the types of goods produced, increasing the amount of land they farmed, and redirecting their time, energy, and resources to producing goods that were oriented toward the market. Although farm families responded differently to the new market demands, and many still maintained traditional methods of production and trade, most were altering their production in response to the needs and demands of the market revolution.

CHAPTER SIX

"The Harbingers of Commerce"

Mid-Hudson Valley
and the Creation of a
Market Society, 1820–1850

In a scene reminiscent of the celebration of King George's ascension to the throne in 1763, Kingston's residents gathered to publicly celebrate once again on November 25, 1826. Rather than marching through the streets of town like crowds did during most previous celebrations, however, this group moved along the banks of Rondout Creek, and in small boats on the creek's waters. As in past celebrations, toasts were offered, bands played, cannons roared, and a benediction was given by the pastor of the Kingston Reformed church. However, this was no celebration of a political figure, military victory, or a religious or national holiday. This day the people of Kingston were celebrating the initial voyage along the recently constructed Delaware and Hudson Canal. The *Ulster Sentinel* called the journey "a proud day for the County of Ulster, for on that day her bosom was opened to the harbingers of Commerce."[1]

Ostensibly, the celebration was the completion of the Delaware and Hudson Canal. Begun in 1824, and not fully completed until 1831, the canal was, much like the Erie to the north, a technological triumph. Hundreds of laborers worked for seven years blasting stone, felling trees, pulling stumps, digging ditches, and constructing a one-hundred-mile-long "artificial river," connecting the Hudson River to northern Pennsylvania.[2]

In fact, though, this day was just as much a celebration of commerce, or more specifically, the new leading role Kingstonians hoped their town was to play in reaping the benefits of the bounty of western New York and Pennsylvania. A flotilla of small boats made their way down the Rondout where they were "saluted

115

with a discharge of cannon from the Heights." Unlike parades of the past, this entourage was not led by Kingston's Board of Directors, leading citizens of the town, military heros or the like, but by Mr. Bolton, a Pennsylvanian and president of the Delaware & Hudson Canal Company, and Mr. Stebbins, the company's director (also a Pennsylvanian) as well as the Kingston Order of Freemasons.

Although the canal's opening was not completely auspicious, since the boat carrying the dignitaries was detained "at length" on her first stop in the lock "owing to the numbers that weighed her down and the premature opening of the lock below," it was clear to most observers that this was the beginning of a new era for both Kingston and the mid–Hudson Valley. As the reporter covering the event wrote, back-river valley communities, "which had slept for ages in silence" were now connected to the Hudson River and "opened to the harbingers of Commerce."[3]

The people of Kingston accurately envisioned their future. Their town did become a leading market entrepot in the years after 1826, and indeed the town was dramatically transformed in size, scope, and economic development. As Kingston's hinterland grew, so too did the town, and the community's economy diversified. In 1817 some twenty dry goods stores serviced the Kingston population of 2,400 people living in 150 dwelling houses (not much larger than the other towns in Ulster). The majority of these residents were directly engaged in agriculture, and much of the rest of the population were artisans and shopkeepers who serviced these farmers.[4] By 1850, the population of the town surpassed 13,000, the overwhelming majority of whom were *not* farmers but laborers involved in nonagricultural and generally nonmanufacturing work.[5]

Nevertheless, most communities in the mid-valley did not undergo such changes. Indeed, the small agricultural towns of New Paltz, Marbletown, and Rochester, among others, remained essentially small agricultural towns. The majority of the households in these communities were composed of farm families and remained so past the Civil War. This was representative of the northeastern United States generally. However, even these farm households altered the types of agricultural production in which they were involved, and experienced the impact of the commercial market in ways they had not earlier. This new experience was true of many Kingston farmers as well. An exploration of the Hudson Valley's development during the nineteenth century reveals the diverse impacts of the "market" and "transportation" revolutions on long-established farm communities.

FROM CORPORATE COMMUNITY
TO BOOSTER TOWN:
KINGSTON, 1800–1850

Through the early nineteenth century, with little competition from western farmers, farm families in Ulster County produced and traded agricultural goods much as they had throughout the eighteenth century; smaller farmers alternating and combining home production with neighborhood trade, and larger producers doing the same but also selling commercially. However, the completion of various transportation systems in the early nineteenth century challenged the mid-valley's once dominant position in grain production, and by extension, challenged farm families' traditional production and trade practices. Furthermore, this new competition offered challenges to the economic community that had shaped life in these small towns. Through the early nineteenth century, community standards and corporation policies had continued to regulate private economic activity in valley towns. This regulation sought to protect emerging economic interests and prevent the worst excesses of unfettered market development.[6] Town authorities continued to regulate the prices and quality of goods, to supervise markets and financial exchanges, as well as regulate interest rates for money loaned to the town's poor. Further, in Kingston, the "assize of bread" and maximum prices on other staple products continued at least through the 1830s, and probably beyond.[7]

Little of this legislation was an attempt to prevent commercial development; indeed, the majority of the population of Kingston, and the Hudson Valley generally, were small farmers or artisans who were well aware of, and participated in, the growing agricultural market. Corporation initiatives had from the earliest days of its organization attempted to facilitate the community's easy involvement in the river trade. The corporation routinely appropriated funds for repairing docks, maintaining roads leading to the river, and keeping the market house in good repair. Further, the corporation donated land and materials for grist and flour mills in town to serve the local farming population, and distributed common land to allow more land to be put under production. Although there were competing economic interests, public policy continued to support and promote the region as an agricultural production center.

Nevertheless, the increased commercial penetration into the countryside of western New York and beyond offered challenges to the mid-valley's once pre-eminent position as a leading agricultural producer. Rumors of the richness and productivity of western lands had reached the valley in the years before the nineteenth century, prompting the "marchants of Kingston," who hoped to gain a share of this agricultural bounty, to build a "rode to Schohary Kill" in 1784. The Kingston Trustees supported the plan and voted £200 of corporation funds for construction. With mid-valley wheat earning high prices on the New York City market, few farmers expressed hostility to the plan, but few expressed support either, and the proposal was eventually abandoned owing to a lack of funding.[8] Shopkeepers, however, realizing the benefits that Kingston's service sector would enjoy if the town controlled this trade, returned to this idea repeatedly over the next several decades.[9]

Even if Kingston's farmers expressed little interest in turnpike building, the larger developments of the transportation revolution were revealing the town's new role in a larger competitive, national market and making clear that competition for the New York grain market would be intense. Storekeepers, millers, coopers, and others within the artisans' community recognized the benefits of processing and packaging produce of western farmers for reshipment to New York City, and the first two decades of the nineteenth century were characterized by a debate among groups that had once shared many common economic goals. This debate, originally centering around building transportation routes to the west, soon involved a reconsideration of many of the economic policies and practices that had characterized Kingston's local political and economic system.

Four times between 1784 and 1817 Kingston's commercial community, supported by many in the service trades, organized substantial efforts for constructing roadways (later canals), into agriculturally rich Delaware County, due west of Kingston. Recognizing the implications of the developing national market, and the fact that Kingston's neighbors, Newburgh and Catskill, had already tapped into western grain supplies with their turnpikes, proponents argued that Kingston must follow their example and establish trade routes to Delaware County.[10] Although Hasbrouck and several shopkeepers incorporated the Delaware Turnpike Company in 1817, they abandoned this effort when few farmers supported it. For the next several years this debate continued with proponents of the pike pleading with farmers not to "neglect their duty" to support the roadway. When farmers did not actively support the call for turnpikes, they were then accused of showing a lack of "public spirit."[11]

By 1820, Kingston's commercial community recognized that the larger structural changes in transportation, represented most dramatically by the imminent completion of the Erie Canal (under construction since 1817), threatened the town's former leading role in the grain trade. Indeed, some believed that Ulster County's role as a leading grain producer was all but finished and declared publicly that developing Delaware County "must eventually effect more for the growth and support of this village [Kingston] than our own county."[12]

As Kingston became more enmeshed in the vagaries of the expanding market system, the consensus that had existed among various economic sectors dissolved. As early as 1799, public debate about the role of the corporation, its control over common land, and the efficacy of local market regulations emerged.[13] In response, the twelve trustees offered their resignations in 1805, but they were refused, and at this time the regulatory powers of the corporation were reduced.[14]

The debate in Kingston, replicated in towns throughout the rural Northeast, represented the growing economic complexity of the town as different groups with opposing interests struggled to promote their economic policies and agendas. Furthermore, it reveals the continued erosion of the corporate unity which had once linked Kingstonians together. In the seventeenth and eighteenth centuries, as Kingston controlled the grain trade, a reciprocity of interests linked the various sectors of the economy together. By the 1810s, the town's economy was far more diverse, and a variety of competing interests struggled for power and position.

Debate continued, however, and in 1816, the trustee's resignations were accepted, the common lands sold, and a new town government officially installed.[15] Although perhaps primarily symbolic, the dismantling of both the corporation and disposal of the common lands represented the recognition that Kingston's corporate identity, a group of people with common unifying social and economic purposes, no longer existed.

Kingston farmers' resistance to turnpikes and canals were not arguments against markets or commerce, but attempts to protect *their* market position, which had been privileged for years by transportation limitations. Although there had never been complete consensus in economic policies, the farming and service sectors had generally worked together because their own economic interests were intertwined. A symbiotic relationship existed that generally benefited all economic constituencies—the regulation and maintenance of a healthy local trade and the promotion of a thriving long-distance commercial trade.

By the 1820s, however, commercial groups could promote their economic interests only by cultivating closer ties with western farmers, the same western farmers whose grain production threatened the livelihoods of Kingston producers. By this time, the generalized nature of the market revolution revealed the larger competitive system within which Kingston now existed. Residents in communities who once shared mutual economic goals gradually realized that their interests had diverged.

Indeed, the desire for economic change had influenced town politics and social order. The movement to incorporate the village of Kingston as a separate entity from the Kingston Corporation, accomplished in 1805, was related to the desire to broaden the commercial powers of the town's regulatory body, powers that would benefit more than just the freeholders of the corporation. The "Directors of the Village of Kingston," the five elected leaders authorized to regulate village affairs, were given the power to tax freeholders and inhabitants, and to use revenues for town improvements, constructing public buildings, and stimulating local industry. Furthermore, the village government would be able to use public funds for improving roads and financing turnpikes.[16]

Through the early nineteenth century the prevailing economic belief of Kingston residents was that the public good of the community could best be served by the corporation trustees who provided economic guidance and maintained ultimate authority over trading practices, prices, wages, common lands, and certain aspects of private economic activity. The diversification of the valley's economy and the growing power of external regional markets challenged the ability of these boards to act as autonomous economic entities, much as it challenged the once interdependent relationships among different economic sectors. Throughout the rural Northeast, many Americans were rejecting not only the economic powers of these boards, but even the public economic philosophy that had sustained them: the belief that communities were corporate bodies with collective economic and social interests.[17]

During the early nineteenth century, the idea that the public good could best be served by private interests, "men in capital and public spirit to take a lead in projecting and promoting such public institutions as are immediately connected w/ the common weal" was gaining support in the mid-valley.[18] Although this belief had prevailed for some time in larger port towns and bustling urban areas where competing economic interests had always struggled with one another in defining public economic policy, it was relatively new for small agricultural communities in rural America where cooperation and interdependence had often prevailed in the economic sphere.

A BOOSTER ECONOMY:
KINGSTON, 1825–1850

Although the Kingston economy boomed following the opening of the canal, in the years before its construction, few would have envisioned the town's dramatic growth. Indeed, available economic indices and contemporary commentators revealed Kingston's unfavorable economic condition in the 1820s. The town's population was declining, farm production was dropping, and western agricultural competition was increasing. By the early 1820s the first shipments of grain from western New York were traveling along the Erie Canal and down the Hudson past Kingston. This grain, of higher quality than the local variety, and produced in larger amounts, earned more on the New York City market than valley wheat and rye.[19] Observers in Kingston, and throughout the valley, watched anxiously.

Although there was real concern, these larger challenges also engendered meaningful debate and discussion about how to counteract the developments that threatened the mid-valley's economy. Central participants in this debate were some of Kingston's leading men of commerce who argued that if their town was to thrive, or even survive, it would have to become more than a mere farming village. These residents, or "boosters" as they were commonly called, emerged in communities throughout the northern United States.[20] Kingston's leading boosters were merchants and shopkeepers who fervently supported their town: Abraham Hasbrouck, Joseph Smith, and John Tappen, among others. These men recognized that in the new competitive environment engendered by the market and transportation revolutions, their town competed with other port communities up and down the Hudson for economic growth. These boosters promoted the economic virtues of their community to obtain outside investment, control over transportation systems, and public funds for internal growth.

Some boosters argued that Kingston should develop its manufacturing base, which had been generally limited to household production, by attracting manufacturing firms to invest in the area. Indeed, one Kingston resident contended in typically inflated booster fashion, that the town was "destined, under the control of the present disposition of enterprise, to become one of the greatest manufacturing and commercial communities on the Hudson."[21] However, prospective manufacturers found the mid–Hudson Valley to be a far less attractive place for industry than areas like southern New England. The mid-valley's west bank, even if under growing economic strain, had few landless or underemployed laborers that would have made the area desirable to potential investors.

Other Kingston residents recognized that their town should take advantage of its propitious location for trade, situated as it was on, or near, four different water transportation systems (the Esopus and Rondout creeks, the Hudson River, and about twenty-five miles away, the Delaware). Contemporary commentators observed that an increasing amount of Kingston's economic activity was fueled by agricultural production outside of town, and some of it outside the county, and encouraged the commercial classes in their town to develop this trade further. As early as 1817 the *Ulster Plebian* asked Kingston residents to draw "their attention to the cultivation of a commercial intercourse with the thickly populated settlements that border on the Delaware and Susquehanna rivers." According to the editors of the paper, Kingston "would and must essentially become, at some future day, the great emporium of that country."[22]

The best ways to increase this trade, of course, were better roadways linking Kingston to farmers in the western part of the county and beyond. Boosters like Hasbrouck, Smith, and others advocated construction of a turnpike that would connect the rich agricultural lands of Delaware County with the Hudson River market through Kingston. These leading men of business argued that the inconvenient transport routes throughout Ulster County "would remain from year to year a barrier to the enterprise of agriculture and commerce." Bad roads, the *Ulster Palladium* argued in 1831, "not only dampen the enterprising spirit of commerce, but would produce the same effect on agriculture and manufacture." The *Ulster Plebian* pointed out that turnpikes would "add materially to the prosperity of the inhabitants of this village." The *Palladium* added, somewhat more grandly, that "all concerned," whether "merchants, mechanics, manufacturers, and agriculturalists, would soon realize its benefits."[23]

One of the most interesting aspects of the call for new transport routes was that it was represented as an act beneficial to the entire Kingston community. The various sectors of the economy were linked together: "agriculture and commerce," "agriculture and manufacture," "all . . . would soon realize its benefits." While farmers in western Ulster and Delaware counties certainly supported the idea for a turnpike (indeed, residents in these areas had petitioned for years for better access to the river market) since it would enable them to transport their produce to market more quickly and efficiently, Kingston farmers were skeptical of the idea of giving western regions the opportunity to compete with them.[24] Those in Kingston supporting the roadway even stated as much by pointing out that it was Delaware County, to the west of Ulster, which "must eventually effect more for the growth and support of this village [Kingston] than our own county."[25]

Small Kingston farmers, realizing that they stood to gain little from supporting the construction of a turnpike and, indeed, that their economic interests might even be threatened, had shown little enthusiasm for such an expensive undertaking. In 1819, after thousands of dollars had been invested by local residents, the proposed Ulster and Delaware Turnpike Road was abandoned because of a lack of local support.[26]

Nevertheless, even as Kingston struggled unsuccessfully to raise the necessary capital to build a turnpike, Kingston's boosters gained a prize that would forever transform their town's economy: The town was chosen in 1823 by a consortium of Pennsylvania coal companies to serve as the eastern terminus of the soon-to-be-built Delaware and Hudson Canal. The canal, which was to run along the Delaware River in southwestern New York, eventually linked southwestern New York and northern Pennsylvania (site of the developing coal-mining industry) to the Atlantic market with Kingston as its nexus. In addition, over 100 miles of hinterland that fronted the Delaware River and the canal was now connected to New York City via Kingston.[27]

The story of the canal's impact on Kingston society and economy has been expertly told by Stuart Blumin, and the details need not be recounted here. However, the canal single-handedly transformed Kingston into the leading commercial entrepôt on the river between New York City and Albany. While other port towns in the valley, such as Poughkeepsie, Newburgh, and

Hudson, witnessed modest growth in population in the thirty years after 1825 (between 15 and 20 percent), Kingston's population grew by almost 300 percent, from 2,475 to over 13,000.[28]

Before the canal's opening in 1826, a mix of farmers, tradesmen, and laborers comprised Kingston's 2,500 residents. Close to 70 percent of the town's population were members of farm families, and most residents had been born in the town or the county. Beginning in earnest during the next decade, the population of the town climbed each year with new immigrants, mostly Irish and Germans, working as unskilled laborers on the canal's docks, unloading cargo, shoveling coal, and transferring goods for river shipment. By 1855, only 30 percent of the town's 13,000 residents had been born in Ulster County, and only 10 percent made their living from farming.[29] Although farming was still practiced in town, Kingston was no longer an agricultural community.

Long before the 1850s, the "corporate community," at least in its eighteenth century form, ceased to exist in Kingston. By mid-century a significant proportion of the town's population were seasonal workers who left in winter to find work in other areas. Farmers and farm laborers formed only 10 percent of the population, and although they carried on their work, they were a declining voice in public debate and affairs. Seventy-five merchants, many of them running specialized stores, had replaced the dozen or so general stores like Hasbrouck's that had once serviced the town's needs. A relatively isolated community of 1,500 people, primarily of Dutch descent, might effectively maintain its relatively homogeneous identity in the eighteenth century. By the 1850s, only 45 percent of Kingstonians were born in the United States, and a mere 20 percent were born in Kingston, and other ethnicities such as the Irish and Germans were becoming far more pronounced in town life than the Dutch.

The Kingston economy increasingly serviced the canal. By the 1850s, the Pennsylvania-owned canal company employed more town workers than any other industry, approximately one-quarter of employed Kingstonians. Hundreds of canal workers, mostly recent immigrants, needed to be housed, fed, clothed, and sold goods. Although long-time Kingstonians sometimes commented disparagingly about their new neighbors—their customs, habits, traditions, and religion—they welcomed their business in local stores, taverns, and boardinghouses.[30] Further, if Kingston residents were unhappy with the way their town was changing, it would have been hard to tell. Local newspapers, public subscriptions, and boosters regularly called for more growth, hoping that Kingston would gain manufacturing and productive industry, rather than the extractive and service-oriented ones that characterized the town's economy.[31] Perhaps few long-time Dutch-American farm families who still lived, worked, and traded in town joined in this call, but by the 1840s, they were only one constituency, indeed one of the smallest in town. In the words of Stuart Blumin, Kingston was transformed from a small, yet bustling, port community to a town on the "urban threshold."

MID-VALLEY FARMERS
AND THE MARKET: 1820–1850

Kingston's dramatic nineteenth century growth, so clearly tied to the market revolution, was replicated in towns throughout the Northeast. Some New York towns, like Rochester and Oswego, became market entrepôts. Others, such as Lynn, and Lowell, Massachusetts, became manufacturing centers. Nevertheless, even as Kingston shed its agricultural character and became a commercial town, farming continued to be the primary livelihood for most people in Ulster County through the 1850s, and the independent farm household the primary unit of production. In 1840, the county produced 225,000 bushels of grain, making it one of the leading counties of grain production in New York. However, only 12,000 bushels were produced by the county's most populous town, Kingston, reflecting the new orientation of that town's economy. Over 90 percent of the county's production came from the smaller agricultural towns where two-thirds of the population lived.[32]

Although it is easy to see the effects of commercial change when examining canal building, growing numbers of wage laborers, and towns like Kingston developing into bustling commercial centers, no less important are the ways that market development affected ordinary farm families in Kingston and smaller towns like New Paltz, Hurley, or Rochester. These families continued to farm family property, although in a very different economic landscape, and were compelled to respond to forces unknown to their parents and grandparents. They did so by bringing more land under cultivation, altering the types of agricultural goods they produced, specializing in cash crops, and increasing manufacturing of certain items for market sale. The more they specialized, of course, the less they produced the items they had formerly made, and the more they became consumers of goods they had once manufactured themselves.

The general outlines of what has been referred to as the nineteenth-century market transformation are fairly clear. Although transportation developments gave valley farms expanded access to the developing New York City urban market, these same developments also brought western agriculture into direct competition with west bank farmers, forcing families to alter the types of goods they produced. Further, valley store shelves were now filled with large quantities of textiles and other ready-made products, once produced locally in the home or village but now produced more cheaply in factories in New England and Pennsylvania. The availability of these inexpensive goods, and since farm families specialized production to earn cash to purchase these goods, helped foster a larger consumer market than had existed earlier.[33]

Unquestionably, the most important factor influencing agricultural production in the mid-valley was increased competition from western agricultural producers who now sent their goods east and south via the thousands of miles of canals and turnpikes that slashed across the state. This competition, added to declining grain returns in the valley resulting from generations of poor farming practices, affected the type of production valley families practiced in the years after 1820.[34]

Indeed, as early as 1833, local commentators were already ranking western wheat as superior to the local Ulster crop. While commenting on the failure of the 1833 crop, the *Ulster Palladium* reported, "Never have we seen such wheat fields as those now waving over the western part of this state," particularly the "granaries of the farmers through the valley of the Mohawk, stretching westwardly to the Garden of the Genesee Country. . . ." The state's own official report stated that the Hudson Valley crop was particularly ravaged.[35]

Although New York farmers produced a variety of grain crops, including rye and corn, wheat had always been the "the principal article for making money. . . ." However, by the 1840s, the New York State Census reported wheat yields in the valley to be below ten bushels an acre, less than half the yields of western New York farmers with whom valley households now competed.[36]

In response to these larger economic trends, Ulster County farmers altered the types of agricultural goods they produced and tended to specialize their production more toward market needs. With less expensive and higher quality wheat entering the New York City market from the west, farmers in Ulster switched to rye production. Ulster wheat production was reduced by half between 1840 and 1850, from 57,277 bushels to only 27,489. In contrast, rye production grew dramatically during these years, almost doubling in the ten-year period between 1840 and 1850, from 169,209 bushels to 305,688.[37] Furthermore, farmers continued to bring more land under cultivation. By 1850, Ulster farmers had improved land amounting to 233,059 acres. Although Ulster ranked only twenty-first of fifty-nine counties in New York in the amount of acres under cultivation, they ranked fourth in the improved to unimproved ratio, revealing the efforts of county residents to bring as much land into production as possible.[38]

Farmers also altered their production of wool and domestic textile manufacturing, increasing wool production early in the century, and then substantially reducing the amount produced by mid-century, in response to New England's growing dominance of that industry. In 1810, Ulster produced 83,150 pounds of wool, and increased this to 117,360 pounds by 1840. However, with the continued influx of inexpensive clothing produced in New England textile mills filling Ulster store shelves, residents had trimmed production to 68,322 pounds by 1850.[39]

With the heightened competition and quickened pace of market change altering Northeastern farming, valley farmers found themselves showered with advice on how to respond to the new market demands. Although farmers relied on their own understanding of market needs to meet these developments, they also heard the advice of a relatively new group—professional agricultural reformers and experts who criticized old methods of farm production and provided ample new suggestions to farm families. The early nineteenth century saw the rise of agricultural fairs and state agricultural societies, both of which aimed to promote improved agricultural techniques as well as new marketing strategies to help valley farmers compete more effectively with western producers.[40]

Although suggestions varied, they tended to fall into two broad categories: First, practical suggestions on what types of production would fetch farmers the highest price for their goods as well as suggestions on techniques to more efficiently produce these products; and second, suggestions regarding the ways farmers conducted their business and affairs.[41]

As early as the 1820s, local reformers were suggesting new forms of progressive agricultural and marketing techniques in order to increase output, develop more efficient production methods, and "to pursue that course which shall be found profitable."[42] Some commentators criticized farmers' market behavior, stating that farmers "neglect making calculations as to the profit and loss attending it [farming]."[43] Agricultural reformers warned about western wheat production and advised mid-valley farmers to alter the types of grain they produced—calling for a switch to rye and corn, and to emphasize dairy and beef production for the growing consumer population of New York City.[44]

Although there was some resistance to these new recommendations, it is clear that farmers in the valley generally heeded their advice, or recognized on their own the need to alter traditional practices. Evidence from mercantile account books reveal farm families in Ulster County once again altered their production to respond to market challenges. However, the way farmers responded to the needs of the market varied from family to family.

Consider the case of Cornelius Acker, a long-time Kingston resident who traded with shopkeeper Abraham Hasbrouck. In the 1820s, Acker produced grain for sale, some barrel staves for trade, but marketed little dairy or fresh food products. By 1839, whether responding to agricultural reformers or his own experiences with changing market needs, he still sold grain (primarily rye), but now produced and sold butter and eggs as well.[45] He had gradually diversified his production in order to satisfy market demand.

Other farm families throughout the valley followed a similar pattern, decreasing their production of grain and increasing their production of beef and dairy products. In 1839, 159 Kingston residents purchased, sold, and traded with merchant Abraham Hasbrouck, still one of Kingston's leading merchants. Hasbrouck, although sixty-six years old, now owned two steamboats that made regular trips down the Hudson. Although agricultural produce had been the "cash crop" of choice for Kingstonians throughout the town's history, this trade had gradually declined over the years. In the eighteenth century, agricultural produce had comprised about 60 percent of the value of goods sold by Hasbrouck's customers.[46] In the 1820s, although this proportion had declined, Hasbrouck's patrons still earned the largest share of their credits from the merchant in agricultural goods, about 45 percent. By 1839 this proportion had decreased precipitously, as farm produce earned only 25 percent of the value of goods sold by Kingston residents.

Further, there were significant changes in the types of goods farmers sold to Hasbrouck. Barrel stave production, an extractive industry, had run its course in Ulster by the late 1830s and staves had disappeared as a source of credits. Three-hundred twenty Hasbrouck customers, over half of the customers who dealt with the merchant, sold staves in 1820, totaling 30 percent of their credits. In 1839, not one Hasbrouck customer marketed staves, although farmers did earn 25 percent of their credits from bulk lumber (see Table 6.3).

The movement away from grain production is revealed clearly in the Hasbrouck account book. Although three-fourths of the agricultural goods farmers sold to Hasbrouck in 1820 were wheat, rye, and flour, these items accounted for only one-fourth of farmers' sales in 1839. Kingston farmers responded to their proximity to the New York City market by diversifying their production and specializing in other agricultural items like butter, cheese, and livestock. The introduction of the steamboat to river travel allowed these goods to reach the city quickly. Butter, rarely sold commercially by Kingston farmers before the 1820s, was valued at 16 percent of all goods traded at Hasbrouck's store. Beef and pork, previously traded in small amounts, were now worth about 13 percent. By the early 1840s, some Ulster farmers were selling fresh milk to New York City as well.[47]

Eggs, exchanged infrequently in 1820, now earned 40 percent of the total value of all agricultural produce traded at Hasbrouck's store. The 1830s witnessed a large increase in poultry raising, and with it the production of eggs for sale. New York led all states in the production of poultry in 1840, and the Hudson Valley counties produced more than any others, again, because of the accessibility of the New York City market[48] (see Table 6.2).

TABLE 6.1

PROPORTIONS OF HASBROUCK ACCOUNTS
WITH CREDITS IN VARIOUS CATEGORIES, 1839

Type of credits	Proportions (%)
Agricultural goods	28.3
Oak wood	7.5
Textiles, clothing	1.0
Service	1.0
Cash payments	32.7
Total cases	159

Source: Hasbrouck Account Books, *vols. 31, 32; New York Historical Society.*

TABLE 6.2

PROPORTIONS OF VALUES OF VARIOUS AGRICULTURAL CREDITS
RECORDED IN HASBROUCK ACCOUNTS, 1839

Type of credits	Proportions (%)
Wheat/flour	23.4
Dairy	15.8
Eggs	40.7
Pork/beef	12.5
Other	7.5
Total value	$1,170.16

Source: Hasbrouck Account Books, *vols. 31, 32; New York Historical Society.*

As in earlier years, those who sent goods to New York City earned far more credits from Hasbrouck then did those who simply exchanged produce at his store. Some thirty-two Kingston residents averaged almost $35 each in agricultural credits, over three times the average for those customers who did not send their produce on Hasbrouck's sloop. This is a dramatic decline, however, from Hasbrouck's 1820 accounts, when sloop customers earned almost seven times as many credits as local customers.

TABLE 6.3

Average Credits for Sloop and Local Customers,
Hasbrouck Customers, 1839

Product	Sloop customer	Local customer
Agricultural	$ 34.75 (32)	$ 11.61 (13)
Textile	11.05 (1)	—
Oak wood	120.60 (6)	102.81 (6)
Service	—	44.57 (1)
Cash	87.58 (14)	34.59 (38)
Total cases	39	120

Source: Hasbrouck Account Books, *vols. 31, 32; New York Historical Society.*

By 1839, other changes were occurring in the *ways* farmers traded and exchanged goods. Farm families were far more likely to use cash in their exchanges than previously. Hasbrouck's accounts reveal a significant increase in the use of cash over time. Only 12 percent of his customers used cash in the eighteenth century, some 25 percent in 1820, but almost one-half of his customers did so in 1839.

Furthermore, valley families were purchasing more consumer goods from Hasbrouck than in previous years. Through the first several decades of the nineteenth century, the majority of Hasbrouck's customers were both producers and consumers—they traded agricultural produce, staves, and other items in exchange for other agricultural goods and some manufactured products that they did not produce. By the 1830s, Hasbrouck and other Kingston storekeepers were stocking and selling far more manufactured products than they had earlier. Household items, finished cloth, shoes, hats, among other necessary products that had once been produced in valley homes were now produced more cheaply in New England factories. Kingston consumers also purchased a variety of nonstaple products, such as coffee, tobacco, and chocolate, as well as "fine china," "silk cloth," among other luxuries.[49] One-half of Hasbrouck's customers traded no goods at the store in 1839, but were *consumers*—they purchased items with cash.

Since Hasbrouck didn't specify what type of good was being purchased, simply a general category such as "food-stuff," "household item," or "sundries," other sources, particularly probate inventories, are most useful in estimating the level of consumption occurring in Ulster County. Table 6.4 illuminates some changes in consumption patterns on the Hudson's west bank during the first third of the nineteenth century. For the most part, there was little difference between the first decade of the century and the fourth, although certain items, such as silverware and clocks, were appearing in far more households than previously, revealing the growing use of more refined products as well as a more "modern" approach to time calculation.[50]

Although this "consumer revolution" certainly reflects one more stage in the changing relationship of households to the market, it should be kept in mind

TABLE 6.4

CONSUMPTION PATTERNS, ULSTER COUNTY, 1806–1835

	1806–1820	1821–1835
Earthenware	68.2%	72.0%
Pewterware	64.4	37.3
Silverware	28.7	38.2
Linens	84.0	82.2
Coffeepots	34.8	41.1
Teapots	44.4	39.5
Knives/forks	61.3	63.3
Clocks	39.8	62.4
Total cases	90	52

Source: Probate Inventories, 1806–1835, Ulster County Clerk's Office.

TABLE 6.5

PROPORTION OF PROBATE INVENTORIES WITH TEXTILE PRODUCTION, ULSTER COUNTY, 1806–1835

	1806–1820	1821–1835
Sheep	14.9	15.2
Looms	43.3%	34.2%
Spinning wheels	76.6%	70.1%
Wool (pounds)	43.8	42.5
Total cases	90	52

Source: Probate Inventories, 1806–1835, Ulster County Clerk's Office.

that it eased many aspects of household production, relieving farm families of much labor-intensive, time-consuming production that had once been done in the home. For example, the availability of inexpensive textiles on Hasbrouck's store shelves convinced many Kingston families to stop manufacturing these products at home and to buy them from the shopkeeper. As Kingstonians purchased more textiles, they reduced the amount of cloth they produced in the home, from 7,687 yards in 1835 to a mere 359 yards by 1855.[51]

Furthermore, fewer Ulster families were producing home textiles in the 1830s. Although the proportion of inventories containing spinning wheels declined slightly from the previous decade, over two-thirds of families possessed wheels. However, the proportion of families owning looms declined far more sharply, from 43.3 percent to 34.2 percent. Families still maintained sheep herds, though, selling wool locally and to agents representing New England mills.

By the mid-1830s, storekeepers in the mid-valley increasingly demanded cash payment for the goods they sold, rather than the previously more common swapping of products. Although it is not clear that Hasbrouck demanded cash, almost one-half of his customers paid some cash in 1839, and one-third of the value of all sales were settled in cash. Joseph Smith, who was challenging Hasbrouck as Kingston's premier retailer, advertised "DRY GOODS, which he will sell as cheap as can be purchased elsewhere in the county for cash or approved credit." Although many stores still advertised like Joseph Field "that every article will be sold at very moderate prices for Cash or Produce," it was increasingly clear that cash was a preferred medium of exchange.[52]

This development was the result of several factors. First, demands on local merchants from their suppliers who preferred cash. Second, with the increasingly specialized nature of retail in the 1830s and 1840s, many shopkeepers were simply not equipped to market produce or goods, and so they demanded cash, the one medium that was negotiable. Third, and perhaps most important, the increasing availability of a reliable, stable currency trusted by both shopkeepers and farmers.[53]

Nevertheless, in order to obtain the necessary cash to purchase textiles, other necessities, and even "luxuries," families had to increase their production of, and specialization in, marketable products. As families specialized in market goods and drew the additional income this offered, they also were able to increase their purchase of ready-made goods at local stores. As this process replicated itself throughout the rural Northeast, a consumer market for finished products continued to expand. Furthermore, much like with barrel-stave production in the 1820s, farm families began to devote more labor and time to producing goods specifically targeted to commercial markets, not neighborhood barter.[54]

The growing use of cash, the increasing market specialization of Ulster farmers, along with the expanding supply of ready-made products from New England, all combined to challenge and alter the traditional practices of local trade and barter. Hudson Valley farmers had infrequently used cash in the eighteenth and early nineteenth centuries, primarily because it was unreliable, inflationary, and generally unnecessary. This lack of a reliable circulating medium put much more emphasis on the credibility and character of the trading partners themselves. Most neighborhood trade, whether between farmers or between farmers and the local storekeeper, was conducted in social settings in which personal and family reputation, as well as personal relations, all helped structure trading behavior.

The increasing use of cash offered challenges to the rural economic culture that had structured local exchange among neighbors. On the one hand, the purchase of a product with cash essentially completed the exchange once both parties were satisfied. Ostensibly, the months, even years, of lingering indebtedness that had once characterized relations between shopkeepers and customers, as well as between fellow farmers, were no longer necessary. Although local accounts reveal that accounts continued to be "unsettled" for long periods of time, and cash was often used alongside of promises of future goods or services, cash use was clearly increasing and bartering decreasing.[55]

Nevertheless, if an "impersonal" medium, such as cash, replaced many of the personal obligations and duties that characterized exchange between friends and neighbors, it also offered opportunities to farmers of meager means who might otherwise be seen as risky trading partners. A farmer offering cash for a product being sold by a shopkeeper did not have to worry about whether he might be perceived as unreliable or untrustworthy. The web of cultural assumptions involving exchange, questions of whether to sell on credit, and the haggling often involved in bartering between neighbors were simply not necessary when a buyer with cash appeared at a shopkeeper's counter. Past reliability as well as future responsibility were no longer important variables contextualizing who to trade with and under what conditions. Cash, if reliable and trusted by its users, removed most, if not all, traditional personal obligations, questions of character, and social responsibilities among neighbors, or among strangers, that had once characterized economic behavior.[56]

Although many farm households still traded with neighbors, swapping goods and labor with each other, delaying payment for months, even years, the economic and social significance of this once important means of neighborly interaction was declining. Contemporary commentaries reveal families were just as likely to sell to each other for money, and more likely to simply purchase goods from the local shopkeeper. As the president of the New York Agricultural Society observed in 1851, "Time and Labor have become cash articles and [the farmer] neither lends them or barters them" but "now sells for money."[57]

The long-term implications for the rural economic culture that had shaped relations within communities and among trading partners were profound, although in the short-term, traditional and customary neighborhood exchange continued side-by-side with more commercial practices, the two sometimes intersecting. Over many years, the intricate web of economic interdependence that had linked neighbors to one another slowly eroded. By no means had this occurred by mid-century, and the continued prominence of certain communal endeavors like neighborhood "barn-raisings," "huskings," and "bees" reveal the persistence of interdependent neighborly relations.[58] Nevertheless, barter and trade between neighbors became less frequent with the growing reliance on cash and abundance of inexpensive, ready-made goods at local stores.

In sum, the years 1820 through 1850 further reshaped farm life throughout the northeastern United States, and the mid-valley in particular. Although most Ulster County residents continued farming, many moved away from grain production and specialized in more profitable dairy production and various forms of rural manufacturing. The more families specialized, the more they depended upon purchasing goods they had once produced or traded for in order to make ends meet. Furthermore, shopkeepers and even many farmers began requesting cash for their sales. Although cash had always been used in the valley, the proportion of farm families that used cash at local stores doubled between the early 1820s and the late 1830s.

Although the goals of farm families seemed not to have changed much, since subsisting, acquiring consumer goods, and adding more landholdings to pass onto future generations remained the primary objective of most farm families, the strategies employed to do so changed considerably. Families devoted more time and energy to producing goods for market sale, and in responding to market shifts in ways they had not done so earlier. They produced a smaller variety of goods for home use and local trade since much of this could now be purchased more cheaply at local stores.

In the process, larger regional markets were shaping the lives of mid-valley residents in unprecedented ways. In the eighteenth century, the average mid-valley farm family consumed food produced on their own farm, wore clothing produced by the family or neighbors, and purchased products generally made locally. Although they purchased necessities and some luxuries from local shopkeepers, mercantile accounts reveal these sales were limited.

After 1820, farmers produced primarily for long-distance markets and not neighborhood trade, purchased clothing and many other goods that were factory-made outside the region, in New England, and used coal from Pennsylvania mines to heat their homes. Purchases at local stores were more often for necessities (textiles, shoes, food, etc.) than luxuries, and although families still traded with each other, this once primary form of economic interdependence was now secondary to more commercial relations. Although a "comfortable subsistence" remained the goal for many families, the method by which this was achieved was shaped by a level of market dependence and orientation unknown to an earlier generation.

A Diversified Economy and Society

THE MID–HUDSON VALLEY
AT MID-CENTURY

On September 4, 1852, a few dozen local Katsban (Saugerties) residents gathered at the store of Cornelius Persens. Persens was running no special "sale" that day, and if he had been a price gouger from an earlier time, he might have feared a riot. No, these Ulster families had come to Persens's store for another traditional community celebration, a "moving bee." Indeed, Persens and his neighbors spent much of the day moving his store "back from the road about 50 feet." Persens entertained his neighbors for their efforts: drams of ale for the men, and lighter fare for the women and children. Throughout the day, as the men worked, Persens carried on his business of selling and bartering "broadcloths," "tammies," "persians and pelongs," and a wide variety of other household items.[1]

This "bee" suggests, both symbolically and practically, the role the market economy and a still vibrant communal economy continued to play in mid-nineteenth century Ulster. On the one hand, while he and his neighbors literally moved the store, Persens continued to do business with the gathered crowd, selling goods whose prices were shaped by market forces. Nevertheless, these commercial transactions were taking place this day within the context of a more "communal" undertaking—a neighborly work detail where no wages were offered but in which sociability prevailed. As in most economic activities on the Hudson's west bank by the 1850s, at points the "market economy" and "communal economy" intersected, and other points, existed side-by-side.

Long before this day in 1852, a market economy had begun to shape the economic lives of the people that resided on the Hudson, and the towns they resided in. A larger regional market system dictated the products valley farmers could profitably produce and sell, and the prices they would earn for that produce. Further, this larger market allowed manufactured goods and various raw materials produced throughout the Northeast and mid-Atlantic to make their way onto valley store shelves, further influencing what local residents produced, and perhaps more important, what they consumed.

Nevertheless, many aspects of a communal economy continued to exist, an economy where social considerations and neighborly interdependence continued to thrive. There is no mention in the accounts of the bee that any of the participants saw any contradiction between the two activities that day—commercial sales and a neighborly work detail—although they undoubtedly viewed them as different. No one demanded wages or goods for their services, but they probably expected some future consideration from Persens that went beyond the refreshments served that afternoon. Perhaps a special item sold at discount, or an extension of credit if the family found itself on "hard times." In this way, market and communal forces intersected, reinforcing and even benefiting each other. Even in the 1850s, with the increasing strength of the market economy, less commercial and more communal networks were still at work. Perhaps, as Paul Clemens has suggested for rural Pennsylvania, these neighborly relations "actually strengthened as market relationships—cash sales and wage labor—figured more prominently in the rural economy."[2]

In many ways the folks who came to Persens that afternoon lived and worked much like their parents and grandparents had done. Most farmed family property and lived in small towns and villages that dotted the river valley, and which, as late as 1850, remained just that—small farm towns. During the period that the Kingston economy and population expanded from 3,000 residents in 1820 to over 13,000 in 1850, most other Ulster towns retained their relatively small populations. In 1790, the population of New Windsor was 1,819, and by 1850 it had grown by only 600 people, to 2,457. New Paltz followed a similar pattern: its population was 2,309 in 1790, but only 2,729 as late a 1850.[3]

For a generation beyond 1850, most residents of Ulster County earned their livelihoods from agriculture, as did most people who lived in the United States. Families still sold surplus to market and bartered with neighbors. But, like Kingston farm households, these families altered their production to meet market needs; switching production from grain to wooden staves in the 1820s, and to butter and cheese when it became more profitable to do so in the 1830s and 1840s. Most families remained farmers, albeit it in a far more competitive, market-directed economy.

Much like Kingston, each of these towns had changed too, but the market's impact was less pronounced. Since many families in the backcountry dealt less regularly with commercial markets, they responded less rapidly to market demands. For example, through the mid-1830s, fully one-half of New Paltz shopkeeper Garret DuBois's trading partners settled their accounts by bartering other goods. Marbletown tailor Jacobus Cole accepted almost one-half his payment for services rendered during the 1830s in goods: coffee, bread, potatoes, salt, and cinnamon, among many other items. Indeed, his book of accounts reads very much like Marbletown account books from the 1730s![4]

Further, these towns *looked* much like what they had decades earlier. New Windsor's Edward McGraw wrote that during the 1830s, his town's "farms were rough, the farming implements rude, and the people generally poor." This commentary seems little different from Richard Smith's observations seventy years earlier when he characterized the town as having only "some trade" and the grain growing in the area as "indifferent." Furthermore, the farmland he noted as "broken, stony and few places proper for the Plow." Peter Stansbury commented in the 1820s that Rochester looked much like it had when it had been settled over one hundred years earlier, the "dwellings of the inhabitants are mere log huts" with "half-burnt trees to disfigure the fields."[5]

Nevertheless, the mid–Hudson Valley was a far different place in 1850 from what it had been in 1750, or even 1820 for that matter. Valley farmers had altered their production and consumption patterns in response to the transportation and industrial developments of the nineteenth century, and once begun this process repeated itself every few years, as increased western competition and new demands from urban markets compelled farmers to routinely alter the types of goods they produced. Although mid-valley farmers had always responded to market forces in the eighteenth century, their control of the grain trade and the relatively primitive state of market development had allowed them to produce and sell the same way for generations.

Not all families responded to the new economic developments in the same way, however. Some farmers increased agricultural production, specialized in dairy or grain production, purchased additional lands of neighbors and became commercial farmers. This group remained a minority of the Ulster County population, however. Quite simply, many families, whether in bustling Kingston or quiet Marbletown, could not compete as commercial agricultural producers and were economically unable to produce at this level. For the most part, it was the "busy, successful, farmers" who figure so prominently in the accounts of some historical analyses, who became large market producers.[6] Analysis of the economic activities of the many farmers who were neither so busy nor so successful yields a more varied portrait of rural economic behavior, one that highlights the need to exercise caution when making generalizations based upon the experience of families at the vanguard of commercial production.

Even if most farm families did not become large agricultural producers, the market revolution had a significant impact on their lives. No longer able to competitively produce and trade grain and flour, farm families diversified their production, turning to various forms of rural manufacturing or specializing in various cash crops in order to maintain their standard of living. This production brought even these smaller households closer to the market than they had been in the eighteenth century, as they now responded to new demands and opportunities that had not existed earlier.

However, unlike their New England neighbors who increasingly made ends meet by laboring for wages in rural outwork networks, valley farm families remained relatively independent of this form of productive relations. The putting-out systems that dominated the New England countryside were characterized by farm families weaving cloth, binding shoes, and making hats in the employment of rural manufacturers. Although the work was done in the home, it was under the direction and control of the employer who owned the raw materials being worked with. By specializing in stave manufacturing and dairying, Hudson Valley farm households maintained a significant degree of control in their production, since the goods being produced and sold were theirs, and they could generally fit this work into the farm schedule. Further, families traded and sold staves and butter with shopkeepers much like they had grain, earning cash or credits in shopkeepers' accounts.

Nevertheless, unlike much of the production and trade farmers engaged in during the eighteenth century, which was often with neighbors or with shopkeepers with whom they just as often bartered as sold to, the production of staves, grain, and dairy after the 1820s was primarily for market sale. Families no longer engaged in diversified farming, when they had produced much of the food they ate and clothing they wore, but devoted their time toward producing specialized products for market sale. Although on the surface this production looked little different from the methods households had used for years, families were focusing more of their labor and time toward market involvement.

Furthermore, the more families specialized their production and the less they produced a variety of goods for sale or home use, the more they purchased less expensive ready-made goods from local shopkeepers, further expanding the market for consumer goods throughout the Northeast. In addition, families were far more likely to use cash in this more commercial economy, and demand cash for the goods they produced.

These changes altered the economic culture that structured town life. Although families continued to trade and barter with neighbors and shopkeepers in smaller towns, and even in bustling Kingston, this centerpiece of eighteenth-century rural economic culture declined in practice and significance. As residents purchased more goods from shopkeepers with cash, families relied less on one another for labor and goods. Although farmers' accounts reveal the persistence of these neighborhood networks, they were less pronounced.

In the process, the very nature of community changed as well. Although eighteenth-century valley towns boards had promoted economic growth within communities and encouraged river trade to New York City, they had also emphasized the significance of community needs over individual ones, public demands over private needs. The new town governments that replaced the corporation boards during the years 1780 through 1810 did not continue to act as policy formulators in promoting economic guidance and direction. This role was provided by private, commercial entities, such as the Delaware & Hudson Canal Company and the Ulster County Bank, firms representing distinct economic interests, but also, from the perspective of many town residents, economic potential for communities being transformed by the market revolution.

In the eighteenth century, the Kingston Corporation, like other town boards in the mid-valley, had the power to regulate the public market, halt exportation of goods outside of town, set interest rates, cap prices on goods, and even regulate commercial exchanges between private individuals. In 1742, the Kingston Corporation warned Cornelius DeLameter, the owner of the town's most profitable gristmill, that they would close his mill if he did not comply with their wishes concerning a land dispute bordering his property. He did so. In 1783, Cornelius Schoonmaker, one of Kingston's most powerful and wealthy merchants, and a trustee of the corporation that year, was threatened with a fine if he did not allow the trustees to examine goods being transported on his sloop. There was suspicion that Abraham Brinckerhoff was attempting "to transport a parcel of boards to New York" for which he had not received the "liberty" to do so. Both DeLameter and Schoonmaker bowed to the wishes of the "Corporation of the Freeholders of Kingston."[7]

By the 1840s, the arbiter of economic activity in Kingston was not the town government, but the Delaware & Hudson Canal Company, a private corporation headquartered in Pennsylvania. The D & H, like the old Kingston Corporation, existed to serve its stockholders. However, while the stockholders of the Kingston Corporation had been the freeholders of the town, few stockholders of the canal company were in Kingston; indeed, most were in Philadelphia and New York City. Although it employed several thousand Kingstonians in the 1840s and 1850s, few employees of the canal company were long-time Kingston residents. The economic measures the D & H Canal Company followed—managing the canal, setting carrying costs, regulating wages of workers—were taken in response to the needs of its stockholders, not residents of the town or mid-valley generally. The Kingston Board of Directors had no regulatory power over the Delaware & Hudson Canal, even if a large part of the canal's operations were centered in town and it was the most important economic institution in the community, or the mid-valley for that matter. Those measures might, or might not, benefit local residents. In either case, the Delaware & Hudson would probably be generally unaware of, and perhaps unconcerned with, the needs or opinions of Kingston residents.

By the 1840s, the health of the Kingston economy depended upon the interests of a company with no real ties within the town. In short, the major economic decisions of the town were made not by the town government, wealthy Kingstonians, or even the state government for that matter, but by a private company located over 100 miles away.[8] Although influential Kingstonian Cornelius DeLameter might be forced to submit before the dictates of a powerful town government in 1742, it is difficult to imagine the Kingston Board of Directors summoning Peter Bolton, the President of the D & H Canal Company (and a resident of Philadelphia, for that matter) before their board in the 1840s. It is even more difficult to imagine him complying.

Nevertheless, it would be a romanticized vision of the past to interpret this process as mere community declension since a new community-based economic boosterism and voluntarism had developed within these towns as residents joined together to compete *as* towns with other communities for control over transportation systems and industry that would bring economic prosperity back into their communities. Furthermore, although a more powerful market was reshaping economic life, the mid–Hudson Valley was far from what could be categorized as a free enterprise or free market economy or society. Many economic regulations continued to shape the way residents within towns transacted business with one another.

The Kingston Board of Directors, the town board that replaced the old Kingston Corporation, continued to regulate prices on necessary items, specifically the "assize of bread" into the mid-nineteenth century, and distributed poor relief and capped interest rates as well. Furthermore, a second public market was added in Kingston in the 1830s, where the directors appointed a supervisor to maintain quality standards, monitor price maximums, hours of operation, and weights and measures.[9] In addition, few mid-nineteenth-century valley farmers and tradesmen were "liberal individualists," at least not in the late-nineteenth-century sense of the term. Nevertheless, some residents certainly showed a greater enterprising temperament to take chances, had a larger capacity to absorb risks, and enjoyed larger landholdings and access to labor than smaller neighbors.

Generally, mid-valley residents lived, worked, and traded in what can best be described as a transitional economy, not yet wholly capitalistic nor truly communal. Kin, community, and neighborhood networks still exerted power in the economic sphere and in town residents dealings with one another, but did so within the framework of a market economy that had existed since the earliest days of set-tlement. Nevertheless, the market's growing strength reshaped the relationships of these towns with the larger national economy, and by extension, affected the eco-nomic and social relationships that existed among residents within their small communities and the nature and autonomy of these local economies.

Some viewed the economic developments occurring around them as threat-ening. One Ulster farmer complained of the changing economy, that it "benefits the manufacturer solely, to whom that system compels the producer to pay trib-ute, and thus they set down the Farmer, a mere dependent purchaser."[10] Others, mindful of the declining importance of agriculture in the Northeast, reminded neighbors that farmers composed seventy percent of the population of New York "to which all owe their prosperity."[11]

Others welcomed the developments, lauding the opportunities the competi-tive market system offered and publicly called for more economic growth.[12] Ulti-mately, although some families viewed the changes occurring as positive and oth-ers as negative, most farm families restructured and altered their production and economic practices to meet the needs of the market economy, recognizing both the challenge, as well as the opportunity, that now existed. The ways individual families might do this could vary, since a variety of concerns, not simply market ones, continued to influence a farm household's producing and consuming habits. However, even if more families were responsive to markets than they had been ear-lier, the goals of their production and trade were much the same as their parents and grandparents before them: to subsist, use cash earned from market produc-tion to acquire consumer goods, and transmit legacies to their children. Never-theless, the ways in which they did so, the communities in which they lived, and the economic relations that shaped everyday life had changed considerably.

Notes

Introduction

1. "Presidential Address of Horatio Seymour to New York State Agricultural Society, 1851," reprinted in Danhof, *Changes in Agriculture*, pp. 21–22; Bruce Levine, *Half Slave–Half Free: The Roots of the Civil War* (New York: Hill and Wang, 1992), p. 55.

2. Rothenberg, *From Market-Places to a Market Economy*, pp. 53–55; Christopher Clark, *The Roots of Rural Capitalism*, pp. 59–77.

3. Rothenberg, *From Market-Places*, pp. 80–95. Even Christopher Clark, who disagrees with many of Rothenberg's analyses and conclusions, confirms the increase in market production. See his *Roots of Rural Capitalism*, pp. 146–50. Clemens and Simler, "Rural Labor and the Farm Household," p. 111; Lemon, *The Best Poor Man's Country*, pp. 27–29.

4. See Hal Barron, "Listening to the Silent Majority," pp. 5–8.

5. Rothenberg, "The Market and Massachusetts Farmers," p. 312. Perkins, "The Entrepreneurial Spirit," 160–86.

6. Lemon, "Agriculture and Society," 93, 88–89; and his "Comment on James Henretta's 'Families and Farms'," 688–96.

7. Henretta, "Families and Farms," 3–30; Merrill "Cash Is Good to Eat," 52–56; ibid., "The Political Economy of Agrarian America."

8. Henretta, "Families and Farms," 16–19. The quote is from page 19. See also Henretta, "A Reply to James T. Lemon," *William and Mary Quarterly* 37, 3rd Ser. (October 1980), p. 696.

9. Rothenberg, *From Market-Places*; Clark, *Roots of Rural Capitalism*; Vickers, *Farmers and Fishermen*; Clemens and Simler, "Rural Labor," pp. 106–43.

10. Rothenberg, *From Market-Places*, pp. 80–147.

11. Ibid., 82–89; 95–101; 149–50.

12. Clark, *Roots of Rural Capitalism*, pp. 21–58; and Clark, "Household Economy," p. 175. See also Robert Mutch, "Yeoman and Merchant," 279–302.

13. Vickers, *Farmers and Fishermen*, p. 206.

14. Clemens and Simler, "Rural Labor," p. 111.

15. See Barron, "Listening to the Silent Majority," pp. 5–8.

16. Clark, *The Roots of Rural Capitalism*, pp. 317–29; Allan Kulikoff, *Agrarian Origins*, pp. 13–33; Dublin, *Transforming Women's Work*, pp. 71–75.

17. Rothenberg, *From Market-Places*, pp. 59–69. See Vickers's criticisms of the unrepresentativeness of farmbooks in *Farmers and Fishermen*, pp. 297–98, n. 53. Gloria Main's phrase, which was not a criticism of these sources, is contained in her "Gender, Work, and Wages in Colonial New England," *William and Mary Quarterly* 51, 3rd Ser. (1994): 45.

18. See especially Rothenberg, *From Market-Places*, chapters 2 and 3.

19. See, for example, Clemens and Simler, "Rural Labor," pp. 106–43; and Henretta, "Families and Farms," 3–30.

20. Donald Parkerson's *The Agricultural Transition*, one of the few studies to examine New York, is focused exclusively on agricultural life in the mid-nineteenth century. See also Breugel, "Rise of a Market Society."

21. On horizontal and vertical linkages, see Clark-Smith's "Food Rioters," 29–30; and Lynne Taylor, "Food Riots Revisited," *Journal of Social History* (1996): 487–88.

22. For the European "moral economy," see E. P. Thompson, "The Moral Economy" and "Moral Economy Reviewed," *Customs in Common: Studies in Traditional Popular Culture* (New York: The New Press, 1993). For a useful corrective in the North American context, see Vickers, "Competency and Competition," 3–33.

23. For overviews of this important period in North American economic and social history see Sellers, *The Market Revolution*; Taylor, *The Transportation Revolution*.

24. Washington Irving quoted in *History of the Delaware & Hudson Canal Company, 1823–1923* (Albany, N.Y.: J. B. Lyons, Co., 1925), pp. 109–110.

25. *The New York Times*, 13 March 2000, "Plans for Industrial Revival Divide River Towns": 1.

Chapter One
"A Very Beautiful and Fertile Wheatland"

1. Kalm, *Travels in North America*, pp. 326–31; Smith, *Journal from New York to Albany*, 1:489–90.

2. Kalm, ibid., p. 335, 647; Smith, ibid., 1:9.

3. Population estimates are based on Michael Kammen, *Colonial New York*, pp. 38, 44.

4. Oliver Rink, *Holland on the Hudson* (Ithaca: Cornell University Press, 1986), chapters 1 and 2; Goodfriend, *Before the Melting Pot*, pp. 8–10.

5. The Van der Donck statement can be found in Burke, *Mohawk Frontier*, p. 7. Population calculations are based on Rink, ibid., pp. 157–58.

6. Schenectady's history is recounted in Burke, ibid. The quotations are found on pp. 221, 217. Other New York towns, like Newtown, followed a different, less contentious pattern of development. See Jessica Kross-Ehlrich, *Evolution of an American Town: Newtown, New York, 1664–1775* (Philadelphia: Temple University Press, 1983).

7. The Van Gaasbeck quote is cited in Blumin, *Urban Threshold*, p. 16; the second quote is from Roeloff Swarthout, cited in Zimm, *Southeastern New York*, p. 58.

8. Kammen, *Colonial New York*, pp. 145–47. On powers of the Duzine (not officially established until 1713), see Hugo Freer Papers, Haviland-Heidgerd Collection, Elting Memorial Library, New Paltz, N.Y.; LeFevre, *History of New Paltz*, Chapter 1; Abraham Hasbrouck Sr. Diary, pp. 1–5, and Papers of the Duzine, 1703–1821. See also Sylvester, *History of Ulster County*, pp. 214–15, 164, and *Olde Ulster*, Vol. 3, pp. 46–47.

9. Sung Bok Kim, *Landlord and Tenant in Colonial New York*, (Chapel Hill: University of North Carolina Press, 1978); Douglas Edward Leach, *The Northern Colonial Frontier* (New York: Holt, Rinehart, and Wilson, 1966), pp. 21–22; the Bellomont quote is contained in Patricia Bonomi, *A Factious People*, p. 6.

10. Bielinski, "People of Colonial Albany," pp. 23, n.17.

11. Stephen Innes was speaking of the settlers in Springfield, Massachusetts, in his *Labor in a New Land*, pp. xvii, 180.

12. *Colden Papers*, V. 51, pp. 30–31.

13. About two-thirds of those preparing wills and testaments in Ulster County in the years before the American Revolution did so in Dutch, the remainder was a split between English and French. See Narrett, "Men's Wills," pp. 98–99.

14. On the "Dutchness" of Hudson Valley towns see Records of Town Court at Kingston, 1688–1774, *Ulster County Records*, reel 50, Paul Klapper Library, Queens College, New York. For church denominations, see Papers of Marbletown Church (for Marbletown), Ulster County Records, reel 1. See also Cohen, "How Dutch," 43–60.

15. Lefevre, *History of New Paltz*, pp. 134–39; Narrett, "Men's Wills and Women's Property," pp. 100–101.

16. On methods of land distribution and settlement in New England towns in the seventeenth century see Lockridge, *New England Town*, pp. 8–10. Bonomi, *A Factious People*, details the methods by which town grants were obtained in New York, pp. 32–34.

17. New Paltz Patent, 1677, is reprinted in *Olde Ulster* (1905) vol. 1, pp. 110–14; Papers of the Duzine.

18. Marius Schoonmaker, *History of Kingston*, pp. 197–98; Records of Highway Commissioners of Ulster County, vol. 2, pp. 39–50; *Ulster County Supervisor's Minutes, 1710–1730*, entries for 16 February 1711 and 4 February 1715, describing road and highway repair, and tax assessments for same. For this type of communal behavior in other New York towns see Langdon G. Wright, "In Search of Peace and Harmony," 10–11.

19. On Kingston's fertility, see letter of Laurentius Van Gaasbeck in *Olde Ulster*, vol. 3, p. 53. The poor land of New Windsor is described in "The Recollections of Edward McGraw" in Ruttenber, *A History of New Windsor*, p. 48, and R. Smith, *Journal from New York to Albany*, vol. 1:489–90.

20. Wright, "In Search of Peace and Harmony," pp. 10–12.

CHAPTER TWO
"ONE BODY CORPORATE AND POLITIQUE"

1. This description of Kingston's celebration of King George's coronation is based on the account published in *New York Gazette*, 16 February 1761.

2. David Underdown, *Revel, Riot, and Rebellion: Popular Politics and Culture in England, 1603–1660* (New York: Oxford University Press, 1989), Chapter 3.

3. Kingston Patent of 1687 is reprinted in Schoonmaker, *History of Kingston*, pp. 510–15, and is contained within the Records of the Corporation of the Town of Kingston, Trustees Minutes, 1736–1816 (hereafter referred to as "Trustees Minutes"), "Trustees Minutes, 1688–1713," and "1736–1816"; and Records of the Town Court, 7 October 1713–February 1737 (hereafter referred to as "Trustees Minutes" as well). There were distinctions among the towns. New Paltz's civil affairs were controlled by a town government while land ownership and economic affairs were under the authority of the Duzine, the elected board of twelve. Into the late eighteenth century, Rochester's "Six Men" controlled common land and its distribution as well as civil and criminal affairs, but competing civil authorities usurped these latter powers over time. See Countryman, *People in Revolution: The American Revolution*, pp. 29–30.

4. Kingston Patent of 1687; New Paltz Patent, 1677 in *Olde Ulster*, vol. 1, pp. 110–14. Kingston's history before 1687 can be retraced in Fried, *Early History of Kingston and Ulster County*.

5. Kingston Patent. Jurisdiction was to be limited to "all Actions under five pounds." Berthold Fernow, ed., *Documents Relating to the Colonial History*, 13:459.

6. Ibid., pp. 3–4. Charles Z. Lincoln, ed., *Colonial Laws of New York from 1664 to the Revolution*, 5 vols. (Albany, 1894), 1:121–22, 540, details the relationship between towns and the county supervisors. See also Bonomi, "Local Government in Colonial New York," pp. 42–43; 33–36. The powers of the Kingston Corporation were not common to all New York towns. See Jessica Kross-Ehrlich, *Evolution of an American Town*, pp. 55–56. However, the Kingston Corporation controlled criminal cases at least through 1753. See "Trustees Minutes," 2 May 1753, 27 July 1753, U.C.C.O., and Schoonmaker, *History of Kingston*, pp. 198–99, 385.

7. Ibid., pp. 194–98.

8. "New Paltz Patent, 1677," in *Olde Ulster* (1905) vol. 1, pp. 110–14; Marbletowns' "Twelve Men" limited the use of common wood, stone, and other items to freeholders, see Countryman, *People in Revolution*, pp. 29–30; "Kingston Patent," pp. 3–6.

9. "Kingston Patent," p. 4; The process for becoming a "freeman" in Kingston is described in the "Trustees Minutes," 17 February 1721, NYHS, and "Trustees Minutes," 14 March 1750, U.C.C.O.

10. "Trustees Minutes," 12 April 1771, U.C.C.O. For an excellent discussion of the legal and political aspects of commonalties see Blackmar, *Manhattan for Rent*, pp. 152–53. See also Countryman, *People in Revolution*, p. 30.

11. *Olde Ulster*, vol. 3, pp. 46–48. For selected examples of Kingston freemen losing their rights to common holdings see "Trustees Minutes," 18 August 1770, 23 September 1783, 14 May 1789.

12. *Colonial Laws*, vol. 1, pp. 121–22.

13. "Trustees Minutes," 15 March 1737, 14 March 1740, 10 March 1753, 13 March 1761, U.C.C.O. For New Paltz, see Papers of the Duzine, 1703–1821.

14. The data on Kingston freeholders serving in public office is found in Bonomi, "Local Government," pp. 41–43.

15. The corporation's defense of private households from lawsuits challenging corporation grants can be reviewed in "Trustees Minutes," 14 August 1741, and 20 December 1751, U.C.C.O.

16. The 1688 and 1786 ordinances are in "Trustees Minutes," 12 February 1689, 17 January 1786, U.C.C.O. The act of 1721 is in "Trustees Minutes," 17 February 1721, NYHS.

17. The warning out of the Kinderhook stranger is contained within "Trustees Minutes," 7 February 1736, NYHS. Thomas Chase is found in "Trustees Minutes," 5 December 1788, U.C.C.O. See also 12 September 1789, U.C.C.O.

18. "Trustees Minutes," 23 November 1744. For additional examples of "warning-out" see 20 May 1747, 14 February 1753, and 8 December 1769, all in U.C.C.O.

19. For the attempt to restrict newcomers in Long Island communities see Kross-Ehrlich, *Evolution of an American Town*, pp. 63–64.

20. For Rochester, see Sylvester, *History of Ulster County*, p. 215; for Marbletown, ibid., pp. 276–77. Although it varied from town to town, seventeenth-century New England communities generally made religious belief a prerequisite in becoming a town freeholder. See Lockridge, *A New England Town*, pp. 23–29.

21. The Hardenbergh lawsuit, which lasted some five years, can be traced in "Trustees Minutes," 14 August 1741, 24 November 1742, 17 August 1745, and Schoonmaker, *History of Kingston*, pp. 129–32.

22. The dispute with landholders in the county of Albany lasted over ten years, from 1751 through 1762. See "Trustees Minutes," 20 December 1751, 4 October 1762, U.C.C.O.

23. Untitled document, 20 October 1727, Kingston Papers, CV 10181–17, New York State Library.

24. "Trustees Minutes," 17 February 1719, NYHS, detail the fines for transgressions against the corporation. For interest rates, "Trustees Minutes," 2 March 1728, NYHS. This rate was reduced to 5 percent in 1750, but raised back to 6 percent in 1752. "Trustees Minutes," 10 December 1750, 8 November 1752, U.C.C.O. For the "assize of bread" see "Trustees Minutes," 12 April 1779, U.C.C.O., and Kingston Board of Directors Minutes, 8 November 1806, Kingston City Hall.

25. "Trustees Minutes," 5 April 1751, 13 March 1746.

26. "Trustees Minutes," 21 November 1757, 16 June 1784, 23 September 1783, U.C.C.O.

27. The Wood lawsuit is found in Schoonmaker, *History of Kingston,* pp. 185–86. See also "Trustees Minutes," 25 August 1737, 14 May 1740, and 18 August 1770, U.C.C.O., detailing other corporation mediation of private disputes.

28. Kingston Board of Directors Minutes," 8 November 1806. Although this event occurred in 1806, beyond the scope of coverage of much of this chapter, it reveals the extent to which this corporate power continued beyond the eighteenth century. Bogardus estimated his damages at $1,000, but the town offered $500.

29. Kingston Patent, pp. 1–2.

30. On this point, see Matson, "'Damned Scoundrels' and 'Libertisme of Trade,'" 390–91.

31. In 1790 Ulster, 3,495 of 4,590 farmers owned their own freehold, and as late as 1815, 70.4 percent did so. These figures are contained within the Census for the State of New York for 1855 (Albany: 1857). Compare this large proportion of freehold farmers with Pennsylvania, where some 25 to 30 percent of householders were tenants. Simler, "Tenancy in Colonial Pennsylvania," 542–44; 550–51; 569.

32. Kalm, p. 335, 647.

33. See Roelof Swarthout's 1662 observations on the potential of Kingston-area production in Zimm, *Southeastern New York,* p. 58; see Governor Francis Lovelace's encouragement of grain production in Lovelace to Kingston Corporation, 25 October 1671 in Fernow, ed., *Documents Relating to the Colonial History of New York,* p. 460.

34. Rev. Laurentius van Gaasbeck considered the area the central grain-producing region, Blumin, *Urban Threshold,* p. 16; Kalm, *Travels in New York,* pp. 335, 647; Smith, *Journal from New York to Albany,* 1:9

35. The most thorough analysis of regulation during the colonial period is Matson, "'Damned Scoundrels' and 'Libertisme of Trade,'" 400–403, 410–11, and Robert Ritchie, *The Duke's Province: A Study of New York Politics and Society, 1664–1691* (Chapel Hill: University of North Carolina Press, 1977), pp. 190–95.

36. Fernow, *Documents,* vol. 13, p. 460; Schoonmaker, *History of Kingston,* pp. 82–83.

37. "Trustees Minutes," April 1736, NYHS, describe the building of the public docks; "Trustees Minutes," 27 July 1753, and 19 October 1753, U.C.C.O., describe the public market.

38. On corporation land grants for private mills see "Trustees Minutes," 30 May 1739, 17 February 1742 (flour mills); 2 November 1750 (sawmill); 19 October 1753 (gristmill); 13 May 1757 (sawmill), U.C.C.O.

39. Examples of requests for "liberty to transport and sell outside of said township" can be found in "Trustees Minutes," 8 January 1741 (wood); 5 June 1747 (boards); 1 April 1782 (fish); 17 January 1786 (chestnut wood), U.C.C.O.

40. "Trustees Minutes," 11 February 1785, 27 August 1783, U.C.C.O. Masten, although fined £5, had "two pounds ten shillings remitted him, as he has been his own Informer."

41. "Trustees Minutes," 7 March 1786, U.C.C.O.

42. "Trustees Minutes," 12 February 1748, 21 September 1789, U.C.C.O.

43. Ulster's consumers complaints of shopkeepers' prices can be reviewed in "Trustees Minutes," 4 November 1757, 24 February 1783, U.C.C.O.; and in Force, *American Archives*, 5:635, 638. Ulster shopkeepers' complaints can be sampled in Thomas Ellison to Col. T. Ellison, Ellison Papers, 14 March 1775, and 13 June 1775, Ulster County Collection.

44. A sampling of disputes over access to land, fishing rights, and other resources can be reviewed in "Trustees Minutes," 14 May 1740, 5 March 1745, 13 March 1778, 1 April 1782, U.C.C.O.

45. Gunn, *Decline of Authority*, pp. 30–33.

46. Countryman, *A People in Revolution*, pp. 56–59. See also, Matson, *Merchants and Empire*.

47. "Trustees Minutes," 27 July 1753, describes the market at Hendrick Sleght's. Petrus Smedes was appointed the first "manager of the market." See "Trustees Minutes," 19 October 1753, 29 January 1790, U.C.C.O., for various aspects of market supervision.

48. LeFevre, *History of New Paltz*, pp. 66–77, outlines the regulatory powers of the Duzine in New Paltz. For New Windsor price regulation, see Samuel Brewster to the New York Provisional Congress, 31 May 1776, in Force, *American Archives*, 5:638. For the assize in Kingston, see "Trustees Minutes," 12 April 1779, U.C.C.O.; "Kingston Board of Directors Minutes, 20 April 1807, 14 May 1819.

49. For price ceilings on corporation wheat see "Trustees Minutes," 22 March 1772, 6 February 1785, 20 January 1790, U.C.C.O. For restrictions on its use, see 19 February 1790, U.C.C.O.

50. For regulation of usury see "Trustees Minutes," 2 March 1728, NYHS. This rate was reduced to 5 percent in 1750, but raised back to 6 percent in 1752. "Trustees Minutes," 10 December 1750, 8 November 1752, U.C.C.O.

51. For an analysis of seventeenth-century New England Puritans, useful here is Innes, *Creating the Commonwealth*, p. 174.

52. "Trustees Minutes," 2 March 1728, NYHS.

53. *Olde Ulster*, vol. 1, p. 326, 12 February 1664 for the Blanshan fine; for Hurley, see *Olde Ulster*, vol. 3, pp. 205–206.

54. "Trustees Minutes," 12 June 1783 (DuMond); 20 February 1784 (Roosa); 21 September 1789, U.C.C.O.

55. "Trustees Minutes," 28 May 1739, 12 September 1783, U.C.C.O.

56. "Trustees Minutes," 15 January 1790, U.C.C.O.

57. "Trustees Minutes," 24 June 1774, 6 February 1745, U.C.C.O.

58. For examples of county-wide poor relief see Ulster County Supervisors Minutes, 1710–1731, 27 February 1713; for New Paltz and Marlborough see Sylvester, *History of Ulster County*, pp. 84, 13.

59. "Trustees Minutes," 20 February 1784, 28 March 1786, 15 January 1790, U.C.C.O.

60. The flour embargo can be found in "Trustees Minutes," 12 February 1748, U.C.C.O. The meaning and occurrence of eighteenth century riots is discussed in Chapter 4.

61. Although some parallels to what E. P. Thompson has described as a "moral economy" exist in the Hudson Valley, one should be careful not to draw too many similarities between the valley, where a large proportion of residents owned land and supplied their own dietary needs, and the European one, characterized by large, urban populations. E. P. Thompson, "The Moral Economy of the English Crowd in the Eighteenth Century," *Past and Present* 50 (February 1971): 76–136. The most persuasive discussions of a moral economy in eighteenth-century America are Countryman, *American Revolution*, pp. 78–79, 143–45, and Clark-Smith, "Food Rioters in Revolutionary America," 9–15.

62. On the fluidity of ethnic identities in colonial New York, see Goodfriend, *Before the Melting Pot*, pp. 187–99; Kenney, *Stubborn for Liberty*, pp. 69–70. Pointer, *Protestant Pluralism*, pp. 2–3, describes the internal Dutch migration of the early eighteenth century.

63. LeFevre, *History of New Paltz*, pp. 134–39; On the changing languages in New Paltz, see David Narrett, "Men's Wills and Women's Property," pp. 100–101.

64. For churches in Ulster County see *Olde Ulster*, vol. 8, p. 23; vol. 10, p. 91; and Pointer, *Protestant Pluralism*, pp. 4–8.

65. On the tenaciousness of the Dutch in holding on to their heritage see Bonomi, *A Factious People*, pp. 26–28, and Kenney, *Stubborn for Liberty*, pp. 69–90. On the power of the Dutch churches see Goodfriend, *Before the Melting Pot*, pp. 82–83.

66. Ongoing corporation assistance for the Kingston church can be followed in "Trustee Minutes" 19 April 1749, 25 January 1751, 29 March 1753, 1 March 1768, U.C.C.O., and Schoonmaker, *History of Kingston*, pp. 210–212.

67. John Murrin, "English Rights as Ethnic Aggression," in *Authority and Resistance in Early New York*, William Pencak and Conrad E. Wright, eds., pp. 58–59.

68. Randall Balmer, "Schism on Long Island: The Dutch Reformed Church, Lord Cornbury, and the Politics of Anglicization," in ibid., pp. 105–106, 101–102; *Olde Ulster*, vol. 5, pp. 301–304.

69. Kenney, *Stubborn for Liberty*, pp. 91–134. The petition is described in "Trustees Minutes," 27 August 1779, U.C.C.O.

70. Countryman, *A People in Revolution*, pp. 26–28.

71. In 1773, the first year the Kingston Academy was incorporated, five of its twenty-two trustees were also trustees of the corporation. Nine of the twenty-two served at some point as trustees of the Corporation. Compare "Records of Kingston Academy, 1773–1804" in *Olde Ulster* (1913) vol. 9, p. 324, with "Trustees Minutes," 8 March 1773, U.C.C.O.

72. For social and legal relations between husbands and wives see Norton, "White Women's Experience," pp. 593–619.

73. Wall, *Fierce Communion:*, pp. ix.

74. Ibid., pp. 9, 76, 82; "Kingston Court Records, 1661–1667," *New York Historical Manuscripts: Dutch* (Baltimore, 1976), pp. 478–79.

75. "Proceedings of Courts of Ulster County, 1746," U.C. reel 50, Historical Documents Collection, Queens College, New York, details the Marbletown act; Sylvester, *History of Ulster County*, p. 13, discusses the New Paltz laws, and p. 84, the sale of poor children in Marlborough. The Kingston action is contained in the "Trustees Records," 8 December 1769, U.C.C.O.

76. Bonomi, *Factious People*, pp. 28.

77. Ibid., p. 27.

78. *Olde Ulster*, pp. 37–47; Pointer, *Protestant Pluralism*, pp. 34–35.

79. Schoonmaker, *History of Kingston*, pp. 198–99.

80. "Trustees Minutes," 2 May 1753, 15 February 1760, 8 March 1773, UCCO; Schoonmaker, *History of Kingston*, pp. 198–99.

81. T. H. Breen, "The Baubles of Britain," 73–77; Shammas, *Pre-Industrial Consumer*, pp. 55–59.

Chapter Three
"A Comfortable Subsistence"

1. McCusker and Menard, *The Economy of British America*, pp. 205–206; Perkins, *Economy of Colonial America*, pp. 19–44.

2. For thorough discussions of local trade and the meaning it held for its participants see Clark, *Roots of Rural Capitalism*, pp. 30–33; Bettye Hobbes Pruitt, "Self-Sufficiency and the Agricultural Economy of Eighteenth-Century Massachusetts," *William and Mary Quarterly* 41 (1984): 354–62; Kulikoff, *Agrarian Origins*, pp. 19–23.

3. For regulation during the colonial period see Matson, "'Damned Scoundrels' and 'Libertisme of Trade,'" 400–403, 410–11. For late-eighteenth-century state regulation see Gunn, *Decline of Authority*, pp. 118–19; for early nineteenth, Miller, *Enterprise of a Free People*, pp. 10–11.

4. On tenantry see Kim, *Landlord and Tenant*, pp. 39–40; 235–37; Ellis, *Farmers and Landlords*, Chapter 4.

5. Schumacher, *Northern Farmer*, p. 37; Bidwell and Falconer, *History of Agriculture*, p. 115; Ellis, *Farmers and Landlords*, p. 104. Landholding records for seventy-two Ulster residents reveal an average holding of 182 acres for the years 1760 through 1780. Ulster County Deed Records, vol. 6 (FF) 1737–1770 and 7 (GG) 1765–1780, and the Trustees of Kingston Record of Conveyances &c., 1729–1764, and Trustees of Kingston Record of Conveyances, 1767–1798.

6. Important discussions of rural life include Clemens and Simler, "Rural Labor," pp. 106–43; Weiman, "Families, Farms, and Rural Society"; Vickers, *Farmers and Fishermen*, pp. 25–28.

7. Dwight, *Travels in New England* 1:18; "Will of Caleb Dill," New Windsor, Ulster County, 23 February 1786, in Anjou, *Ulster County* 1:10; Jacobus Cole Account Book, entry in May 1817.

8. Daniel Vickers' provocative work has informed my understanding of eighteenth-century rural economic culture. See his *Farmers and Fishermen*, pp. 14–28; 258–597. See also Baker and Paterson, "Farmers' Adaptations to Markets," pp. 95–96; and Merrill, "Political Economy," Chapters 2 and 3.

9. Pruitt, "Self-Sufficiency," 354–62

10. Weiman, "Families, Farms, and Rural Society," p. 257.

11. Henretta, *Origins of American Capitalism*; Weiman, ibid., pp. 257–58.

12. Charles DeWitt Daybook and William Pick Account Book; Diary of Abraham Hasbrouck Sr.

13. Bidwell and Falconer, *History of Agriculture*, pp. 125–26; William Smith, *Journal from New York to Albany*, 1:491–92. For the introduction of "modernizing" tools, see Henretta, *The Evolution of American Society*, pp. 18–19; Ulysses Hedrick, *A History of Agriculture in the State of New York* (New York, 1933), pp. 64–83, 287–306.

14. Schumacher, *Northern Farmer and His Market*, p. 11; Bidwell and Falconer, *History of Agriculture*, p. 24; Henretta, *Evolution of American Society*, p. 15.

15. Discussion of agricultural practices in the valley are based on the following farm daybooks: Charles DeWitt Daybook, William Pick Accounts, and Jacobus Cole Account Book. The quote is from DeWitt Daybook, 10 October 1773.

16. Three hundred ninety-four probate inventories from Ulster County from the period 1760 through 1850 serve as the basis for my analysis of agricultural and household production. Eighty-seven inventories are from Kingston and three hundred seven are from

the twelve other towns. Ulster County Surrogate Court, Kingston, New York, Boxes 9–49. These records are also available on microfilm from the National Genealogical Society, Salt Lake City, Utah, reels #0941026–0941048, 0940811–0940829.

17. Thirty of fifty-four surviving inventories for the years 1776–1790 recorded wheat in production, averaging 102.6 bushels, while thirteen recorded rye, averaging 67 bushels. Nineteen of the inventories record acreage of grain, averaging 9.7 acres; Ulster County Probate Inventories, 1776–1791. Schumacher, *Northern Farmer*, pp. ii, 37–41.

18. Lee A. Craig, "The Value of Household Labor in Antebellum Northern Agriculture," *Journal of Economic History* 51 (1991): 78.

19. This and the previous paragraph on rural labor in the valley are based on the Christoffel Kiersted Account Book, 1742–1747; Daybook of Cornelius Jansen, 1787; Account Book of Daniel Osterhoudt, 1791–1836, all in the Account Book Collection, Kingston Senate House. Barbara Clark Smith provides an excellent descriptive analysis of the daily workings of the early American farm household in her *After the Revolution*, pp. 51–57. See also, Joan Jensen, *Loosening the Bonds*, pp. 83–93.

20. Kiersted Account Book, 1742–1747, Kingston Senate House Museum; Inventory and Account of Abraham Bevier (1763) in Ulster County Wills and Inventories, Ulster Country Clerk's Office, Kingston, New York.

21. Blackmar, *Manhattan for Rent*, pp. 54–55; for comparisons to Massachusetts see Vickers, *Farmers and Fishermen*, pp. 64–68.

22. Discussion of Ulster County families swapping labor is found in "Recollections of Edward McGraw," p. 49, in Ruttenber, *A History of New Windsor*. The Plough Accounts are found in William Pick Account Book.

23. Jacobus Cole Account Book. See entries from May 1797 through March 1807, detailing this laborer's various work relations with employers.

24. For accounts of slave life in the mid–Hudson Valley see Groth, "Slaveholders and Manumission," 33–50. See also Margaret Washington, ed., *Narrative of Sojourner Truth* (New York, 1993), pp. 6–8. Truth lived the first thirty years of her life as an Ulster County slave.

25. Governor Moore to Board of Trade, 1767, quoted in Victor Clark, *History of Manufacturers in the United States*, 2 vols. (New York, 1929), 1:16–17.

26. Ulrich, "Martha Ballard and her Girls," p. 90.

27. On New York textile production, see Governor Moore to Board of Trade, 1767, in Clark, *History of Manufacturers*, 1:16; Smith, *Journal from New York To Albany*, pp. 491–92; Brink, *Early History of Saugerties*, pp. 226–27.

28. Milling Accounts of Richard Davis, 1821–1824 (contained in Davis's probate inventory, Rochester, 1823), Ulster County Clerk's Office; Ralph LeFevre, *History of New Paltz*, p. 216.

29. Cott, *Bonds of Womanhood*, p. 26; Ulrich, "Martha Ballard," pp. 70–105; Norton, "White Women's Experience," 593–619.

30. Jacobus Cole Book of Accounts, 1789–1831; Vickers, "Competency and Competition," 5–10.

31. Cadwallader Colden to Board of Trade, 1723, in Edmund O'Callaghan, ed., *Documents Relative to the Colonial History of New York*, 15 vols. (Albany: State of New York, 1856–1887), 5:685–88.

32. On behavior of Ulster County farmers see Thomas Ellison to Col. Thomas Ellison, 13 June 1775, Ellison Box, NYHS. On New York farmers generally, see Matson "'Damned Scoundrels' and 'Libertisme of Trade,'" pp. 409–11; Henretta, *Origins of American Capitalism*, pp. 264–66.

33. For an overview of the importance of commercial markets for early American farmers in other northern regions see Rothenberg, *From Market-Places to a Market Economy*, pp. 80–110.

34. As late as 1697, parts of western Ulster County were prohibited from exporting grain outside of the county. See "Petition of the Inhabitants of Ulster to his Excellency Edmund Andros to Transport and Import," MSS Ulster County, NYHS.

35. On the business relationships that existed among city and upriver merchants, see Thomas Ellison to Col. Thomas Ellison, New York, 14 March 1775, Ellison Box. New York Historical Society (NYHS); Diary of Abraham Hasbrouck Sr.; Benjamin Snyder Account Book.

36. The record of eighteenth-century sloop trips from Kingston can be found in *Ulster Plebian*, 22 November 1817; the Ellisons' ship in Ellison Papers, NYHS; Ben Snyder's trips from North Kingston (Saugerties) to New York are in the Benjamin Snyder Day and Sloop Book.

37. Several storekeepers attempted to link up the rich agricultural lands of Schohary Kill to Kingston in 1784, but little support could be found for the expensive undertaking. Subscription Roll, 16 November 1784, Folder 3036, Kingston Senate House Museum; "Trustees Minutes," 12 June 1783, UCCO.

38. McCusker and Menard, *Economy of British America*, pp. 189–98; Kammen, *Colonial New York*, p. 167; Ellis, *History of New York State*, pp. 50–60, 71–88.

39. Harrington, *New York Merchants*, pp. 169–72; Gary M. Walton and James F. Shepherd, *The Economic Rise of Early America* (New York: Cambridge University Press, 1979), pp. 75–77; Colden to Board of Trade, 1723, in *Letters and Papers*, 5:685–88.

40. On marketing opportunities for New York farmers see Matson, "'Damned Scoundrels' and 'Libertisme of Trade,'" pp. 391–92, 408–409.

41. For biographical information on Snyder see Evers, *Woodstock*, pp. 48–52; and Brink, *Early History of Saugerties*, pp. 117–25.

42. The Benjamin Snyder Day and Sloop Book, 1774–1777, actually goes into 1777. However, this final year is incomplete, so it has been excluded from analysis.

43. Fred Anderson, *A People's Army*, pp. 28–35. See also Henretta, "Families and Farms," pp. 19–26; Merrill, "Cash Is Good to Eat," pp. 52–55; Clark, "Household Economy," pp. 172–75.

44. Background information on Short was obtained from Benjamin Snyder Account Book.

45. The quote is from David Clarkson's chapman, 1732, cited in Matson "'Damned Scoundrels' and 'Libertism of Trade,'" pp. 29–30 (unpublished manuscript). See also Thomas Ellison Jr. to Col. Thomas Ellison, 28 February 1765; 26 March 1774, Ellison Papers, NYHS.

46. See Ellison's attempts to stay one step ahead of his customers by meeting their price in New Windsor, and still gain a profit in his dealings with city merchants: Thomas Ellison Jr. to Col. Thomas Ellison, 14 March 1775 and 13 June 1775, Ellison Papers, NYHS.

47. John Hathorn to New York Provincial Congress, 2 December 1776, cited in Ruttenber, *History of New Windsor*, pp. 67–68. These riots are discussed in greater detail in Chapter 4.

48. On local trade, see Clark, *Roots of Rural Capitalism*, pp. 30–33; Pruitt, "Self-sufficiency and the Agricultural Economy," pp. 354–62; Merrill, "Political Economy," Chapter 3; Kulikoff, *Agrarian Origins*, pp. 19–23.

49. Kingston *Rising Sun*, 24 February 1797.

50. New Windsor shopkeeper Mrs. Jonathon Lawrence had her merchandise seized by her farm neighbors, who accused her of price gouging. Force, *American Archives* 5:635, 638.

51. Account of Jacobus Bush in Account Book of Jarman and William Pick, 1765–1798; Petrus Hendricks in Osterhoudt Account Book, 1791–1820.

52. Frederick Westbrook Daybook, 1779–1782, Account Book Collection, Kingston Senate House Museum; John Masten Account Book, 1781–1828.

53. Ellis, *Farmers and Landlords*, pp. 148–49.

54. See accounts of Adam Snyder, George Minteny, and Abraham Newkirk in Jarman and William Pick, Account Book, 1765–1798.

55. Accounts of James Paul in William Van Gaasbeck, Account Book, 1790–1808.

56. Accounts of Johanis Suyland, Jacob Brinck, and Cornelius Cole in Cole, Book of Accounts, 1789–1831.

57. Benjamin Snyder Account Book, 1768–1795.

58. Pick, Account Book, 1765–1798.

59. Ibid.

60. "Trustees Minutes," 8 March 1780, 7 March 1786, UCCO. On the goals and nature of local trade, see Merrill, "Cash Is Good to Eat," pp. 50–56; Clark, *Roots of Rural Capitalism*, pp. 21–58; Kulikoff, *Agrarian Origins*, pp. 24–26.

Chapter Four
"We Are Daily Alarmed, and Our Streets Filled with Mobs"

1. There are voluminous studies examining the Revolutionary War in New York, although one must start with Becker's *Political Parties in the Province of New York, 1760–1776*. Also important is Alexander Flick, *American Revolution in New York* (Albany: State University of New York, 1926); Mason, *The Road to Independence*. The most thorough, province-wide study is Countryman, *A People in Revolution*.

2. For the significance of rioting in the revolutionary period, see Clark-Smith, "Food Rioters"; Countryman, *A People in Revolution*, pp. 55–71.

3. Countryman, ibid., pp. 72–98; Mason, *Road to Independence*, pp. 134–77.

4. Becker, *Political Parties*, pp. 42–69.

5. Letter from an anonymous Kingston farmer in Force, *American Archives*, 1:1230.

6. Resolves of New Windsor Committee in ibid., 2:131–33.

7. Papers of the Duzine, 1703–1821; LeFevre, *A History of New Paltz*, pp. 113–114, describes the voting methods for the New Paltz committee.

8. Minutes of 14 March 1775, New Windsor Town Meeting, in Force, *American Archives*, 2:131–33.

9. The resolves and proclamations of New Paltz and Rochester can be sampled in ibid., 2:832–33, 1100, 1183–84, 1201.

10. All six members of New Windsor Committee of Observation appear on the New Windsor Civil List for 1775. The committee list can be found in ibid., 2:131–32, and the Civil List of New Windsor Officials in E. M. Ruttenber, *History of New Windsor*, p. 20. See Kingston Committee of Observation, 9 May 1775, in Force, *American Archives*, 2:833, and compare to "Trustees Minutes," 12 March 1771, 10 March 1774, and 14 March 1775, UCCO.

11. "Ulster County Committee Minutes," 7 April 1775, in Force, *American Archives*, 2:298–99.

12. "Resolves of the Ulster Association, 1775," in ibid., 2:132–33.

13. The pamphlet was also burned in Marbletown, see ibid., 1:1100, 1183–84; 1201.

14. Robert Boyd to George Clinton, 3 July 1776, *Clinton Papers*, 1:244–47; Margaret Crooke to Clinton, 15 September 1779 and Clinton to Crooke, 24 September 1779, in ibid., 5:280–81.

15. Cadwallader Colden Jr., to Ulster County Committee, 27 June 1776, in Force, *American Archives*, 6:1112.

16. "Trustees Minutes, 1783–1795," UCCO; *Inventory of Archives in Kingston* (Albany: State of New York, 1911), p. 15; LeFever, *History of New Paltz*, pp. 42–43.

17. Compare this to the customers of Benjamin Snyder, William Van Gaasbeck, and Jacobus Cole (Chapter 3), and Abraham Hasbrouck (Chapter 5). All of these merchants' customers continued to earn a majority of their credits in agricultural goods.

18. Jarman and William Pick Account Book, 1741–1826.

19. Roger Weiss, "The Issue of Paper Money in the American Colonies, 1720–1774," *Journal of Economic History* (December 1970): 770–85; Joseph Ernst, "The Currency Act Repeal Movement: A Study of Imperial Politics and Revolutionary Crisis, 1764–1769," *William and Mary Quarterly* (April 1968): 177–211.

20. Curtis Nettels, *The Emergence of a National Economy, 1775–1815* (New York: Rinehart and Co., 1962), pp. 23–24; Flick, *American Revolution in New York*, pp. 109–15; "Proceedings of the New York Committee of Safety," in Fernow, ed., *Documents Relating to the Colonial History* 15:24–34.

21. For the various currency issues see the *Journals of the Provincial Congress, Provincial Convention, Committee of Safety and Council of Safety of the State of New York 1775, 1776, 1777,* 2 vols. (Albany: State of New York, 1842) 2 vols., 1:455–57. See also, Flick, *American Revolution in New York*, p. 124.

22. For the nonimportation agreements in Ulster see Ulster County Association, 6 January 1775 in Force, *American Archives*, 1:1100–1101. For the general background and purpose behind the nonimportation movement see Pauline Maier, *From Resistance to Revolution* (New York: Vintage, 1972), pp. 137–38. For two excellent studies of community self-regulation, see John L. Brooke, *Heart of the Commonwealth: Society and Political Culture in Worcester County, Massachusetts, 1713–1861* (New York: Cambridge University Press, 1989), pp. 189–223, and Peter C. Mancall, *Valley of Opportunity: Economic Culture along the Upper Susquehanna, 1700–1800* (Ithaca: Cornell University Press, 1991), pp. 131–33.

23. Alphonse Clearwater, *History of Ulster County*, pp. 281–82; Sylvester, *History of Ulster County*, p. 202.

24. Some of the prices were firmly set by the Congress, such as wheat at 13s per bushel, and "good merchantable wheat flour" at £1 16s per hundred gross weight. Other prices, such as leather and various animal skins, were set "in the proportion of the price they usually bore to raw hides." See the *Journals of the Provincial Congress*, 1:455–57, 3 April 1778, for a full listing of the regulation of prices.

25. Regulation of laborer's wages is recorded in ibid. 1:455.

26. Ulster's call for new price controls can be found in Ulster County Association Instructions to Assemblymen, 1779, Matthew Visscher Folder, Albany Institute; Ulster County to New York State Legislature, 1782, Box 4239, New York State Library, Albany, New York.

27. Ulster County Committee Minutes, 7 April 1775, in Force, *American Archives*, 2:298. Low to Ulster County Committee, 6 June 1775; Minutes of Ulster County Committee, in ibid., 2:917–18. A lively and colorful debate between Low and the committee

chairman, Johannes Sleght, can be sampled in Jacobus Low to New York Committee, 30 April 1775; Ulster County Committee Minutes, 10 May 1775, both in ibid., 2:448; 3:548–49.

28. Force, ibid., 5:635, 638–39.

29. "Ulster County Committee to New York Convention," 18 November 1776, *Provincial Congress*, pp. 229–30; Countryman, *People in Revolution*, p. 182.

30. Clark-Smith, "Food Rioters," p. 15.

31. Correspondence of John Hathorn, 2 December 1776, in Ruttenber, *History of New Windsor*, pp. 67–68.

32. Ibid., p. 67.

33. Countryman, *People in Revolution*, pp. 144–48; Eric Foner, *Tom Paine and Revolutionary America* (New York: Oxford University Press, 1976), Chapter 4.

34. For a thorough discussion of the political implications of revolutionary rioting, see Clark Smith's "Food Rioters." For suspicions that Ellison was unpatriotic because of his economic dealings see Boyd to Clinton, 3 July 1776, *Clinton Papers*, 1:244–47.

35. James H. Kip to James Caldwell, New Windsor, 14 July 1777, *Journals of the Provincial Congress*, 1:506.

36. New York Convention Proceedings, August 1776, in Force, *American Archives*, 1:1542–43.

37. Linda Kerber, *Women of the Republic: Intellect and Ideology in Revolutionary America*, (Chapel Hill: University Press of North Carolina, 1980), p. 44, and Mary Beth Norton, *Liberty's Daughters: The Revolutionary Experience of American Women, 1750–1800*, (Boston: Scott, Foresman and Company, 1980).

38. Sean Wilentz describes this changing view of political economy among some skilled craftsmen in New York in his *Chants Democratic: New York City and the Rise of the American Working Class, 1788–1850* (New York: Oxford University Press, 1984), pp. 61–103.

39. For New York farming interests that supported both inflationary policies and paper currency, see Matson, "Liberty, Jealousy, and Union," pp. 114–15, and for those rural New Yorkers opposed see Countryman, *People in Revolution*, pp. 180–82.

40. Clark-Smith, "Food Rioters," p. 29; Countryman, *American Revolution*, pp. 78–79.

41. The extent of Ulster County's production for the war can be seen in George Clinton's report for 1778, where he argued that the entire west bank, "Having long been the seat of the war," had been "ravaged plundered and greatly exhausted." Clinton to F. M. Dana, 17 February 1778, *Clinton Papers*, 2:824–25. Indeed, in 1778, the Continental Army was fed almost exclusively on Ulster wheat. See *Olde Ulster*, 3:365–69.

42. Louis C. Hatch, *The Administration of the American Revolutionary Army*, (New York, 1904), pp. 86–115; Flick, *American Revolution*, pp. 179–202.

43. For background on Elmendorph see, Probated Inventories for Ulster County, Ulster County Surrogate Court Office, Kingston, N.Y.; 1798 Kingston Tax Assessment, NYHS; E. Wayne Carp, *To Starve the Army at Pleasure: Continental Army Administration and American Political Culture, 1775–1783* (Chapel Hill: University of North Carolina Press, 1984), pp. 33–73.

44. This analysis is based on the sixty-two probate inventories for the years 1776–1791 located in the Ulster County Surrogate Court Office.

45. The quote is from Henretta, "War for Independence," 78–79.

46. James Shepherd and Gary M. Walton, *Shipping, Maritime Trade, and the Economic Development of Colonial North America* (New York: Cambridge University Press, 1972), pp. 110–13, 182; Perkins and Walton, *A Prosperous People*, pp. 29–36.

47. "Ulster County Committee Resolves," 14 March 1775 in Force, *American Archives*, 2:132.

48. Flick, *American Revolution in New York*, p. 184.

49. See the inventories of Cornelius Wynkoop (Hurly, 1793), James McClaughry (New Windsor, 1790), Roeloff Eltinge (New Paltz, 1795) in Probated Inventories and Accounts of Ulster County, 1776–1820.

50. Frederick Westbrook, Daybook, 1779–1782, Account Book Collection, Kingston Senate House Museum.

51. On the connection between textile and dairy production see Joan Jensen, *Loosening the Bonds*, pp. 87–88.

52. Flick, *American Revolution in New York*, p. 187. See also the reports of the commissaries of clothing in *Clinton Papers*. Commissar John Henry worked out of Shawangunk, see his report 26 August 1778, in ibid., 3:693; 4:31–32. Commissar Peter Curtenius was in charge of the store in Walkill. See his report in ibid., 3:692.

53. Henretta, "War for American Independence," pp. 81–86; Virginia Harrington discusses New York merchants fondness for provincial bonds and real estate, not manufacturing, in *New York Merchant*, Chapter 4.

54. For the Duer and Parker plans see Duer to William Alexander, 15 June 1781, Alexander Papers, NYHS; Daniel Parker to Duer, 26 June 1781, Duer Papers, NYHS. For Smith's store, still in operation in 1785, see Duer Papers, Box 8, NYHS.

Chapter Five
"The Farmer Now Sells for Money"

1. Kingston farmers averaged 11.6 acres from 1791–1820. Farmers throughout Ulster County averaged 13.3 during the same period; seventeen of ninety probate inventories (1791–1805) record iron tools. Ulster County Probate Inventories and Accounts, UCCO.

2. Daniel Osterhoudt, Account Book, 1791–1836, Account Book, Jacobus Cole, 1789–1831, KSHM. Ten of Osterhoudt's thirty customers settled at least some portion of their debt with spinning, as did ten of Cole's forty-nine customers.

3. "Recollections of Edward McGraw," reprinted in E. M. Ruttenber, *A History of New Windsor*, pp. 48–49.

4. This analysis is based on ninety inventories, Ulster County Probate Inventories, 1791–1805, UCCO.

5. Abraham Hasbrouck was one of the wealthiest and most prominent residents of Ulster County. Taxed in the top 2 percent of Kingston residents in 1798, he was one of the original incorporators of the Delaware and Hudson Canal, a founder of the Bank of Kingston, served as a representative to Congress in 1813–1815, and as a member of the State Legislature in 1822. Abraham died in 1845—so did his business, as his son chose not to continue the trade long after his father's death. Sylvester, *The History of Ulster County*, pp. 86; 306–309.

6. The foremost employer of these sources is Rothenberg, *From Market-Places*, pp. 59–69. Gloria Main's phrase is found in her "Gender, Work, and Wages in Colonial New England," *William and Mary Quarterly* 51, 3rd Ser. (1994): 45.

7. On the role of merchants in the eighteenth century, see Nobles, "Rise of Merchants," 3–20, and Thorp, "Doing Business in the Backcountry," 391–92.

8. Vols. 2, 17, and 18, Hasbrouck Account Books. The Hasbrouck accounts for 1839, vols. 31 and 32, are examined in Chapter 6.

9. Advertisement for Hasbrouck's store in *Ulster County Gazette*, 4 January 1800, p. 4.

10. On colonial New York's paper money supply, see Roger Weiss, "The Issue of Paper Money," 770–85; Nettels, *Emergence of a National Economy*, pp. 23–24.

11. Clark, *Roots of Rural Capitalism*, pp. 67–71.

12. On commodity money see Joseph Ernst, *Money and Politics in America, 1755–1775*, (Chapel Hill: University of North Carolina Press, 1973), p. xvi, 21; Matson, "'Damned Scoundrels' and 'Libertisme of Trade,'" p. 409.

13. Wilhelm DuBois was assessed £190, and Peter Burhans £162. The background material for these farmers is based on the Probate Inventories and Accounts of Peter Burhans (1806), Wilhelm DuBois (1810), and Nicholas Hardenbergh (1810), Ulster County Clerk's Office; Ulster County Deed Book, vols. 7 (GG) 1765–1780 and 8 (HH) 1780–1790; Records of the Corporation of the Town of Kingston, Vol. 3 (1767–1798) and volume 4 (1798–1816), UCCO; 1798 Tax Assessments, NYHS.

14. Altogether, families who dealt with Hasbrouck in 1799 averaged 6.2 members, with 3.2 men and 3.0 women per family. Twenty years later families who dealt with Hasbrouck reversed their gender composition, averaging 2.9 men and 3.2 women.

15. Shammas, *The Pre-Industrial Consumer*, pp. 52–68.

16. The material on customers' purchases is based on a sampling of forty-nine customers (26 percent) who dealt with Hasbrouck in 1799. This analysis could not be employed for 1820 because Hasbrouck recorded most purchases as "sundries," making it impossible to differentiate among purchases.

17. L. Ray Gunn, *Decline of Authority*, pp. 36–37; Blumin, *The Urban Threshold*, Chapter 3.

18. Bidwell and Falconer, *History of Agriculture*, p. 87; Charles DeWitt describes these problems as early as the 1760s and 1770s. See *Day Book and Diary of Charles DeWitt, 1749–1780*, NYHS; Ulysses Hedrick, *A History of Agriculture in the State of New York* (New York: Rinehart and Co., 1933), pp. 332–36.

19. Andrea Zimmerman, "Nineteenth-Century Wheat Production in Four New York State Regions," *Hudson Valley Regional Review* (September 1988): 59–60; David Ellis, *Farmers and Landlords*, pp. 186–87.

20. Kingston farmers moved from 11.1 acres (six of fourteen inventories) in the period 1776–1790 to 11.6 acres from 1791–1820 (eleven of forty-nine). Farmers throughout Ulster County increased their acreage under cultivation from 9.1 to 13.3 during the same period. Probate Inventories and Accounts.

21. Twenty-one percent of Hasbrouck's customers spent approximately £1,800 of cash in 1815, and 24 percent of customers spent £2,200 in 1825. In 1820, 20.4 percent of Hasbrouck's customers spent £1,627 of paper money. See Murray Rothbard, *The Panic of 1819: Reactions and Policies* (New York: Cambridge University Press, 1962), pp. 14–17; Sellers, *The Market Revolution*, pp. 135–38.

22. Rothenberg, *From Market-Places*, pp. 80–95; Charles Post, "Agrarian Origins of U.S. Capitalism," 395–96.

23. Clemens and Simler, "Rural Labor and the Farm Household," p. 111; Lemon, *The Best Poor Man's Country*, pp. 27–29.

24. Michael Merrill, "The Transformation of Ulster County, 1750–1850" (unpublished paper, 1985); Rolla Milton Tryon, *Household Manufactures in the United States, 1640–1860* (Chicago: University of Chicago Press, 1917), pp. 170–72; 250–52; 288–89; Henretta, "The War for Independence," pp. 73–74.

25. Hedrick, *A History of Agriculture in the State of New York*, pp. 196–97, details the growth of commercial sheep raising in the valley, while David Ellis, *History of New York State*, pp. 168, 272, explores dairy and livestock production.

26. Charles Cochrane, *A History of the Town of Marlborough*; Sylvester, *History of Ulster County*, pp. 96–97; Woolsey, *History of the Town of Marlborough*, pp. 247–49.

27. Thomas Dublin, *Transforming Women's Work: New England Lives in the Industrial Revolution* (Ithaca: Cornell University Press, 1994), Chapter 2.

28. Thirty-six percent of William Pick's customers used cash in the 1820s, but 54 percent of William Van Gaasbeck's customers did the same. *Account Book of William Pick; Van Gaasbeck Account Book*.

29. *Hasbrouck Accounts*, 1811–1827, NYHS.

30. Mary Blewett, *Men, Women and Work: Class, Gender, and Protest in the New England Shoe Industry, 1780–1910*, (Urbana: University of Illinois Press, 1988), pp. 3–19; Dublin, *Transforming Women's Work*, Chapter 2.

31. Hedrick, *History of Agriculture in New York*, p. 138; Edwin Tunis, *The Colonial Craftsmen and the Beginnings of American Industry* (New York: Crowel, 1965), pp. 22–23.

32. Clark, *Roots of Rural Capitalism*, pp. 185–89; Dublin, "Rural Putting-Out Work," 571–73.

33. Joan Jensen, *Loosening the Bonds*; Osterud, *Bonds of Community*.

34. Jensen, *Loosening the Bonds*, pp. 93–94.

Chapter Six
"The Harbingers of Commerce"

1. The opening of the canal is described in the *Ulster Sentinel*, 29 November 1826.

2. A fine discussion of the canal's construction can be found in Larkin, *New York State Canals*, pp. 72–76. Washington Irving referred to the canal as the "artificial river" in his 1841 summer voyage along the D & H, reprinted in *History of the Delaware & Hudson Canal Company, 1823–1923* (Albany, N.Y.: J. B. Lyons, 1925), pp. 109–10. This phrase was also used by Carol Sheriff, *The Artificial River: The Erie Canal and the Paradox of Progress*, (New York: Hill and Wang, 1996).

3. *Ulster Sentinel*, 29 November 1826

4. The description of shopkeepers and dwelling houses in Kingston is contained in the *Ulster Plebian*, 22 November 1817.

5. Federal Census 1850; Blumin, *Urban Threshold*, pp. 81–87. This figure of 13,000 is based on adding the population of Kingston village (10,232) with Rondout (2,900).

6. For particular legislation as it applied to Kingston and Ulster County, see Alphonse T. Clearwater, *History of Ulster County*, p. 215; Sylvester, *History of Ulster County*, pp. 13, 84. On criticisms of Kingston forestallers see *Kingston Rising Sun*, 24 February 1797.

7. Records of the Kingston Board of Directors (hereafter referred to as "Kingston Directors' Minutes"), 20 April 1807, describes the "assize of bread" in Kingston: "A loaf of superfine wheat flour, when the price of merchantable wheat was 8 shillings per bushel, must weigh 71 ounces." See also ibid., 14 May 1819, Kingston City Hall; ibid., 26 January 1808.

8. "Subscription Roll for 'rode to Schohary Kill,'" 16 November 1784, Kingston Senate House, Folder 3036; "Trustees Minutes," 28 August 1783, 13 August 1784, U.C.C.O.

9. A second attempt to link Kingston via western New York in 1807 proved *somewhat* more successful. Originally hoping to construct a turnpike some 140 miles to Wattles Ferry, Kingston financiers were forced to settle for less than half that distance when financial shortcomings and unfavorable geography prevented its completion. Ibid., 23 August 1803, 26 August 1806, October 1807, U.C.C.O. Schoonmaker, *History of Kingston*, pp. 405–406.

10. "Trustees Minutes," 12 June 1783, 23 August 1803, U.C.C.O.; *Ulster Plebian*, 22 November 1817.

11. Ibid., 28 August 1819; *Ulster Palladium*, 9 March 1821; *Ulster Plebian*, 14 May 1828.

12. *Ulster Palladium*, 9 March 1821.

13. "Trustees Minutes," 13 September 1799; 30 June 1800; 1 April 1803, U.C.C.O.

14. Ibid., 12 May 1805, September 1811, U.C.C.O.; Schoonmaker, *History of Kingston*, p. 184.

15. In fact, the Board of Directors of the Village of Kingston had existed side-by-side with the corporation since 1805, but from 1816 on, it was the sole government in the community. "Kingston Directors' Minutes," 11 May 1805. "Trustees Minutes," 11 October 1816, U.C.C.O.

16. *Inventory of Records in Kingston Area Archives* (Albany, N.Y.: State of New York, 1911), pp. 18–19.

17. See Gregory Nobles, "Rise of Merchants," 16–20; Hall, *The Organization of American Culture*, pp. 53–54.

18. *Ulster Plebian*, 14 May 1828; see also, *Ulster Palladium*, 19 January 1831.

19. From 1820 to 1825, the Kingston population dropped slightly. Ellis, *Farmers and Landlords*, p. 130. On cheaper western grain see ibid., pp. 122–24, and McNall, *History of the Genessee Valley.*

20. On boosterism, see Howard Chudakoff, *Evolution of American Urban Society* (Upper Saddle River, N.J.: Prentice Hall, 1994), pp. 43–44.

21. *Ulster Palladium*, 19 January 1831.

22. *Ulster Plebian*, 22 November 1817.

23. *Ulster Palladium*, 9 March 1831; *Ulster Plebian*, 4 May 1828.

24. "Petition from Shawangunk Farmers, 6 June 1768," and "Petition from Marbletown Farmers, 28 November 1772," in Records of the Highway Commissioners of Ulster County, vol. 1, pp. 88–89, and vol. 2, p. 43.

25. *Ulster Palladium*, 9 March 1831.

26. *Ulster Plebian*, 28 August 1819.

27. For the importance of the Delaware and Hudson Canal on the Kingston economy, see Blumin's *The Urban Threshold*, pp. 50–74. For more general studies of canals and their effect on the New York economy see Nathan Miller, *The Enterprise of a Free People*.

28. Ellis, *Farmers and Landlords*, p. 172. Federal Manuscript Census for 1820 and 1850.

29. Blumin, *Urban Threshold*, pp. 81–83, 87–88.

30. See Diary of Nathaniel Booth, entry of 17 March 1850, KSHM. See also Blumin, *Urban Threshold*, pp. 96–97.

31. *Ulster Republican*, 2 December 1840, 5 July 1848.

32. 1840 Federal Census

33. See Charles Sellers' *The Market Revolution*, Chapters 1 and 2.

34. Bidwell and Falconer, *History of Agriculture in the Northern United States*, p. 87; DeWitt, Daybook, unpaginated. Hedrick, *History of Agriculture*, pp. 332–36.

35. *Ulster Palladium*, 17 July 1833. The state's 1846 report is discussed in Ellis, *Farmers and Landlords*, pp. 184–201.

36. Schumacher, *Northern Farmer*, p. 39, 34; Bidwell and Falconer, *History of Agriculture*, p. 90; Ellis, *Farmers and Landlords*, pp. 168–70, 186–87; Zimmermann, "Nineteenth-Century Wheat Production," *Hudson Valley Regional Review (HVRR)* (1988), pp. 59–60.

37. 1840, 1850 Census. Ulster produced more corn in 1850, some 333,057 bushels, than any other grain crop.

38. Calculations are based on the 1850 Federal Census.

39. Federal Census 1810, 1840, 1850.

40. Baker and Patterson's work on Massachusetts farmers and agricultural reformers has informed my understanding of the importance of these developments for rural New York. See "Farmers' Adaptations to Markets," pp. 99–100. On New York agricultural societies and fairs, see Ellis, *Farmers and Landlords*, pp. 137–42.

41. For examples of the former, see *Ulster Palladium*, 17 July 1833; for the latter, examine ibid., 24 July 1833.

42. Ibid., 3 January 1831.

43. Ibid., 20 March 1833.

44. See various recommendations and criticisms to Ulster farmers in ibid.; ibid., 17 July 1833.

45. Cornelius Acker's accounts are traced in the Hasbrouck Daybooks.

46. I have chosen 1839, the last complete daybook in the merchant's 43-volume set, as a year of analysis in order to examine changes in agricultural production, trade, and sale some twenty years after the 1820 accounts.

47. Hasbrouck, Accounts, 1839, NYHS.

48. Ibid., 1839; Hedrick, *History of Agriculture*, pp. 376–77.

49. Hasbrouck, Accounts.

50. Table 6.4 is based on models and analysis first developed by Paul G. E. Clemens in Clemens and Peter Wacker, *Land Use in Early New Jersey*, pp. 276–81. Bruegel, "'Time that can be relied upon,'" 551–52.

51. Hasbrouck, Accounts, 1839; Blumin, *Urban Threshold*, pp. 61–62.

52. The Smith advertisement is in the *Ulster Palladium*, 8 February 1832. Joseph Field's is in ibid. for 11 April 1832.

53. Wright, "Empire State's Triple Transition," 532, details the growth of New York's banking system and the issuance of a stable currency.

54. Dublin, "Rural Putting-Out Work," 571–73; Jensen, *Loosening the Bonds*, pp. 93–94.

55. Hasbrouck, Accounts; Daniel Holley Account Book, 1828–1835, Reformed Protestant Dutch Church.

56. Wright, "Empire State's Triple Transition," 534–37.

57. Presidential Address of Horatio Seymour to New York State Agricultural Society, 1851, reprinted in Danhof, *Changes in Agriculture*, pp. 21–22; Bruce Levine, *Half Slave–Half Free: The Roots of the Civil War* (New York: Hill and Wang, 1992), p. 55.

58. Brink, *Early History of Saugerties*, pp. 194–95.

Conclusion
A Diversified Economy and Society

1. The "moving bee" is reconstructed from "Notes of Benjamin Brink" and Brink, *Early History of Saugerties*, pp. 194–96.

2. Clemens and Wacker, *Land Use*, pp. 26–27.

3. New York Census of 1782, in E. B. O'Callaghan, *The Documentary History of the State of New York* (Albany, 1850), vol. 3, p. 601; Federal Manuscript Census of Ulster County, 1790, 1820, 1850. The Kingston population of 13,132 is calculated by including the village of Esopus (2,900).

4. Thirty-six of DuBois's seventy-one customers settled some portion of their accounts in goods. Garret DuBois, Account Book, 1828–1835, Huguenot Historical Society; Cole earned 52.3 percent of his payment in the early 1830s in goods, 35 percent in cash, 12.7 percent in services of some kind. Jacobus Cole, Book of Accounts, 1789–1832.

5. The poor land of New Windsor is described in "The Recollections of Edward McGraw" in E. M. Ruttenber, *A History of New Windsor*, pp. 48, 133–35; Smith, "Jour-

nal from New York to Albany," 1:489–90. "Travels of Peter Stansbury," recorded in *Olde Ulster*, vol. 8, pp. 52–53.

6. Rothenberg, *From Market-Places*, pp. 80–111.

7. "Trustees Minutes," 17 February 1742, 28 April 1783, U.C.C.O.

8. Blumin, *Urban Threshold*, pp. 216–18.

9. "Kingston Directors' Minutes," 14 May 1819, 22 May 1827, 22 September 1830, 8 January 1854; *Kingston Archives*, pp. 19–20.

10. *Ulster Palladium*, 6 March 1833.

11. The Ulster farmer's complaint can be found in *Ulster Palladium*, 6 March 1833; J. P. Beekman, Ulster County Secretary of the New York State Agricultural Society, writing in ibid., 30 May 1833.

12. *Ulster Sentinel*, 29 November 1826; *Ulster Palladium*, 9 March 1831; *Ulster Republican*, 2 December 1840.

SELECTED BIBLIOGRAPHY

PRIMARY SOURCES

Unpublished Manuscripts

Assessment Rolls. New Paltz, 1765, 1783. Kingston Senate House Museum. Kingston, N.Y. Kingston, 1798. New York Historical Society. New York. Marbletown, 1794, 1798. New York Historical Society. New York. Hurly, 1798. New York Historical Society. New York.

Cole, Jacobus. Book of Accounts, 1789–1831. Kingston Senate House Museum.

DeWitt, Charles. Daybook. 1749–1780. Ulster County Collection. New York Historical Society. New York.

Elmendorph, Coenraadt. Invoice of Army Supplies, 1778–1779. New York State Archives, Albany, N.Y.

Federal Manuscript Censuses of Ulster County (microfilm). 1800, 1810, 1820, 1830, 1840, 1850.

Hasbrouck, Abraham. Accounts and Daybooks, 1797–1843. New York Historical Society. New York. Vol. 2. 1799. Vol. 17. May 1819–April 1820. Vol. 18. May 1820–April 1821. Vol. 31. April 1838–April 1839. Vol. 32. April 1839–April 1840.

Hasbrouck Sr., Abraham. Diary. Huguenot House Historical Society. New Paltz, N.Y.

Holley, Daniel. Account Book, 1828–1835. Kingston Reformed Protestant Dutch Church, Kingston, N.Y.

Kingston Board of Directors Minutes (Kingston Directors' Minutes). Kingston City Hall. Vol. 1. 1805–1830; Vol. 3. 1854–1863.

Kingston Court Records, March 1751–February 1774. Ulster County Records, reel 50. Queens College. New York.

Kingston Rising Sun.

Livingston, Robert L. Account Book, 1792–1813. Robert R. Livingston Collection. New York Historical Society. New York.

Masten, John. Account Book. Kingston Shoemaker, 1781–1828. New York Historical Society. New York.

Nicholson, Col. John. Account Book, 1775–1777. New York State Archives. Albany, N.Y.

Osterhoudt, Daniel. Account Book, 1791–1836. Account Book Collection. Kingston Senate House Museum. Kingston, N.Y.

Papers of the Duzine, 1703–1821. In New Paltz Town Records, 1677–1880. Huguenot House Historical Society.

Pick, Jarman and William. Account Book, 1726–1741; 1765–1798; 1826–1828, Ulster County Collection. New York Historical Society. New York.

Probated Inventories and Accounts. Boxes 9–49. Ulster County Surrogate Court. Kingston, N.Y.

———. National Genealogical Society. Salt Lake City, Utah. Microfilm Reels #0941026–0941048, 0940811–0940829.

Probated Wills, 1760–1830. Ulster County Court of Probate. New York State Archives. Albany, N.Y.

Records of the Corporation of the Town of Kingston, Trustees Minutes, Ulster County Clerks Office. Kingston, N.Y. Vol. 2. 16 February 1705–4 February 1712. Vol. 4. 1 March 1736–21 February 1783. Vol. 5. 12 March 1783–19 February 1795. Vol. 6. 7 March 1795–3 March 1810. Vol. 7. 8 March 1810–December 1816.

Records of Highway Commissioners of Ulster County, 1722–1795. 2 vols. Ulster County Records, reel 1. Historical Documents Collection. Paul Klapper Library. Queens College. New York.

Records of the Town Court. Proceedings of the Trustees of Kingston. Vol. 3. 7 October 1713–February 1737. New York Historical Society. New York.

Snyder, Benjamin. Account Book, 1768–1795. New York Historical Society. New York.

———. Day and Sloop Book, 1774–1777. New York Historical Society. New York.

Trustees of Kingston Record of Conveyances &c. From the Year 1729 to 1764, inclusive. Volume D. Records Room. Ulster County Clerk's Office.

———. From the Year 1768 to the Year 1798, inclusive. Volume E. Records Room. Ulster County Clerk's Office.

Ulster County Deed Records, Vol. 6 FF 1737–1770; Vol. 7 GG 1765–1780; Vol. 8 HH 1780–1820.Ulster County Clerk's Office, Kingston, New York.

Ulster County Supervisor's Minutes. 1710–August 1730. Ulster County Records, reel 50. Queens College. New York.

———. May 1793–October 1796. Ulster County Records, reel 1. Queens College. New York.

Ulster Palladium.

Ulster Plebian.

Ulster Sentinel.

van Gaasbeck, William. Account Book, 1790–1808. Kingston Senate House Museum, Kingston, N.Y.

Published and Unpublished Personal Papers

Alexander, William. Papers. New York Historical Society. New York.

Clinton, George. *Public Papers of George Clinton, 1777–1804.* 9 vols. Edited by Hugh Hastings. New York: 1899.

Colden, Cadwallader. *The Letters and Papers of Cadwallader Colden.* 9 vols. New York: New York Historical Society, 1918–1937.

DeWitt, Charles. Letters. Kingston Senate House Museum. Kingston, N.Y.

Duer, William. Papers. New York Historical Society. New York.

Ellison Papers. New York Historical Society. New York.

———. Case 2. Washington's Headquarters. Newburgh, N.Y.

Livingston, Robert. Papers. New York Historical Society. New York.

Published Primary Sources

Anjou, Gustave. *Ulster County, New York, Probate Records in the Office of the County Clerk's Office.* 2 vols. New York: 1906.

Kalm, Peter. *Travels in North America: The English Version of 1770.* Edited by Adolph B. Benson. New York: 1987.

Chastellux, Francois Jean. *Travels in North America.* 2 vols. London: 1787.

Crevecoeur, J. Hector St. John. *Letters from an American Farmer.* New York: Penguin Books, 1904.

Dwight, Timothy. *Travels in New England and New York.* 4 vols. Edited by Barbara Miller Solomon. Cambridge, Mass.: 1969.

Force, Peter, ed. *American Archives.* 9 vols. Washington, D.C.: 1837–1853.

Journals of the Provincial Congress, Provincial Committee of Safety, and Council of Safety of the State of New York, 1775–1777. 2 vols. Albany, N.Y.: State of New York, 1842.

Lincoln, Charles Z., ed. *Colonial Laws of New York from 1664 to the Revolution.* 5 vols. Albany, N.Y.: State of New York, 1894.

Olde Ulster. 10 vols. Marbletown, N.Y.: Ulster Historic Society, 1905–1906.

Smith, Richard. "Journal from New York to Albany." In *History of the Valley of the Hudson.* 2 vols. Edited by Nelson Greene. Chicago: 1931.

Wolley, Charles, ed. *A Two Years Journal in New York: 1678–1680.* New York: 1973.

Secondary Sources

Anderson, Fred. *A People's Army: Massachusetts Soldiers in the Seven Years War.* New York: W.W. Norton, 1984.

Appleby, Joyce. "Commercial Farming and the Agrarian Myth in the Early Republic." *Journal of American History* 20 (March 1982).

Baker, Andrew, and Patterson, Holly Izard. "Farmers' Adaptations to Markets in Early-Nineteenth Century Massachusetts." In *The Farm: The Dublin Seminar for New England Folk-Life*. Edited by Peter Benes. Boston: Boston University Press, 1988.

Bailyn, Bernard. *The New England Merchants in the Seventeenth Century*. Cambridge, Mass.: Harvard University Press, 1955.

Balmer, Randall. "Schism on Long Island: The Dutch Reformed Church, Lord Cornbury, and the Politics of Anglicization," in *Authority and Resistance in Early New York*. Edited by William Pencak and Conrad E. Wright. New York: New York Historical Society, 1988.

Barron, Hal S. "Listening to the Silent Majority: Change and Continuity in the Nineteenth Century Rural North," *Agriculture and National Development*. Edited by Lou Ferleger. Ames, Iowa: Iowa State University Press, 1990.

———. *Those Who Stayed Behind: Rural Society in Nineteenth Century New England*. Cambridge, Eng.: Cambridge University Press, 1984.

Beard, Charles. *The Rise of American Civilization*. 2 vols. New York: Macmillan Press, 1927.

Becker, Carl. *The History of Political Parties in the Province of New York, 1760–1776*. Madison, Wisc.: University of Wisconsin, 1909.

Berthoff, Rowland and Murrin, John. "Feudalism, Communalism, and the Yeoman Freeholder: The American Revolution Considered as a Social Accident." In *Essays on the American Revolution*. Edited by Stephen Kurtz and James Hutson. Chapel Hill: University Press of North Carolina, 1973.

Bidwell, Percy Wells, and Falconer, John I. *History of Agriculture in the Northern United States*. Reprint ed. New York: Peter Smith Co., 1941.

Bielinski, Stefan. "Coming and Going in Early America: The People of Colonial Albany and Outmigration." *De Halve Maen* 60 (1987): 2.

———. "The People of Colonial Albany: The Profile of a Community, 1650–1800." In *Authority and Resistance in Early New York*. Edited by William Pencak and Conrad E. Wright. New York: New York Historical Society, 1988.

Blackmar, Elizabeth. *Manhattan for Rent*. Ithaca, N.Y.: Cornell University Press, 1992.

Blewett, Mary H. *Men, Women and Work: Class, Gender, and Protest in the New England Shoe Industry, 1780–1910*. Urbana: Illinois University Press, 1988.

Blumin, Stuart. *The Urban Threshold: Growth and Change in a Nineteenth Century Community*. Chicago: University of Chicago Press, 1976.

Bonomi, Patricia. *A Factious People: Politics and Society in Colonial New York*. New York: Columbia University Press, 1971.

———. "Local Government in Colonial New York: A Base for Republicanism." In *Aspects of Early New York Society and Politics*. Edited by Jacob Judd and Irwin H. Polishook. Tarrytown, N.Y.: Sleepy Hollow Press, 1974.

Breen, T. H. "The Baubles of Britain: The American and Consumer Revolutions of the Eighteenth Century." *Past & Present* 119 (May 1988).

Brenner, Robert. "Agrarian Class Structure and Economic Development in Pre-Industrial Europe." *Past and Present* 70 (February 1976).

Brink, Benjamin Myer. *Early History of Saugerties: 1660–1825.* Kingston, N.Y.: R.W. Anderson, 1902.

Bruchey, Stuart. *The Roots of American Economic Growth, 1607–1861.* New York: Harper Torchbooks, 1965.

Bruegel, Martin. "'Time that can be relied upon': The Evolution of Time Consciousness in the Mid-Hudson Valley, 1790–1860." *Journal of Social History* (Spring 1995).

———. "The Rise of a Market Society in the Hudson River Valley: 1750–1850." Ph.D. diss., Cornell University, 1994.

Burke, Thomas. *The Mohawk Frontier.* Ithaca: Cornell University Press, 1991.

Chazanof, William. "Land Speculation in Eighteenth-Century New York." In *Business Enterprise in Early New York.* Edited by Joseph R. Freese and Jacob Judd. Tarrytown, N.Y.: Sleepy Hollow Press, 1979.

Clark, Christopher. "Household Economy, Market Exchange, and the Rise of Capitalism in the Connecticut Valley, 1800–1860." *Journal of Social History* 13 (Winter 1979): 169–89.

———. *Roots of Rural Capitalism: Western Massachusetts, 1780–1860.* Ithaca: Cornell University Press, 1991.

Clark-Smith, Barbara. "Food Rioters and the American Revolution," *William & Mary Quarterly* (1994): 3–30.

———. *After the Revolution: The Smithsonian History of Everyday Life in the Eighteenth Century.* New York: Smithsonian Press, 1985.

Clearwater, Alphonse. *History of Ulster County.* Kingston, N.Y.: 1907.

Clemens, Paul G. E., and Wacker, Peter. *Land Use in Early New Jersey.* Newark, N.J.: New Jersey Historical Society, 1995.

———, and Simler, Lucy. "Rural Labor and the Farm Household in Chester County, Pennsylvania, 1750–1820." In *Work and Labor in Early America.* Edited by Stephen Innes. Chapel Hill: University of North Carolina Press, 1988.

Cochrane, Charles. *A History of the Town of Marlborough.* New York: 1887.

Cohen, David Steven. "How Dutch Were the Dutch of New Netherland?" *New York History* 62 (1981): 43–60.

———. *The Dutch-American Farm.* New York: New York University Press, 1992.

Cott, Nancy. *The Bonds of Womanhood: Woman's Sphere in New England, 1780–1835.* New Haven: Yale University Press, 1977.

Countryman, Edward, *A People in Revolution: The American Revolution and Political Society in New York, 1760–1790*. Baltimore: Johns Hopkins University Press, 1981.

———. "'Out of the Bounds of the Law': Northern Land Rioters in the Eighteenth Century." In *The American Revolution: Explorations in the Histroy of American Radicalism*. Edited by Alfred Young. DeKalb: Northern Illinois Universtiy Press, 1976.

Craig, Lee A. "The Value of Household Labor in Antebellum Northern Agriculture." *Journal of Economic History* 51 (1991).

Danhof, Clarence. *Changes in Agriculture: The Northern United States, 1820–1870*. Cambridge: Harvard University Press, 1969.

Doerflinger, Thomas M. *A Vigorous Spirit of Enterprise: Merchants and Economic Development in Revolutionary Philadelphia*. Chapel Hill: University Press of North Carolina, 1986.

Dublin, Thomas. "Rural Putting-Out Work in Early Nineteenth Century New England: Women and the Transition to Capitalism in the Countryside." *New England Quarterly* 63 (1991).

———. *Transforming Women's Work: New England Lives in the Industrial Revolution*. Ithaca: Cornell University Press, 1994.

Ehrlich, Jessica Kross. "'To Hear and Try All Causes Betwixt Man and Man': The Town Court of Newtown, 1659–1690." *New York History* (July 1978): 286–87.

———. *Evolution of an American Town: Newtown, New York, 1664–1775*. Philadelphia: Temple University Press, 1983.

Ellis, David M. *A History of New York State*. Ithaca: Cornell University Press, 1967.

———. *Farmers and Landlords in the Hudson-Mohawk Region: 1790–1850*. Ithaca: Cornell University Press, 1967.

Evers, Alf. *Woodstock: History of An American Town*. Woodstock, N.Y.: Overlook Press, 1987.

Ferleger, Lou, ed. *Agriculture and National Development: Views on the Nineteenth Century*. Ames: University of Iowa Press, 1990.

Fernow, Berthold, ed. *Documents Relating to the Colonial History of New York*. 15 vols. Albany, N.Y.: State of New York, 1887.

Fippin, Elmer O. *Rural New York*. Port Washington, N.Y.: Kennikat Press, 1921.

Foner, Eric, *Tom Paine and Revolutionary America*. New York: Oxford University Press, 1976.

Fried, Marc B. *Early History of Kingston and Ulster County, New York*. Marbletown, N.Y.: Ulster County Historical Society, 1974.

Gallman, Robert E., and Wallis, John, eds., *American Economic Growth and Standards of Living Before the Civil War*. Chicago: University of Chicago Press, 1992.

Goodfriend, Joyce. *Before the Melting Pot: Society and Culture in Colonial New York City, 1664–1730*. Princeton: Princeton University Press, 1992.

Grant, Charles. *Democracy in the Connecticut Frontier Town of Kent*. New York: A.M.S. Press, 1961.

Groth, Michael. "Slaveholders and Manumission in Dutchess County, New York." *New York History* 78 (1997): 33–50.

Gunn, L. Ray. *The Decline of Authority: Public Economic Policy and Political Development in New York State, 1800–1860*. Ithaca: Cornell University Press, 1988.

Hacker, Louis. *The Triumph of American Capitalism*. New York: 1940.

Hall, Peter Dobkin. *The Organization of American Culture, 1700–1900: Private Institutions, Elites, and the Origins of American Nationality*. New York: New York University Press, 1982.

Hahn, Steven, and Prude, Jonathan, eds. *The Countryside in the Age of Capitalist Transformation: Essays in the Social History of Rural America*. Chapel Hill: University Press of North Carolina, 1985.

Harrington, Virginia. *The New York Merchants on the Eve of the Revolution*. New York: Columbia University Press, 1935.

Hartz, Louis. *The Liberal Tradition in America*. New York: Harvest, Harcourt Brace, 1955.

Henretta, James. *The Evolution of American Society, 1700–1815*. Lexington, Mass.: D.C. Heath, 1973.

———. "Families and Farms: Mentalité in Pre-Industrial America," *William and Mary Quarterly* #35 3rd Ser. (July 1978): 3–30.

———. *Origins of American Capitalism: Selected Essays*. Boston: Northeastern University Press, 1992.

———. "The War for Independence and American Economic Development." In *The Economy of Early America: The Revolutionary Period, 1763–1790*. Edited by Ronald Hoffman, John McCusker et al. Charlottesville: University Press of Virginia, 1988.

Heyrman, Christine. *Commerce and Culture: The Maritime Communities of Colonial Massachusetts, 1690–1750*. New York: W.W. Norton, 1983.

Hofstadter, Richard. "The Myth of the Happy Yeoman." *American Heritage* 7 (1956): 43–53.

Innes, Stephen. *Creating the Commonwealth: The Economic Culture of Puritan New England*. New York: W.W. Norton, 1995.

———. *Labor in a New Land: Economy and Society in Seventeenth Century Springfield*. Princeton: Princeton University Press, 1983.

———, ed. *Work and Labor in Early America*. Chapel Hill: University of North Caroina Press, 1988.

Jensen, Joan. *Loosening the Bonds: Mid-Atlantic Farm Women, 1750–1850.* New Haven: Yale University Press, 1986.

Kammen, Michael. *Colonial New York: A History.* New York: Charles Scribner's Sons, 1975.

Kenney, Alice P. *Stubborn for Liberty: The Dutch in New York.* Syracuse: Syracuse University Press, 1975.

Kim, Sung Bok. *Landlord and Tenant in Colonial New York: Manorial Society, 1664–1775.* Chapel Hill: University Press of North Carolina, 1978.

Kulikoff, Allan. *Agrarian Origins of American Capitalism.* Charlottesville: University of Virginia Press, 1992.

———. "The Transition to Capitalism in Rural America." *William and Mary Quarterly* 46, 3rd Ser. (January 1989): 120–44.

Larkin, F. Daniel. *New York State Canals: A Short History.* Fleischmanns, N.Y.: Purple Mountain Press, 1998.

LeFevre, Ralph. *A History of New Paltz, New York, and Its Old Families.* Albany: Fort Orange Press, 1903.

Lemon, James T. "Agriculture and Society in Early America." *Agricultural History Review* 35 (1987): 76–94.

———. *The Best Poor Man's Country: A Geographical Study of Early Southeastern Pennsylvania.* New York: W.W. Norton, 1972.

———. "Comment on James Henretta's 'Families and Farms': Mentalité in Pre-Industrial America." *William and Mary Quarterly* 37, 3rd Ser. (1980): 688–96.

Lockridge, Kenneth. *A New England Town: The First Hundred Years.* New York: W.W. Norton, 1970.

Loehr, Rodney. "Self-Sufficiency on the Farm." *Agricultural History* 26 (April 1952): 37–40.

McNall, Neil Adams. *An Agricultural History of the Genesee Valley, 1790–1860.* Philadelphia: University of Pennsylvania Press, 1952.

McCusker, John J., and Menard, Russell R. *The Economy of British America, 1607–1789.* Chapel Hill: University of North Carolina Press, 1985.

Main, Gloria. "Probate Records as a Source for Early American History," *William and Mary Quarterly* 32, 3rd Ser. (January 1975): 89–99.

Matson, Cathy. "'Damned Scoundrels' and 'Libertisme of Trade': Freedom and Regulation in Colonial New York's Fur and Grain Trades." *William and Mary Quarterly* 51 (1994).

———. "Liberty, Jealousy, and Union: The New York Economy in the 1780s." In *New York in the Age of the Constitution.* Edited by Paul Gilje and William Pencak. New York: New York Historical Society, 1992.

——. *Merchants and Empire: Trading in Colonial New York*. Baltimore: Johns Hopkins University Press, 1998.

Mason, Bernard. *The Road to Independence: The American Revolution in New York, 1773–1777*. Lexington: University of Kentucky Press, 1967.

Medick, Hans. "The Proto-Industrial Family Economy: The Structural Function of the Household and Family During the Transition from Peasant Society to Industrial Capitalism." *Social History* 3 (1976).

Mendels, Franklin. "Proto-Industrialization: The First Phase of the Industrialization Process." *Journal of Economic History* 32 (1972): 241–61.

Merrill, Michael. "Cash Is Good to Eat: Self-Sufficiency and Exchange in the Rural Economy of the United States." *Radical History Review* (Winter 1977): 42–72.

——. "The Political Economy of Agrarian America." Ph.D. diss., Columbia University, 1985.

Miller, Nathan. *The Enterprise of a Free People: Aspects of the Economic Development in New York State during the Canal Period, 1792–1838*. Ithaca: Cornell University Press, 1962.

Mutch, Robert. "The Cutting Edge: Colonial America and the Debate about the Transition to Capitalism." *Theory and Society* 9 (November 1980): 847–63.

——. "Yeoman and Merchant in Pre-Industrial America: Eighteenth Century Massachusetts as a Case Study." *Societas* 7 (Autumn 1977): 279–302.

Narrett, David. *Inheritance and Family Life in Colonial New York City*. Ithaca: Cornell University Press, 1992.

——. "Men's Wills and Women's Property Rights in Colonial New York." In *Women in the Age of the American Revolution*. Edited by Ronald Hoffman and Peter Albert. Charlottesville: University Press of Virginia, 1989.

Nash, Gary. *The Urban Crucible: Social Change, Political Consciousness, and the Origins of the American Revolution*. Cambridge: Harvard University Press, 1979.

Nobles, Gregory. "Capitalism in the Countryside: The Transformation of Rural Society in the United States." *Radical History Review* 41 (1988): 163–76.

——. "The Rise of Merchants in Rural Market Towns." *Journal of Social History* 43 (Fall 1990): 3–20.

Norton, Mary Beth. "The Evolution of White Women's Experience in Early America," *American Historical Review* (April 1985): 593–619.

Osterud, Nancy Grey. *Bonds of Community: The Lives of Farm Women in Nineteenth Century New York*. Ithaca: Cornell University Press, 1991.

Parkerson, Donald. *The Agricultural Transition in New York State*. Ames: Iowa State University Press, 1995.

Perkins, Edwin J. *The Economy of Colonial America*. New York: Columbia University Press, 1980.

———. "The Entrepreneurial Spirit in Colonial America: The Foundations of Modern Business History." *Business History Review* 63 (Spring 1989): 160–86.

———, and Walton, Gary M. *A Prosperous People: The Growth of the American Economy.* Englewood Cliffs, N.J.: Prentice-Hall, 1985.

Pointer, Richard. *Protestant Pluralism and the New York Experience: A Study of Eighteenth Century Religious Diversity.* Indianapolis: University of Indiana Press, 1988.

Post, Charles. "Agrarian Origins of U.S. Capitalism: The Transformation of the Northern Countryside Before the Civil War." *Journal of Peasant Studies* 22 (1995).

Prude, Jonathan. *The Coming of Industrial Order: Town and Factory Life in Rural Massachusetts, 1800–1860.* New York: Cambridge University Press, 1983.

———. "Protoindustrialization in the American Context: Response to Jean H. Quataert." *International Labor Working Class History* 33 (Spring 1988).

Rock, Howard. *Artisans of the New Republic: The Tradesmen of New York City in the Age of Jefferson.* New York: New York University Press, 1984.

Rothenberg, Winifred. *From Market-Places to a Market Economy: Transformation of Rural Massachusetts, 1750–1850.* Chicago: University of Chicago Press, 1993.

———. "Emergence of a Capital Market." *Journal of Economic History* 45 (1985): 781–808.

———. "The Emergence of Farm Labor Markets and the Transformation of the Rural Economy: Massachusetts, 1750–1855." *Journal of Economic History* 48 (1988): 537–66.

———. "The Market and Massachusetts Farmers, 1750–1855." *Journal of Economic History* 41 (1981).

Ruttenber, E. M. *A History of New Windsor, Orange County, N.Y.* Newburgh, N.Y.: Historical Society of Newburgh Bay, 1911.

Schoonmaker, Marius. *History of Kingston, New York.* New York: 1888.

Schumacher, George. *The Northern Farmer and His Markets in the Late Colonial Period.* New York: Arno Press, 1975.

Sellers, Charles. *The Market Revolution: Jacksonian America, 1815–1846.* New York: Oxford University Press, 1991.

Shammas, Carol. "Consumer Behavior in Colonial America." *Social Science History* 6 (1982): 67–86.

———. "How Self-Sufficient Was Early America?" *Journal of Interdisciplinary History* 8 (Autumn 1982): 247–73.

———. *The Pre-Industrial Consumer in England and America.* New York: Oxford University Press, 1990.

Simler, Lucy. "Tenancy in Colonial Pennsylvania: The Case of Chester County." *William and Mary Quarterly* 43 (1986): 542–69.

Sylvester, Nathaniel Bartlett. *A History of Ulster County, New York.* Philadelphia: Pleck, 1880.

Taylor, George Rogers. *The Transportation Revolution, 1815–1860.* New York: Rinehart, 1951.

Thorp, Daniel. "Doing Business in the Backcountry: Retail Trade in Colonial Rowan County, North Carolina," *William and Mary Quarterly* 48, 3d Ser. (1991): 382–96.

Ulrich, Laurel Thatcher. "Martha Ballard and Her Girls: Women's Work in Eighteenth-Century Maine." In *Work and Labor in Early America.* Edited by Stephen Innes. Chapel Hill: University Press of North Carolina, 1988.

Vickers, Daniel. "Competency and Competition: Economic Culture in Early America." *The William and Mary Quarterly* 47 (1990): 3–20.

———. *Farmers and Fishermen: Two Centuries of Work in Essex County Massachusetts, 1630–1850.* Chapel Hill: University Press of North Carolina, 1994.

Wall, Helena. *Fierce Communion: Family and Community in Early America.* Cambridge: Harvard University Press, 1990.

Weiman, David. "Families, Farms, and Rural Society in Pre-Industrial America." In *Agrarian Organization in the Century of Industrialization.* Edited by George Grantham and Carol Leonard. *Research in Economic History.* Supplement 5. Greenwich, Conn.: 1989.

Weiss, Rona S. "The Market and Massachusetts Farmers, 1750–1850: A Comment." *Journal of Economic History* 43 (June 1983): 476–77.

White, Philip L. *The Beekmans of New York in Politics and Commerce, 1647–1877.* New York: New York Historical Society, 1956.

Woolsey, C. M. *History of the Town of Marlborough.* Albany, N.Y.: J.B. Lyons, 1908.

Wright, Langdon G. "In Search of Peace and Harmony: New York Communities in the Seventeenth Century." *New York History* 61 (January 1980).

Wright, Robert. "The First Phase of the Empire State's Triple Transition: Banks' Influence on the Market, Democracy, and Federalism in New York, 1776–1836." *Social Science History* 21 (1997).

Young, Alfred, ed. *Dissent: Explorations in the History of American Radicalism.* DeKalb: Northern Illinois University Press, 1968.

Zimm, Louise Hasbrouck. *Southeastern New York.* New York: 1946.

Zuckerman, Michael, *Peaceable Kingdoms: New England Towns in the Eighteenth Century.* New York: Alfred A. Knopf, 1970.

INDEX